AN ELEGANT AND LEARNED DISCOURSE
OF THE LIGHT OF NATURE

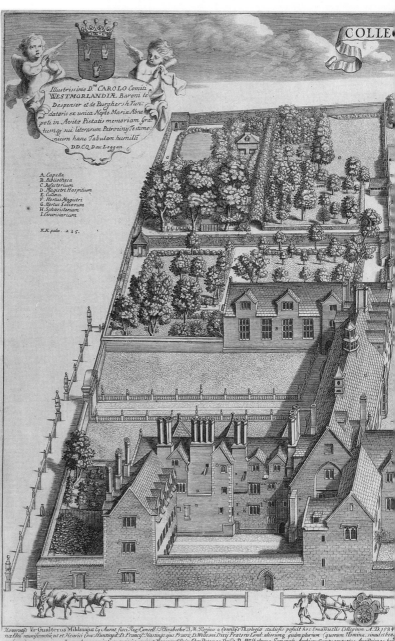

COLLE

Illustrissimo Dⁿⁿ CAROLO Comiti
WESTMORLANDIÆ. Baroni te
Despenser et de Burghersh Furi:
Fidataris ex unica Nepte Maria Abne
poti in Avitæ Pietatis memoriam Gra
tissimiq sui literarum Patrocinij Testimo:
nium hane Tabulam humilli
D.D.C.Q Dav. Loggan

A. Copella
B. Bibliotheca
C. Refectorium
D. Magistri Hospitium
E. Culina
F. Hortus Magistri
G. Hortus Sociorum
H. Sphæristerium
I. Cerevisiarium

K.K. pala. 235.

Honoratiss Vir Gualterus Mildmajus Eq Aurat fisci Reg Cancell Elizabethæ B.M. Reginæ a Consilijs Theologiæ studiosis posuit hoc Emanuelis Collegion A.D 1584 næ Eliz munificentiâ, ut et Henrici Com Huntingd D Franci: Hastings epi Fratri, D Wolhiam Dug Prætoris Lond: aliorumq quàm plurium (quorum Homina simul et bene-res) reperit nepouces, ne columned o, quos inter præcipuè eminēt Reverendiss: in Chr: Pater ac Dnūr D, Wilhelmus Sincrofs Archiep: Cantuar: totiu Ang Primas, huj Vis D Iohan: Pinch novissp viden Hare de Fordwich et Mag Sigilli Ang Cuftor, D: Iof: Hall Norwicen Ep D Wilhem Bedel Ep: Kilmur in Hybernia, Iann Ward et Ric: Nels Arbus, Con: D: etia Fran: Mavesh sp: prime Kilmor nomē Del: Grotio Prouidentia Dublin nec nonD, Franc P Herem nug Capitale Iuucariside Baco Regilla semti Th Ihn Iouis Wilh Professit et linguar Orient im plane eminti Thesaurean instructis Rad Cudworth S.T.P linguæ Hebr: apud Cantabr Profess, et Ioan Wallis Geom Profess hunc iequod Oxon

NUELIS

EMANUEL

rias III. Scholares IV. una cum inferiorum Ordinum Officiarijs. Exinde vero elegantibus Ædificijs, annuisq reditu multo auctius est factum pia ejusd. Regi
one redeuntur) adeo ut jam numerent, qui Socij 34 Scholares studentes praxa 80 Scauero ne etc ✛ (villq hodie, licet recentus paulo fundatu, claros Viros et Scrigu.
Profecss. Laudatiss: nunc s.da ingenu præsidium, post et decus. Hæc etiam Verorum jam functorum nomina incer hujur Colli. Allæmnor debite cum honore sunt recitanda.
issiar. Ant. Tuckney Regnu Præsyss. Mathæw. Pool synopseos Critis sacr. Author Laboriosi. Præter quos gessit idem Coll hodie inter suos numerare post præditum
onnij laude majores Afirit quies sibs D: Wilhd: Temple varijs pro Reg Majestate CAROLI II legatiomib apud exteros functis Edm:Castle S.T.P. hodiernum linquæ Arabit
d Londin, cum atijs quamplurimis, quorum nomina jam nunc in honore sunt, et apud posteros erunt in perpetuum.

Encomiastæ Prerotyp: ad ingen Collegij Magister .
Encomiastæ Johan: Baldenstan S.T.P et

NATURAL LAW AND
ENLIGHTENMENT CLASSICS

Knud Haakonssen
General Editor

NATURAL LAW AND
ENLIGHTENMENT CLASSICS

An Elegant and Learned
Discourse of
the Light of Nature

Nathaniel Culverwell

Edited by Robert A. Greene
and Hugh MacCallum

Foreword by Robert A. Greene

LIBERTY FUND

Indianapolis

© 2001 Liberty Fund, Inc.
Originally published by the University of Toronto Press.
All rights reserved
Printed in the United States of America
Frontispiece by permission of the Houghton Library, Harvard University.

The view of Emmanuel College was published in David Loggan, *Cantabrigia Illustrata* (Cambridge, 1690). Culverwell delivered his *Discourse* in the former chapel of Emmanuel College, identified as "B Bibliotheca" in Loggan's drawing.

06 05 04 03 02 C 5 4 3 2 1
06 05 04 03 02 P 5 4 3 2 1

Library of Congress Cataloging-in-Publication Data
Culverwell, Nathaniel, d. 1651?
An elegant and learned discourse of the light of nature/Nathaniel Culverwell; edited by Robert A. Greene and Hugh MacCallum; foreword by Robert A. Greene.
p. cm.
Originally published: Toronto: University of Toronto Press, 1971.
(Studies and texts/University of Toronto. Dept. of English)
Includes bibliographical references and index.
ISBN 0-86597-327-X (alk. paper)—ISBN 0-86597-328-8 (pbk.)
1. Religion—Philosophy. I. Greene, Robert A.
II. MacCallum, Hugh, 1928– III. Title.
BL51 .C8 2002
211'.6   2001038084

LIBERTY FUND, INC.
8335 Allison Pointe Trail, Suite 300
Indianapolis, IN 46250-1684

CONTENTS

PREFACE

This edition of Culverwell's *Discourse,* edited by Robert A. Greene and Hugh MacCallum, was originally published in 1971 by the University of Toronto Press. The introduction set the work in its historical and philosophical context. This republication substitutes a brief updated foreword by Robert A. Greene for that original introduction. Bracketed page numbers in the text indicate the pagination of the 1971 edition. Bracketed page numbers in the foreword refer to page numbers in this volume. Capitalization of the chapter titles on page 9 and in the text has been modernized. The chapter numbers in the text have been made arabic to be consistent with those on page 9. The following acknowledgments are repeated from the 1971 edition.

The editors wish to express their gratitude to the institutions and libraries that provided assistance, and to the friends who helped them out of difficulties. Leaves of absence from the University of Toronto afforded the opportunity for research abroad, and the Leverhulme Trust, the Canada Council, and the research fund of the University of Toronto supported the project. The work has been published with the aid of grants from the Humanities Research Council, using funds provided by the Canada Council, and from the Publications Fund of the University of Toronto Press.

We wish to recognize a particular debt to the staffs of the British Library and the Huntington Library, where much of the work was done, and to the Librarian of Emmanuel College, Cambridge, Mr. Frank Stubbings, for his generous guidance and advice, which included drawing to our attention the existence of the pulpit from which Culverwell preached his *Discourse.* The complete list of colleagues and friends who contributed to the solution of individual problems is too long for inclusion here, but we desire especially to thank N. J. Endicott, David Gallop, Allan Pritchard, John Rist, Niall Rudd, D. I. B. Smith, and Peter Walsh; K. H. Kuhn and J. W. Wevers were kind enough to check the accuracy of the Hebrew passages in the text. John Brown's nineteenth-century edition of the *Discourse* was of indispensable assistance, and in standing on his shoulders we hope we have avoided the pitfall which Culverwell warned of in his account of the printer who "corrects the old *Errata* of the first Edition, and makes some new Errours in [his] owne." Both editors think with affection of the encouragement offered by the late A. S. P. Woodhouse, and with respect (not unmixed with penitence) of the assistance offered by their wives, Barbara and Mary.

R. A. G.
H. M.

FOREWORD

Emmanuel College and the Cambridge Platonists

Nathaniel Culverwell died at the age of thirty-one in 1651. He had spent eighteen years of his brief life as a student and fellow of Emmanuel College, Cambridge, "that zealous house," as John Evelyn called it. Emmanuel had been established as a Puritan foundation in 1584, and by midcentury its Calvinist ethos had led to its flourishing as the second-largest college in the university. Its influence peaked during the political disruptions of the mid-1640s, when over half the fellows in the university, Emmanuel excepted, were ejected by Parliament for their failure to subscribe to the Solemn League and Covenant, and eleven heads of colleges were removed from their positions. Seven of their replacements came from Emmanuel.

It was during these same years, however, that the Presbyterian Calvinism that had characterized Emmanuel and led to its prominence was beginning to erode, challenged by the new ideas in the preaching and writing of three of Culverwell's contemporaries at the college: Benjamin Whichcote, Ralph Cudworth, and John Smith. Culverwell spent ten, twelve, and eight years, respectively, with them at Emmanuel, and he served as fellow with Whichcote and Cudworth in the early 1640s. Thus he matured intellectually in the collegial company of three of the four major members of that loose federation, the so-called Cambridge Platonists. Henry More of Christ's College was the fourth.

There is no evidence to confirm that Whichcote tutored Culverwell, although their common reliance on scholastic sources and the privileged position in their writings of the biblical verse "The understanding of a man is the candle of the Lord," from Proverbs 20:27, may suggest that possibility. Culverwell is no longer considered a Cambridge Platonist, but his views are strongly linked to Whichcote's, and he clearly shared with the Platonists their new emphasis on the central importance of reason in religious thinking. In any event, he directly experienced this transition in emphasis and intellectual focus at Emmanuel, and his writings reflect it. His first sermons, or commonplaces, in the early 1640s focus on typical Calvinist themes: the necessity of assurance, the nature of justification, man's dependence upon God's free grace. These give way in the later *Discourse of the Light of Nature* to an overriding concern with the emerging and more secular preoccupations of midcentury: the dangers in the ideas of radical sects and enthusiasts, the legitimate and necessary place of reason in religion, the natural law debate.

Culverwell delivered the lectures that constitute his *Discourse* in the college chapel during the academic year 1645–46. They were published posthumously in 1652 by William Dillingham, who dedicated them to the then master, Anthony Tuckney, and the fellows of the college. In his preface to the work, Dillingham asserts that it was written *"on the one hand to vindicate the use of Reason in matters of Religion from the aspersions and prejudices of some weaker ones in those times"* [3], a remark which indicates that the *Discourse* is in part a topical treatise with roots in the furious controversies of its day. The removal of licensing control over printing in 1641 resulted in a surge of religious and political tracts and manifestoes, succinctly described and condemned in the title of a contemporary pamphlet as *Hell Broke Loose.* On August 9, 1644, the Westminster Assembly sent a message to the House of Lords, complaining of the "great Growth and Increase of Anabaptists and Antinomians and other sects"; and in the year in which Culverwell wrote and delivered his *Discourse,* Thomas Edwards was composing his *Gangraena* (1646), the most famous and thorough of the English catalogues of heresy.

It is no surprise, then, to find Culverwell deploring "those black and prodigious Errors, that cover and bespot the face of these times" [125] in the midst of the English civil war, including those on both ends of the spectrum of religious argument. At one extreme, there was the "blundering *Antinomian*" who transformed the traditional Calvinist assertion of man's utter depravity into the conviction that redemption of the elect by God's free grace released them from conventional moral obligations and justified scandalously licentious behavior. At the opposite pole, Culverwell criticizes the Arminianism that "pleads for it self under the specious notion of God's love to mankinde" [14], a reference to Samuel Hoard's *God's Love to Mankind* (1633), an Arminian rejection of Calvinist predestination. The legitimate claims of reason in religious matters should not be suspect, Culverwell argues, because they can be misused and distorted by such extremists. Culverwell's plan for the *Discourse* was to develop a moderate and judicious defense of reason and natural law *"standing in the midst between two adversaries of extreme perswasions,"* in Dillingham's words [4]. Had he lived to complete the work, he would have argued that "all the Moral Law is founded in natural and common light, in the light of *Reason*" and that "there's nothing in the mysteries of the Gospel contrary to the light of *Reason;* nothing repugnant to this light that shines from *the Candle of the Lord*" [16].

In addition to resisting antinomian libertinism on one side and liberalizing Arminianism on the other, Culverwell clearly intended to respond to Francis Bacon's call for "a temperate and careful treatise . . . which as a kind of divine logic, should lay down proper precepts touching the use of human reason in theology." In the first sentence of the *Discourse,* he echoes Bacon's *Advancement of Learning* in declaring that distinguishing the provenances of faith and reason is the task that he has set himself: "to give unto *Reason* the things that are *Reasons,* and unto *Faith* the things that are *Faiths*" [10]. Although, unlike the Cambridge Platonists, he quotes or refers to Bacon's writings frequently enough to indicate considerable knowledge and approval of the Baconian gospel, the spirit of the *Discourse* is basically at odds with Bacon's plan for man's intellectual progress. In his emphasis upon scholastic psychology and his indebtedness to Aristotle, Aquinas, and Suarez, as well as in his flourishing rhetoric and richly metaphorical style, Culverwell does not forward the Great Instauration. Accordingly, although the seed for Culverwell's *Discourse* may have been sown by Bacon's call for new works to fill the gaps in human knowledge, the result might well have dismayed him.

The Argument of the Discourse

Delivered as a series of separate sermonlike lectures to students on a specific biblical text, Proverbs 20:27, the *Discourse* nevertheless presents a continuous and progressive argument. This style of lecturing to students was practiced generally in Cambridge at the time and is exemplified by John Sherman's *A Greek in the Temple: Some Common-places delivered in Trinity College Chapel upon Acts XVII, part of the 28 verse* (Cambridge, 1641). The more rhetorical and poetic passages in the *Discourse* reflect the additional influence of the commonplace and declamation. Unfortunately, Culverwell followed the tradition of the ostentatious declamation in quoting generously from Latin and Greek sources, a habit that has dismayed the student and daunted the scholar.

The general outline of the argument is clear. The first chapter contains a statement of the theme of the whole work. Reason and faith are distinct lights, yet they are not opposed; they are complementary and harmonious. Reason is the image of God in man, and to deny right reason is to deny our relation to God. Chapter 2 concludes the prologue by analyzing the text from Proverbs, "The understanding of a man is the candle of the Lord," which serves as a touchstone for the whole argument. Culverwell understands the verse to be an endorsement and celebration of the light of nature, that is, reason.

The first of the two major divisions of the work, chapters 3 through 10, now begins. Chapter 3 defines nature in two ways: first, it is God himself, or what the scholastics called *natura naturans;* second, nature is the principle of operation of any entity, whether spiritual or material. In chapters 4 through 7, law is defined as a measure of moral acts which has as its end the common good; it finds its authority in the will of the lawgiver. The eternal law is the fountain of all other laws: its end is to regulate all things, commanding good and forbidding evil. It is founded in God's reason and formalized by God's will, and it is promulgated both by the law of nature and by direct revelation from God. The law of nature applies only to rational beings who are capable of a formal and legal obligation, "for where there is no Liberty, there's no Law" [44]. God thus publishes his law through reason, the inward scripture or candle of the Lord. Chapters 8 through 10 deal with the light of nature and the related question of how the law of nature is discovered. That discovery is made by "that intellectual eye which God has fram'd and made exactly proportionable to this Light" [71] and confirmed by the consent of nations.

The first half of the *Discourse* dealt with "How *The Understanding of a man is the Candle of the Lord*"; the second half, chapters 11 through 18, considers a different question: "What this *Candle of the Lord* discovers" [16]. This question entails an examination of the powers, nature, and limitations of the light of reason.

Chapters 11 through 13, the first of the three subdivisions, emphasize the limitations of reason, which is described as a "derivative" and a "diminutive" light. The soul does not possess innate ideas. It enters the world as a *tabula rasa* and discovers common notions by observing and comparing sense impressions, and thus it discerns the rational order imposed by God on creation. Accordingly, the argument continues in chapters 14 through 16, reason can serve as a guide to truth. Reason may be limited, but it is "certain" and "directive" despite the attacks of ancient and modern skeptics. Far from being extinguished by faith, reason is completed by it. The final section, chapters 17 and 18, confirms this endorsement of reason, calling it a "pleasant" and "ascendant" light.

Suárez

The antinomian and Arminian writers and Francis Bacon form part of the circle of influences surrounding Culverwell's *Discourse*. Closer to the center lies the *De Legibus, ac Deo Legislatore* (1612) by Francisco Suárez, the Spanish Jesuit. Despite Culverwell's expressed indignation at the logic-chopping of the scholastics, "their works are like so many raging seas, full of perpetual tossings, and disquietings, and foamings, and sometimes casting up mire and dirt" [15], the *Discourse of the Light of Nature* is essentially a Protestant blossom on the scholastic tree; its fundamental philosophic position and spirit are derived from Suárez and Thomas Aquinas.

Chapters 4 through 7 of the *Discourse* examine the nature of law itself, the eternal law, and the definition and extent of natural law. These chapters contain the philosophic keystone of the work, and they support the views of the light of reason and its place in the divine economy which form the substance of later sections. Culverwell follows the arguments of Suárez on these questions, while omitting many of his subtleties and distinctions, and accepts his definitions and conclusions virtually without exception. For example, his quotations of Thomistic definitions of law in chapter 4 are repeated from Suárez and then qualified by Suárez's own restatement of them. The notes make this indebtedness clear.

In chapter 6 John Selden's recently published *De Jure Naturali* (1640), and Hugo Grotius's *De Jure Belli ac Pacis* (1625), are mined for appropriate quotations to illustrate or buttress the points at issue and are at times cited in their own right, but the major insights of the chapter are again derived from Suárez. Natural law, Culverwell asserts, is "intrinsecal and essential to a rational creature"; only an intellectual creature is "capable of a moral government" [40]. Suárez is quite correct, therefore, in rejecting the distinction which the *Institutes* and *Digest* of Justinian draw between the law of nature, common to man and irrational creatures, and the law of nations, the specific rule of men—a distinction also repudiated by Grotius and Selden. Plato, Aristotle, Cicero, and Plutarch are all brought forward to endorse the conclusion that "the Law of *Nature* is built upon Reason," to testify to the "harmony that is between *Nature* and *Law*," and to repeat the substance of Culverwell's view that "the Law of *Nature* is a streaming out of Light from *the Candle of the Lord*" [47]. The final pages of chapter 6 are then taken up with a consideration, based almost entirely upon Suárez, of the precedence of the divine intellect or will in the establishment of law.

This scholastic dilemma, finding popular expression in the conundrum of whether God wills things because they are good or whether things are good because God wills them, appears close to being tautological, but it had already had a long history when Culverwell considered it. The tradition of emphasizing the divine volition as the ultimate determinant of moral good, the voluntarism of William of Ockham, has been traced through his fourteenth-century disciples Pierre d'Ailly and Jean Gerson to both Calvin and Luther, and it is an emphasis encountered frequently in Puritan theologians. The realist position of Thomas Aquinas, which stressed God's rationality and the inherent rationality and morality of the laws governing the universe, was reexpressed for the Elizabethans in Richard Hooker's *Of the Laws of Ecclesiastical Polity.* "They err, therefore," says Hooker, "who think that of the will of God to do this or that, there is no reason besides his will."

Suárez's subtle solution to this inherited problem was to argue that law is founded in reason and formalized by will, or, in Culverwell's words: "This law of Nature having a firme and unshaken foundation in the necessity and conveniency of its materials, becomes formally valid and vigorous by the minde and command of the Supreme Law-giver; So as that all the strength and nerves, and binding virtue of this Law are rooted and fasten'd partly in the excellency and equity of the commands themselves, but they principally depend upon the Sovereignty and Authority of God himself" [71]. As the immutable essences of things created by divine reason and discoverable by human reason are the foundation for natural obligations incumbent upon men, so the divine will by its command creates moral obligations which bind men in a formal and, technically speaking, legal way.

The clearest understanding of Culverwell's judicious balancing of the divine attributes is provided by the impressive conclusion to chapter 11, which rises to a sustained endorsement of reason comparable to the paragraphs of Hooker and traceable, like those, to scholastic sources. Here the subtle distinctions of Suárez are transformed by Culverwell's metaphoric vigor into the humanistic assertion that, "The more men exercise reason, the more they resemble God himself" [117]. Arguing from the premise that "The understanding of God thus being fill'd with light, his Will also must needs be rational" [114], Culverwell concludes that the separation of these attributes is misleading. "Now the understanding of God being so vast and infinite, and his will being so commensurate and proportion'd to it, nay all one with it; all those Decrees of his that are the Eternal product and results of his minde and will, must needs be rational also; For in them his understanding and will met together, his truth and goodnesse kissed each other" [115]. Such emphasis upon the divine reason and reluctance to oppose it to the divine will are thoroughly Thomistic. "All law," Thomas asserts, "proceeds from the reason and will of the law-giver; the Divine and natural laws from the reasonable will of God; the human law from the will of man, regulated by reason."

The Candle of the Lord

Another legacy from the Middle Ages is evident in a distinctive feature of the *Discourse* that sets it apart from other classic works on the natural law: Culverwell's imaginative and literary incorporation into his argument of the metaphor of the candle of the Lord. Proverbs 20:27 has been frequently cited as a kind of shibboleth for the Cambridge Platonists as a group, but the fact is that it was Whichcote and Culverwell alone who wove it into the texture of their thinking and writing on the light and law of nature, and who revived and explored its special medieval significance. Whichcote was clearly the first to make the metaphor a prominent and integral part of his anthropology and theology in his preaching at Trinity Church in the 1630s. In fact, it was so prominent that he and his former tutor at Emmanuel, the Calvinist Anthony Tuckney, engaged in public controversy over it in three successive Cambridge commencement addresses from 1650 to 1652. None of Whichcote's writings, however, were published until after his death in 1683, and so it was Culverwell's *Discourse,* published four times from 1652 to 1669, frequently plagiarized and echoed, that established the candle of the Lord as a resonant and popular metaphor for right reason and the light of nature.

Both Whichcote and Culverwell viewed man's reason as more than a dry Baconian light, more than a discursive faculty to "reckon with" in Hobbes's words. Ancient Judaic tradition had read the expression "the spirit of man" to mean "the higher region of the soul," and the light of the candle of the Lord was identified by Dionysius of Richel in the fifteenth century with synderesis, that "pure part of conscience" or spark of man's deiform nature remaining after the Fall that enabled mankind (*contra* Calvin) to recognize and pursue the good and to be repelled by evil. Rhetorically adapting such ancient wisdom to present philosophical and pastoral needs, and echoing Dionysius' commentary on Proverbs 20:27, Whichcote spoke of reason or the candle of the Lord as *res illuminata, illuminans,* a thing lighted by God and lighting the way to God, the discoverer of the moral "principles of first inscription," or the natural law. Culverwell expresses the same idea in concluding that the light of the candle is an ascendant light: "The Candle of the Lord it came from him, and 'twould faine returne to him" [184]. On that humanistic and affirmative note, Culverwell concludes his persuasive and eloquent encomium of reason, delivered at a surprising time in an unexpected place.

The Text

The copy-text is the British Library copy shelf-mark 1113.d.1, with the addition of Richard Culverwell's letter from E.676.(1). William Dillingham's corrections ("the most material escapes of the impression") listed on a prefatory page of the first edition have been incorporated. Dillingham was an experienced editor of considerable reputation among his contemporaries. In 1658 he gave a first edition of the *Discourse* to the library of Emmanuel College, where it remains today, inscribing it "Collegio Emmanuele Dedit G. D."

Certain typographical alterations have been made silently: modern *s* (for long *s*) and *w* (for *vv*, both capital and lowercase) are used throughout; random italics and wrong-font letters are corrected, and ligature capitals as well as Renaissance Greek contractions have been regularized. All other departures from the copy-text are recorded in the textual notes. Emendations have been made sparingly—in a few cases where the spelling of the 1652 edition is incorrect, eccentric even by seventeenth-century standards, or confusing, that of the second edition of 1654 has been used. Punctuation and syntax have been altered only where the first edition would positively mislead the reader, and all such cases have been recorded. As the textual notes indicate, there are only a few instances, marked "(ed.)," where the second edition of 1654 fails to provide a satisfactory alternative reading.

The second edition, however, has no textual authority. Collation reveals that it was based on the first edition and that no manuscript intervened in its publication. Although some care was taken in the second edition to correct obvious slips made in the first, only half of Dillingham's corrections were incorporated ([125] to end), perhaps as the result of employing two printers, Thomas Roycroft and E[dward] M[ottershead?]; the table of contents was reproduced with the page numbers of the first edition. Selective collation of the third (1661) and fourth (1669) editions reveals that they too are without textual authority, the fourth having been set up from the third and the third from the first.

After Culverwell's death, Dillingham first published one of his commonplaces under the title *Spiritual Opticks,* (Cambridge, 1651). The *Discourse* itself was published together with eight such exercises, including *Spiritual Opticks,* in 1652: AN / ELEGANT / And Learned / DISCOURSE / Of the / Light of Nature, / With several other / TREATISES: /

	The Schisme.		*Mount Ebal.*	
	The Act of Oblivion.		*The White Stone.*	
Viz.	*The Childes Returne.*		*Spiritual Opticks.*	
	The Panting Soul.		*The Worth of Souls.*	

[rule] By NATHANIEL CULVERWEL, Master of Arts, and / lately Fellow of EMANUEL *Colledge* in CAMBRIDGE, [rule] *Imprimatur,* EDM. CALAMY. [rule] *London.* Printed by *T. R.* and *E. M.* for *John Rothwell* at the Sun / and Fountain in *Pauls* Church-yard. 1652. Sigs. A4, [a]4, Aa–Ee4, A–X4, Y2, Z4, Aa–Dd4.

Signature "a" appears to have been reserved for further prefatory material, including Richard Culverwell's letter dated eight days after Dillingham's "To the Reader." Richard's letter is missing in some copies of the first edition and is bound sometimes before, sometimes after, the table of contents, perhaps suggesting that it arrived late at the printer.

This volume was reprinted at London in 1654 and 1661. The copyright was transferred to Thomas Williams, October 30, 1663, and he printed the fourth edition at Oxford [London] in 1669. The *Discourse* has been reprinted twice since the seventeenth century: John Brown edited the text in 1857 and published it at Edinburgh with a prefatory critical essay by John Cairns; E. T. Campagnac reprinted the Oxford edition of 1669, omitting chapters 2, 12, 13, 14, 17, and 18 in *The Cambridge Platonists* (Oxford, 1901).

The principles for translating foreign-language quotations which John Worthington adopted in his edition of John Smith's *Discourses* (London, 1660) have been adhered to in the present work: "It seemed expedient to render the Latine, but especially the Hebrew and Greek, Quotations into English; (except in such places where, the substance and main importance of the Quotations being insinuated in the neighboring words, a Translation was less needful)." Accordingly, all foreign phrases, with the exception of a few obvious Latin tags, have been translated if Culverwell did not himself translate or closely paraphrase them.

Further Reading

Beiser, Frederick. "Culverwell, Nathaniel." In *Routledge Encyclopedia of Philosophy*, ed. Edward Craig, vol. 2, 750–52. London, 1998.

Culverwell, Nathaniel. "Introduction." In *An Elegant and Learned Discourse of the Light of Nature*, ed. Robert A. Greene and Hugh MacCallum. Toronto, 1971.

Darwall, Stephen. *The British Moralists and the Internal "Ought" 1640–1740*, 23–52. Cambridge, 1995.

Dockrill, D. W. "The Heritage of Patristic Platonism in Seventeenth Century English Philosophical Theology." In *The Cambridge Platonists in Philosophical Context*, ed. G. A. J. Rogers, J. M. Vienne, and Y. C. Zarka. Dordrecht, 1997.

Gewirth, Alan. "Cambridge Platonists." In *The Cambridge Dictionary of Philosophy*, ed. Robert Audi, 99–101. Cambridge, 1995.

Greene, Robert A. "Whichcote, the Candle of the Lord and Synderesis." *Journal of the History of Ideas* 51 (1991): 617–44.

AN ELEGANT AND LEARNED DISCOURSE
OF THE LIGHT OF NATURE

The Epistle Dedicatory
To the Reverend and Learned

ANTHONY TUCKNEY

D. D. Master of *Emmanuel* Colledge
In
CAMBRIDGE,
And to the *Fellows* of that Religious
and happy Foundation.

Honoured Sirs,

[5] The many testimonies of your real affection towards this pious and learned Authour, (especially while he lay under the discipline of so sad a Providence) deserve all thankful acknowledgement, and grateful commemoration: which I doubt not but himself would have made in most ample manner, had it pleased God to have granted him longer life, and farther opportunity. But since Divine Providence hath otherwayes disposed; I thought it no solecisme in friendship to undertake the Executorship of his desires, and so farre to own his debt of gratitude, as to endeavour some Publike acknowledgement of it, though the greatnesse of your benefits admit not of just recompence and satisfaction. Having therefore the disposal of his papers committed to me by his nearest and dearest friends, and finding them to be of such worth and excellency as ought not to be smothered in obscurity; I interpreted this a fit opportunity to let both your selves and others understand, how deep an impression your kindnesse to him hath left in the apprehensions and memories of those his friends, whom God and Nature had given the advantage of being more peculiarly interested in his welfare. Upon which account I do here present you with this Elegant issue of his noble and gallant abilities; which, besides the relation it hath to you by the Fathers side, would gladly intitle it self unto your acceptance and protection, as having been *conceived* in

I

your Colledge, and delivered in your Chappel; and therefore hopes that you, who with much delight were sometimes ear-*witnesses* of it, will now become its *Susceptours.*[1]

And thus having lodged it in its Mothers armes, I leave it to her embraces. On whose behalf I shall only offer up this serious and hearty wish; That as, by the blessing of heaven upon her fruitful womb, she hath been made a Mother of many profitable instruments both in Church and Common-wealth: so God would be pleased to make good her name unto her, and delight still to use her as the handmaid-instrument of his glory; that he would lay her topstone in his blessing, as her foundation was laid in his fear.

So prayes
The meanest of her sonnes,
and
Your humble servant
WILLIAM DILLINGHAM.

Aug. 10.
1652.

TO THE READER

Courteous Reader;

[6] *Not many moneths have passed since I sent abroad into the world a little Treatise, which knew it self by the name of* Spiritual Opticks, *with intention only to make some discovery of the mindes and affections of men towards pieces of that Nature; which having met somewhere (it seemes) with kinde entertainment, and acceptance beyond its expectation; hath now perswaded all its fellows into a resolution to take wing, and adventure themselves upon thy candour and ingenuity. I intend not here to hang out Ivy; nor with my Canvase to preface this cloth of gold. The work is weaved of Sunne-beams, to hang any thing before it, were but to obscure it; yet something here must needs be said for mine own discharge, and thy better satisfaction. Know therefore, (gentle Reader) that these pieces were first intended as Scholastick Exercises in a Colledge-Chappel, and therefore more properly suited to such an Auditory; yet I make no question but some of them, the* White Stone *especially, may be read with much profit, by those who are of meaner capacities, and lesse refined intellectuals. The* Discourse of the Light of Nature *(which, though here it beare the torch before the rest, is younger brother to them all) was written above six yeers ago; the designe of it was, as on the one hand to vindicate the use of Reason in matters of Religion from the aspersions and prejudices of some weaker ones in those times, who, having entertained erroneous opinions, which they were no way able to defend, were taught by their more cunning seducers to wink hard, and except against all offensive weapons: so on the other hand to chastise the sawcinesse of* Socinus *and his followers, who dare set* Hagar *above her Mistresse,*[1] *and make* Faith *waite at the elbow of corrupt & distorted* Reason; *to take off the head of that uncircumcised Philistim with his own sword, but better sharpened;*[2] *and then to lay it up behinde the Ephod in the Sanctuary.*[3] *An enterprise I confesse, of no*

3

small import; which yet he hoped, with Gods assistance, to have effected by giving unto Reason *the things that are* Reasons, *and unto* Faith *the things that are* Faiths. *And had the world been favoured with his longer life, the height of his parts, and the earnest he gave, had bespoken very ample expectations in those who knew and heard him: But it pleased God (having first melted him with his love, and then chastised him, though somewhat sharply) to take him to himself; from the contemplation of the* Light of Nature, *to the enjoyment of one* supernatural, *that* φῶς ἀπρόσιτον,[4] Light inaccessible, *which none can see and live; and to translate him from snuffing a* Candle* [7] *here, to be made partaker of the inheritance of the Saints* in Light. *So that all he finisht towards that undertaking was this* Discourse of the Light of Nature *in general, not descending so low as to shew how the Moral Law was founded in it, or that Gospel-revelation doth not extinguish it. Wherein, if, standing in the midst between two adversaries of extreme perswasions, while he opposes the one, he seeme to favour the other more than is meet; when thou shalt observe him at another time to declare as much against the other, thou wilt then be of another minde. Judge candidly, and take his opinion, as thou wouldst do his picture, sitting; not from a luxuriant expression (wherein he alwayes allowed for the shrinking) but from his declared judgement, when he speaks professedly of such a subject. For instance, if any expression seeme to lift Reason up too high; you may, if you please, otherwhere hear it confesse and bewail its own weaknesse;* [chap. 12.] *you may see it bow the head and worship, and then lay it self down quietly at the feet of* Faith; [chap. 18.] *So that if thou reade but the whole discourse, thou wilt easily perceive (as himself would often affirme) that he abhorred the very thought of advancing the power of Nature into the throne of Free-Grace, or by the light of Nature in the least measure to eclipse that of Faith.*

I would not willingly by any Prolepsis *forestall thy reading, yet if thou shouldst desire a foretast of the Authours stile, I would turne thee to the beginning of the seventeenth chapter; never was light so bespangled; never did it triumph in greater bravery of expression. But I detaine thee too long. Let this suffice thee as a course* List *to a finer* Webb; *or as waste paper to defend this* Book *from the injury of its covers.*

Farewell.

Cambr. *Aug.* 10.
1652.

Courteous READER

[8] This Discourse, which had my Brother[1] for the Author; might justly have expected me to have been the publisher: And I should think my self inexcusable, in this particular, did not the remote distance of my present abode, and the frequent avocations from study, by attendance upon my Ministery, together with the ruines of a crazy body, somewhat apologize in my behalfe.

That is obvious and πολυθρύλητον [often repeated] in every mans mouth, that the Brother should raise up seed to the Brother;[2] but here, lo a friend that is neerer then a brother, who reares up this living monument, to the memory of his deceased friend.

In this Treatise we may perceive, how the Gentiles Candle out-went us with our Sun-beams: How they guided only by the glimmering twilight of Nature, out-stript us who are surrounded with the rayes of Supernatural light, of revealed truth. Thou may'st here finde *Plato* to be a *Moses Atticissans*,[3] and *Aratus, Menander,* and *Epimenides* called into the Court, to bring in their suffrages to Saint *Pauls* Doctrine.[4]

Here we may finde Reason like a *Gibeonite* hewing wood, and drawing water for the Sanctuary:[5] *Jethro* giving counsell to *Moses*.[6] God draws us with the cords of a man; he drew profest Star-gazers with a Star to Christ. *Galen* a Physician was wrought upon, by some Anatomicall observations to tune an hymne to the praise of his Creatour, though otherwise Atheist enough.

Reason though not permitted (with an over-daring *Pompey*)[7] to rush into the Holy of Holies, yet may be allowed to be a Proselyte of the gate, and with those devote Greeks, to worship in the Court of the Gentiles.[8]

Naturall Light, or the Law written in the heart, emproved by that γνωστὸν θεοῦ[9] [which may be known of God] which is written in the book of the creature in capitall letters, so that he that runnes may read, is that which this Treatise beares witnesse to; where these Διόσκουροι [Gem-

5

ini], those heaven-borne-lights are set up in the soul of man, like those twin flames on the Marriners shroud, they presage a happy voyage to the fair Havens.

As for the bosome-secrets of God, Gospel-mysteries, the Mercy-seat it self into which the Angels desire παρακύψαι[10] [to look into], Reasons plum-line will prove too short to fathome them; here we must cry with the Apostle ὦ βάθος[11] [O the depth]! Reason may not come into these Seas, except she strike her top-saile; here we may say with *Aristotle,* at the brinke of *Euripus,* not being able to [9] give an account of the ebbes and flowes, *If I can't comprehend thee, thou shalt me.*

It is storied of *Democritus,* that he put out his eyes that he might con-template the better:[12] I do not counsel you to do so; but if you would wink with one, the eye of Reason (captivate every thought to the obedience of Christ) you might with that other of Faith, take the better aime at the marke, to obtaine the price of the high calling in Jesus Christ.[13]

Possibly an expression or two (more there are not) may seem to speak too much in Reasons behalfe; but if well examined, will prove nothing to the prejudice of free Grace: The whole scope of the book endeavouring to fil those landmarks and just bounds betwixt Religion, and Reason, which some (too superciliously brow-beating the hand-maid, and others too much magnifying her) have removed.

These exercises suit well with the place where, and the auditours to whom they were delivered, but like *Aristotles* ἀχροάσεις φυσικαί [physical lectures] these are not for vulgar eares; These Lucubrations are so elabo-rate, that they smell of the Lamp, *The Candle of the Lord.*

As concerning the Author of this Treatise, how great his parts were, and how well improved (as it may appear by this work) so they were fully known, and the losse of them sufficiently bewailed by those among whom he lived and conversed; and yet I must say of him ἀνθρώπινόν τι ἔπαθεν[14] [he suffered that which is common to man]: And as it is hard for men to be under affliction, but they are liable to censures, *Luke* 13.2, 4. so it fared with him, who was looked upon by some, as one whose eyes were lofty, and whose eye-lids lifted up;[15] who bare himself too high upon a conceit of his parts (although they that knew him intimately, are most willing to be his compurgatours[16] in this particular.) Thus prone are we to think the staffe under the water crooked, though we know it to be straight: However, turne thine eyes inward, and censure not thine own fault so severely in others. Cast not the first stone, except thou finde thy self without this fault: dare not to search too curiously into ἀνεξιχνιάστους ὅδους [the untraceable ways] of God;[17] But rather learn that lesson of the Apostles in that elegant Paranomasy, μὴ ὑπερφρονεῖν παρ᾽ ὃ δεῖ φρονεῖν, ἀλλὰ φρονεῖν εἰς τὸ σωφρονεῖν [not to think of himself more highly than he ought to think; but to think soberly]. *Rom.* 12. *v.* 3.

Thus not willing longer to detain thee from the perusall of this Discourse; I commend both thee and it to the blessing of God, and rest

From my study at
Grundisburgh in
the County of *Suffolk.*
August, 18. 1652.

Thine to serve thee in any
spirituall work, or labour
of love,
RICH. CULVERWEL.

The *Discourse of the Light of Nature*

conteines

A DISCOURSE

Of the Light of Nature.

PROVERBS 20. 27.

נד יהוה נשמת אדם   *Mens hominis lucerna Domini,*
The understanding of a man is the Candle of the Lord.
Φῶς κυρίου, πνοὴ ἀνθρήπων.   Septuag. *λύχνος κυρίου.*
Aqu. Symm.   Theod. Λαμπτὴρ κυρίου.   Sic. alii.[1]

∞ CHAPTER I ∞

The Porch, or Introduction

[13] Tis a work that requires our choycest thoughts, the exactest discussion that can be; a thing very material and desirable, to give unto *Reason* the things that are *Reasons,* and unto *Faith* the things that are *Faiths;*[2] to give *Faith* her full scope and latitude, and to give *Reason* also her just bounds and limits; this is the first-born, but the other has the blessing.[3] And yet there is not such a vast *hiatus* neither, such a *μέγα χάσμα*[4] [great gulf] between them as some would imagine: there is no such implacable antipathy, no such irreconcileable jarring between them, as some do fancy to themselves; they may very well salute one another, *ἀγίῳ φιλήματι,*[5] *osculo Pacis* [with a holy kiss, the kiss of peace]; *Reason* and *Faith* may kisse each other.[6] There is a twin-light springing from both, and they both spring from the same fountain of light, and they both sweetly conspire in the same end, the glory of that being from which they shine, & the welfare & happines of that being upon which they shine. So that to blaspheme *Reason,* 'tis to

reproach heaven it self, and to dishonour the God of *Reason,* to question the beauty of his Image, and by a strange ingratitude to slight this great and Royal gift of our Creator. For 'tis he that set up these two great Luminaries in every heavenly soul, *the Sun to rule the day, and the Moon to rule the night;*[7] and though there be some kinde of creatures that will bark at this lesser light, and others so severely critical, as that they make mountains of those spots and freckles which they see in her face; yet others know how to be thankful for her weaker beams, and will follow the least light of Gods setting up, though it be but *the Candle of the Lord.*

But some are so strangely prejudic'd against *Reason,* and that upon sufficient reason too (as they think) which yet involves a flat contradiction, as that they look upon it not as *the Candle of the Lord,* but as on some blazing Comet that portends present ruine to the Church, and to the soul, and carries a fatal and venemous influence along with it. And because the unruly head of *Socinus* and [14] his followers[8] by their meer pretences to *Reason,* have made shipwrack of *Faith,* and have been very injurious to the Gospel; therefore these weak and staggering apprehensions, are afraid of understanding any thing, and think that the very name of *Reason,* especially in a Pulpit, in matters of Religion, must needs have at least a thousand heresies couch't in it. If you do but offer to make a Syllogisme, they'l strait way cry it down for carnal reasoning. What would these men have? Would they be banisht from their own essences? Would they forfeit and renounce their understandings? Or have they any to forfeit or disclaime? would they put out this *Candle of the Lord,* intellectuals of his own lighting? or have they any to put out? would they creep into some lower species, and go a grazing with *Nebuchadnezar* among the beasts of the field?[9] or are they not there already? Or if they themselves can be willing to be so shamefully degraded, do they think that all others too are bound to follow their example? Oh, what hard thoughts have these of Religion? do they look upon it only as on a bird of prey, that comes to peck out the eyes of men? Is this all the nobility that it gives, that men by vertue of it must be beheaded presently? do's it chop off the intellectuals at one blow? Lets hear awhile what are the offences of *Reason;* are they so hainous and capital? what has it done? what lawes has it violated? whose commands has it broken? what did it ever do against the crown and dignity of heaven, or

against the peace and tranquillity of men? Why are a weak and perverse
generation, so angry and displeased with it? Is it because this daughter of
the morning is fallen from her primitive glory? from her original vigour
and perfection? Far be it from me to extenuate that great and fatal over-
throw, which the sons of men had in their first and original apostasie from
their God; that under which the whole Creation sigh's and groanes:[10] but
this we are sure, it did not annihilate the soul, it did not destroy the essence, the powers and faculties, nor the operations of the soul; though it
did defile them, and disorder them, and every way indispose them.

Well then, because the eye of *Reason* is weakened, and vitiated, will they
therefore pluck it out immediately? and must *Leah* be hated upon no other
account, but because she is blear-ey'd?[11] The whole head is wounded, and
akes, and is there no other way but to cut it off? *The Candle of the Lord*
do's not shine so clearly as it was wont, must it therfore be extinguisht
presently? is it not better to enjoy the faint and languishing light of this
Candle of the Lord, rather then to be in palpable and disconsolate darknesse? There are indeed but a few seminal sparks left in the ashes, and must
there be whole floods of water cast on them to quench them? 'Tis but an
old imperfect Manuscript, with some broken periods, some letters worn
out, must they therefore with an unmerciful indignation rend it and tear
it asunder? 'Tis granted that the picture has lost its glosse and beauty, the
oriency of its colours, the elegancy of its lineaments, the [15] comelinesse of
its proportion; must it therefore be totally defac'd? must it be made one
great blot? and must the very frame of it be broken in pieces? Would you
perswade the Lutanist to cut all his strings in sunder, because they are out
of tune? and will you break the Bowe upon no other account, but because
it's unbended? because men have not so much of *Reason* as they should,
will they therefore resolve to have none at all? will you throw away your
gold, because it's mixt with drosse? Thy very being that's imperfect too,
thy graces, they are imperfect, wilt thou refuse these also? And then consider, that the very apprehending the weaknes of *Reason,* even this in some
measure comes from *Reason. Reason,* when awaken'd, it feels her own
wounds, it hears her own jarrings, she sees the dimnesse of her own sight.
'Tis a glasse that discovers its own spots, and must it therefore be broke in
peices? *Reason* her self has made many sad complaints unto you; she has

told you often, and that with teares in her eyes, what a great shipwrack she has suffered, what goods she has lost, how hardly she escaped with a poor decayed being; she has shewn you often some broken reliques as the sad remembrancers of her former ruines; she told you how that when she swam for her life, she had nothing but two or three Jewels about her, two or three common notions; and would you rob her of them also? is this all your tendernesse and compassion? Is this your kindness to your friend? will you trample upon her now she is so low? Is this a sufficient cause to give her a Bill of divorcement,[12] because she has lost her former beauty and fruitfulnesse?

Or is *Reason* thus offensive to them, because she cannot grasp and comprehend the things of God? Vain men, will they pluck out their eyes because they cannot look upon the Sun in his brightnesse and glory? What though *Reason* cannot reach to the depths, to the bottomes of the Ocean, may it not therefore swim and hold up the head as well as it can? What though it cannot enter into the *Sanctum Sanctorum,* and pierce within the Veile; may it not notwithstanding lie in the Porch, *at the gate of the Temple called beautiful, and be a door-keeper in the house of its God?*[13] Its wings are clipt indeed, it cannot flie so high as it might have done, it cannot flie so swiftly, so strongly as once it could, will they not therefore allow it to move, to stirre, to flutter up and down as well as it can? the turrets and pinacles of the stately structure are fallen, will they therefore demolish the whole fabrick, and shake the very foundations of it? and down with it to the ground? though it be not a *Jacobs* ladder to climbe up to heaven by, yet may they not use it as a staffe to walk upon earth withall? and then *Reason* it self knows this also and acknowledges, that 'tis dazled with the Majesty and glory of God; that it cannot pierce into his mysterious and unsearchable wayes; it never was so vain as to go about to measure immensity by its own finite Compasse, or to span out absolute eternity by its own more imperfect duration. True *Reason* did never go about to comprize the Bible in its own Nutshel. And if [16] *Reason be content* with its own sphere, why should it not have the liberty of its proper motion?

Is it because it opposes the things of God, and wrangles against the mysteries of salvation, is it therefore excluded? An heinous and frequent accusation indeed, but nothing more false and injurious; and if it had been an open enemy that had done her this wrong, why then she could have born it; but it's thou her friend and companion, ye have took sweet counsel together, and have entred into the house of God as friends,[14] 'tis you that have your dependance upon her; that cannot speak one word to purpose against her, without her help and assistance. What mean you thus to revile your most intimate and inseparable self? why do you thus slander your own beings? would you have all this to be true which you say? Name but the time if you can, when ever right *Reason* did oppose one jot or *apex* of the word of God. Certainly, these men speak of distorted *Reason* all this while. Surely they do not speak of *the Candle of the Lord*, but of some shadow and appearance of it. But if they tell us that all *Reason* is distorted, whether then is theirs so, in telling us so? if they say that they do not know this by *Reason*, but by the Word of God; whether then is their *Reason*, when it acknowledges the Word of God? whether is it then distorted, or no? Besides, if there were no right *Reason* in the world, what difference between sobriety and madnesse, between these men and wiser ones? how then were the heathen left without excuse,[15] who had nothing to see by but this *Candle of the Lord?* and how do's this thrust men below sensitive creatures, for better have no *Reason* at all, then such as do's perpetually deceive them, and delude them.

Or do's *Reason* thus displease them, because the blackest Errours sometimes come under the fair disguise of so beautiful a name, and have some tincture of *Reason* in them? But truly this is so farre from being a disparagement to *Reason,* as that 'tis no small commendation of it, for πρόσωπον χρὴ θέμεν τηλαυγὲς,[16] Men love to put a plausible title, a winning frontispiece upon the foulest Errours. Thus licentiousnesse would faine be called by the name of liberty, and all dissolutenesse would faine be countenanced and secured under the Patronage and protection of free-grace. Thus wickednesse would willingly forget its own name, and adopt it self into the family of goodnesse. Thus *Arminianisme* pleads for it self under the specious notion of Gods love to mankinde.[17] Thus that silly Errour of *Antinomianisme* will needs stile it self an *Evangelical Honey-comb.* Thus all irregularities and anomalies in Church affairs must pride themselves in those glittering titles of a *New Light, A Gospel way, An Heaven upon Earth.*[18] No wonder then that some also pretend to *Reason,* who yet run out of it, and beyond it, and besides it; but must none therefore come near it? because *Socinus* has burnt his wings at this *Candle of the Lord,* must none therefore make use of it?

May he not be conquer'd with his own weapons, and beat out of his own [17] strong holds? and may not the head of an uncircumcised Philistine be cut off with his own sword?[19]

Or lastly, are they thus afraid of *Reason,* because by vertue of this, men of wit and subtilty will presently argue and dispute them into an Errour, so as that they shall not be able to disintangle a truth, though in it self it be never so plaine and unquestionable? But first, *Reason* it self tells them that it may be thus, and so prepares and fortifies them against such a tryal; and then, this only shews that some mens *Reason* is not so well advanc'd and improv'd, either as it might be, or as others is; a sharper edge would quickly cut such difficulties asunder. Some have more refined and clarifi'd intellectuals, more vigorous and sparkling eyes then others, and one soul differs from another in glory; and that reason which can make some shift to maintain Errour, might with a great deal lesse sweat and pains maintain a truth.

There's no question but that *Bellarmin,*[20] and the rest of the learned Papists could have if they had pleased, far more easily defended the Protestant Religion then that of their own. Besides, the vigour and triumph of *Reason* is principally to be seen in those first-born beames, those pure and unspotted irradiations that shine from it; I mean those first bublings up of common principles that are own'd and acknowledg'd by all; and those evident, and kindly derivations that flow from them. *Reason* shews her face more amiably and pleasantly in a pure and cleare streame, then in those mudded and troubled waters, in which the Schoolmen (that have leasure enough) are always fishing. Nay, some of their works are like so many raging seas, full of perpetual tossings, and disquietings, and foamings, and sometimes casting up mire and dirt;[21] and yet these vast and voluminous *Leviathans* love to sport therein, and that which is most intolerable, these grand σοφοì [wise men], that seem'd so zealous for *Reason,* at length in expresse termes disclaime it; and in a most blindfold and confused manner, cry up their great *Diana,*[22] their Idol of Transubstantiation; and the Lutherans are very fierce against *Reason* too, much upon the same account, because it would never allow of that other monstrous and misshapen lump of Consubstantiation.

But why have I all this while beaten the air, and spilt words upon the ground? why do I speak to such as are incurable and incapable? for if we speak *Reason* to them, that's that which they so much disclaim: if we do not speak *Reason* to them, that were to disclaime it too.

But I speak to men, to Christians, to the friends of learning, to the professors of *Reason:* to such as put this Candle of the Lord into a golden Candlestick, and poure continual Oile into it. Yet lest any among you Athenians, should erect an Altar to an unknown God;[23] lest you should ignorantly worship him, we will declare him to you.

[18] And that which we have now said may serve as a Porch and preamble, to what we shall speak hereafter out of these words.

Where we shall see

1. How *The understanding of a man is the Candle of the Lord.*

2. What this *Candle of the Lord* discovers; where we shall finde

1. That all the Moral Law is founded in natural and common light, in the light of *Reason.*

2. That there's nothing in the mysteries of the Gospel contrary to the light of *Reason;* nothing repugnant to this light that shines from *the Candle of the Lord.* [24]

CHAPTER 2

The Explication of the Words

[19] Now as for the words themselves, we cannot better judge of the fitnesse of this expression, then by considering who it was that spoke it.

Now these words were spoke by him that had a large portion of intellectuals, one that was ἔξοχος ἀνθρώπων κεφαλῇ[1] [an intellectual superior among men], they were spoken by *Solomon* in whom *the Candle of the Lord* did shine very clearly; one that had ask'd this as the choisest favour that he could expect from the bounty of heaven; to have a glorious lamp of knowledge shine in his soul for the enlightning of it. And though the envious Jews would fain perswade the world that he lighted his candle at hell it self, for they esteemed him no better then a Magician; as they esteemed him also that was greater then *Solomon;* yet we know very well, that *Solomons* was a purer Candle then to be lighted at a Lake of fire and brimstone; 'twas not of Lucifers setting up, but it came from the Father of lights,[2] 'twas lighted with Sun-beams from heaven.

And 'tis a modest and humble expression in him to call his understanding *the Candle of the Lord,* when as the world look'd upon him as a star of the first magnitude, nay as a Sun shining in the firmament, gilding the world with knowledge, scattering beams of light, sparkling out in wise and proverbial sayings, so that the bordering Princes and Nations are ready to adore such an orient light; and the Queen of the South thinks it no small happinesse to sit under the shadow of it. But yet to be sensible of his own narrow sphere, of his own finite compasse and influence, did not at all take from his lustre, but did rather set it off, and adde to his glory.

Thus that wise man among the Heathen *Socrates* did so farre complain of the weaknesse of his candle-light, as that he tels us his lamp would shew him nothing but his own darknesse. And though a wiser then *Socrates* be

17

here, yet he is much in the same measure sensible of the dimnesse of his own intellectuals. And yet he was one that had made many discoveries with this *Candle of the Lord,* he had searcht into the mines, and several veins of knowledge; he had searcht into the hid treasures of wisdom, he had searcht into the depth of State-affairs, he had searched into the bowels of natural causes, into the *Magnalia & Mysteria* [mighty things and mysteries] of Nature; as if among many other wives he had espoused *Nature* also to himself, he had searcht into [20] the several tempers and intellectual complexions of men; he had searcht long enough with this *Candle of the Lord,* to see if he could finde any good under the Sun, he went with his *Candle* to finde out a *summum bonum;* he searcht into all the corners of being; and at length being sufficiently wearied, you may see him sitting down; you may hear him complaining that he had but spent and wasted *the Candle of the Lord* in vaine; for so much is implyed in רעוח רוה[3] [feeding on wind], this was but *depastio spiritus* [vexation of spirit], as he himself calls it.[4]

Yet he was one that shewed others how they might make better improvement of their intellectual lamp; and this was his wisest advice that he gave upon his most mature and concocted thoughts, this was *tanquam mox emoriturae lucernae supremus fulgor* [the final gleam of a dying light]: that men would only follow this *Candle of the Lord,* as it directs them in the wayes of God, which are wayes of sweetnesse and pleasantnesse,[5] for this was נל האדם[6] [the whole duty of man] the very end why God set up such a light in the soul, that it might search out his Creatour with it.

And as for the minde of the words, though one would think they were very clear, and shining with their own light, yet interpreters are pleased to cloud them, to turn light it self into a *Chaos,* and to cast darknesse upon the face of the Text; like some unskilful ones, while they go about to snuff the Candle, they put it out, but we'l try whether it can be blown in again.

We shall reduce their several meanings to these three heads.

1. Some would have it thus. *The Candle of the Lord is in the understanding of a man,* as if the words did run thus, בנשמח אדם נר יחוח *Lucerna Domini in mente hominis,*[7] that is, God with his Candle discovers the very thoughts and intentions of men, he searches into every corner of the heart; he has *lucernam in corde* [a light in the heart], he spies out every Atome, he perceives the first starting of a motion, the first peeping out of a thought, but this, though it be very true, yet is nothing to the purpose here.

2. Some glosse upon the words thus, the understanding of man when 'tis enlightned with supernatural knowledge, is then *the Candle of the Lord:* but these do rather dictate to *Solomon,* and tell him what they would have him say; they do rather frame and fashion a Proverb to themselves, then explain his meaning: and these are they that are afraid to give natural light, and natural reason their due. But

3. I shall fully agree with them that take this for the proper and genuine meaning of the place, that God hath breathed into all the sons of men Reasonable souls which may serve as so many Candles to enlighten and direct them in the searching out their Creatour, in the discovering of other inferiour beings, and themselves also; and this is that which is here implyed by נשמח אדם [the understanding of a man], that same *spiraculum vitae*[8] [breath of life], nay that [21] same immortal breath, that same rational breath quickened by God himself, and flowing from him as a pure derivation from his own being, and thus the Hebr. Doctors do still look upon this word נשמח [breath], as that which does expresse τὸν νοῦν *animam rationis participem*[9] [the rational soul, the soul sharing reason], and (as they observe) it has a plain vicinity with שמים[10] [heaven], but to be sure the being is derived from thence whether the word be or no. So then נשמח [breath] it points out the supreme region, the very top and flower of a reasonable soul, τὴν τῆς Ψυχῆς κορυφήν; as נפש [soul] does speak nothing but the dregs and bottome of it, the inferiour and sensitive soul.[11] The Apostle *Paul* in his learned speech to the Athenians mentions them both, and calls them very significantly, ζωὴν καὶ πνοήν[12] [life and breath], and so some also take that other place of the Apostle in that accurate discourse of his to the Corinthians,[13] that which he calls Ψυχὴν ζῶσαν [living soul], they call it היח נפש [living soul], and that which he termes πνεῦμα ζωοποιοῦν [quickening spirit], they render it נשמח חיים [breath of life], though it be true also that sometimes they take the word נפש [soul] in a more generical sense, for thus they tell us, there are in man 3 נשמוח[14] [souls]. (1) הצמוחה the vegetable soul, a soul in the bud, the very blossome and flower of life. (2) הנהמיח *anima bruti* [the animal soul], a soul looking out at the window of sense. (3) החנמח נפש a soul sparkling and glittering with intellectuals, a soul crowned with light, and this is the same with נשמח [breath]. Now as for that other word רוח[15] [spirit] though sometimes the minde of man his intellectual part be exprest by it, yet the word in its own

nature is a great deal more large and comprehensive, and as it extends to some material beings, so it reaches to all spirituals; hence רוח יהוה רוח הקוש [the spirit of God: the spirit of holiness], and the Angels both good and bad frequently come under this name, but when 'tis put for the minde and spirit of man, yet I finde it very well differenced from נשמה [breath] for רוח [spirit] doth properly import *impetum animi, motum mentis,* the vigour and energy of the soul, τὸν θυμὸν [vitality], rather then τὸν νοῦν[16] [the mind], and the Hebrew Doctors are pleased to tell us the several situations of these, רוח they say is *in corde* [in the heart], נשמה *in cerebro* [in the brain], נפש *in hepate*[17] [in the liver]. Now though I know that some places in the New Testament which speak of soul and spirit meet with this interpretation, that spirit there is the purest eminency, the most refined part of the soul; yet this is not at all prejudicial to what we now speak of; for first, they may take it for the regenerate part of the soul, that which the Apostle cals the new creature;[18] or else (2) suppose it be spoke of the soul in its natural condition, 'tis worth the considering then whether it would not be better rendered by נשמה [breath] then רוח [spirit], as נשמה here[19] is rendered the spirit of a man; but (3) grant that רוח be more answerable to it, and that רוח should have the worth and precedency of נשמה which yet will scarce ever be shewn or explained; [22] yet this is very sure and unquestionable, that נשמה does very properly speak a reasonable soul, and that the more peculiarly, because when *Moses* speaks of that very moment when 'twas created, and breathed into man, he calls it נשמח חיים[20] [the breath of life] and the Arab. interpreter keeps as close to the words, as so vast a Dialect will give leave, and stiles it נסמח אלחיאה *halitus vitae*[21] [the breath of life]. And 'tis somewhat worth the wond'ring at that that learned interpreter of *Genesis,*[22] who is so well verst in Rabbinical writings should yet expound that of the sensitive; but they run as far into the other extreme that would understand נשמה of a soul advanc'd above it self by supernatural principles, and I think this sense will scarce be owned by any that can construe Hebrew.

So then, these words are a brief commendation of natural Light, of the Light of *Reason.* For the farther clearing of which we must enquire. (1) What *Nature* is. (2) What the *Law* of Nature is. (3) What the *Light* of Nature is.

CHAPTER 3

What Nature Is

[23] The words being to be understood of *Lumen Naturale* [natural light], according to the mindes of the best and most interpreters; it will be very needful to enquire what *Nature* is, and here we will be sure not to speak one word for *Nature,* which shall in the least measure tend to the eclipsing of *Grace;* nay, nothing but what shall make for the greater brightening and amplifying of the free Grace and distinguishing goodnesse of God in Christ; and nothing but what an *Augustin,* or a *Bradwardin*[1] those great Patrons of Grace would willingly set their seals unto.

Well then, as for *Nature,* though it be not far from any one of us, though it be so intimate to our very beings; though it be printed and engraved upon our essences, and not upon ours only, but upon the whole Creation; and though we put all the letters and Characters of it together as well as we can, yet we shall finde it hard enough, to spell it out, and read what it is; for as it is in corporeal vision, the too much approximation and vicinity of an object do's stop up and hinder sight, so 'tis also many times in Intellectual Opticks; we see something better at a distance; the soul cannot so easily see its own face, nor so fully explain its own nature. We need some Scholiast or Interpreter, to comment upon our own beings, and to acquaint us with our own Idiomes; and I meet with many Authors that speak of the light of *Nature,* but I can scarce finde one that tells us what it is. Those famous and learned *Triumviri;*[2] SELDEN, that has made it his work to write *De Jure Naturali;* and *Grotius* that has said somewhat of it in his book *De Jure Belli & Pacis:* and *Salmasius* that has toucht it in his late Treatise *De Coma,* and in his little Dialogue subordinate to it, in either of which, if he had pleased, he might have described it without a digression; yet none of these (as far as I can finde) give us the least adumbration of it; which notwithstanding was the rather to be expected from them, because the Philosophers had left it in such a cloudy and obscured manner, as if they had never seen *Nature* face to face, but only through a glasse darkly, and in a riddle. And as we reade of a Painter that represented *Nature* appearing to *Aristotle* with a veile and mask upon her face; so truly *Aristotle* himself painted her as he saw her, with her veile on, for he shews her only wrapt up and muffled in matter and forme, whereas methinks he that could set Intelligences to the wheele to spin out time and [24] motion, should have allowed them also some natural ability for performing so famous a task and imployment, which his head set them about. And truly why Angelical beings should be banished from the Common-wealth of *Nature;* nay, why they should not properly belong to Physicks as well as other particular beings; or why bodies only should engrosse and monopolize natural Philosophy, and why a soul cannot be admitted into it, unlesse it bring a certificate and *commendamus* from the body, is a thing altogether unaccountable, unlesse it be resolved into a meer Arbitrary determination, and a Philosophical kinde of Tyranny.

And yet *Aristotles* description of *Nature*[3] has been held very sacred, and some of the Schoolmen do even dote upon it. *Aquinas* tells us in plain termes, *Deridendi sunt, qui volunt Aristotelis definitionem corrigere*[4] [those who desire to correct Aristotle's definition should be laughed at]. The truth is, I make no question but that *Aristotles* definition is very commensurate to what he meant by *Nature;* but that he had the true and adaequate notion of *Nature,* this I think *Aquinas* himself can scarce prove; and I would fain have him to explain what it is for a thing *innotescere lumine Naturae*[5] [to become known by the light of nature], if *Nature* be only *principium motus & quietis* [the origin of motion and rest]. Yet *Plutarch* also in this point seems to compromise with *Aristotle,* and after a good, specious and hopeful Preface, where he saies that he must needs tell us what *Nature* is, after all this preparation he does most palpably restrain it to corporeal beings, and then votes it to be ἀρχὴ κινήσεως, καὶ ἐρημίας[6] [the origin of motion and the absence of it]. And *Empedocles,* (as he is quoted by him) will needs exercise his Poetry and make some Verses upon *Nature,* and you would think at the first dash that they were in a good lofty straine, for thus

he sings—φύσις οὐδενὸς ἐστὶν ἑκάστου, θνητῶν οὐδὲ τὶς οὐλομένη θα-
νάτοιο γενέθλη.⁷ 'Twas not of a mortal withering off-spring, nor of a fading Genealogy; but yet truly his Poetical raptures were not so high as to
elevate him above a body, for he presently sinks into ὕλη, he falls down
into matter, and makes *Nature* nothing else but that which is ingenerable
and incorruptible in material beings; just as the Peripateticks speak of their
materia prima. But *Plato* who was more spiritual in his Philosophy, chides
some of his contemporaries, and is extreamly displeased with them, and
that very justly, for they were degenerated into a most stupid Atheisme,
and resolved all beings into one of these three Originals, that they were
either διὰ φύσιν, διὰ τύχην, διὰ τέχνην.⁸ They were either the workmanship of *Nature,* or of *Fortune,* or of *Art.* Now as for the first and chief corporeal beings, they made them the productions of *Nature,* that is, (say
they) they sprung from eternity into being by their own *impetus,* and by
their own vertue and efficacy, ἀπὸ τινὸς αἰτίας αὐτομάτης,⁹ like so many
natural *automata,* they were the principles of their own being and motion,
and this they [25] laid down for one of their axiomes. Τὰ μὲν μέγιστα καὶ
κάλλιστα ἀπεργάζεσθαι φύσιν, καὶ τυχὴν τὰ δὲ σμικρότερα τέχνην.¹⁰ All
the Master-pieces of being, the most lovely and beautiful pictures were
drawn by *Nature,* and *Fortune;* and *Art* only could reach to some poor rudiments, to some shadows, and weaker imitations, which you will be
somewhat amazed at when you hear by and by what these τὰ σμικρότερα
[weaker imitations] were.

The foundation of being, that they said was *Natural;* the mutation and
disposing of being, that they made the imployment of *Fortune;* and then
they said the work of Art was to finde out Laws, and Morality, and Religion, and a Deity; these were the τὰ σμικρότερα [weaker imitations] they
spake of before.

But that Divine Philosopher does most admirably discover the prodigious folly of this opinion, and demonstrate the impossibility of it in that
excellent discourse of his, in his 10 *De Legibus.* Where he does most clearly
and convincingly shew, that those things, which they say were framed by
Art; were in duration infinitely before that which they call *Nature,* that
Ψυχὴ ἐστι πρεσβυτέρα σώματος:¹¹ that spirituals have the seniority of
corporeals. This he makes to appear by their (1) πρωτοκινησία (2) αὐτο-

κινησία (3) ἀλλοκινησία, for these three though they be not expressely
mentioned in him, yet they may very easily be collected from him.[12] Souls
they move themselves, and they move bodies too, and therefore must
needs be first in motion; so that νοῦς, καὶ τέχνη, καὶ νόμος τῶν σκληρῶν,
καὶ μαλακῶν, καὶ βαρέων καὶ κουφῶν πρότερα ἂν εἴη.[13] Reason and Religion, Laws and Prudence must needs be before density and rarity, before
gravity & levity, before all conditions and dimensions of bodies. And Laws
and Religion they are indeed τοῦ νοῦ γεννήματα[14] [the products of the
mind]; that is, the contrivances and productions of that eternal νοῦς &
λόγος [Mind and Reason] the wisdome of God himself.

So that all that *Plato* will allow to *Nature,* amounts to no more then
this, that it is not δημιουργὸς[15] *opifex rerum* [the creator of things], but
only *Dei* δημιουργοῦντος *famula & ministra* [the handmaid and servant of
the creating God]; *As the eyes of a servant wait upon his master, and as the
eyes of an handmaiden look up to her mistris, so wait her eyes upon the Lord
her God.*[16] And he doth fully resolve and determine that God is the soul of
the world, and *Nature* but the body; which must be took only *in sensu
florido,* in a flourishing and Rhetorical sense: that God is the fountain of
being, and *Nature* but the chanel; that he is the kernel of being, and *Nature* but the shell. Yet herein *Plato* was defective, that he did not correct
and reform the abuse of this word *Nature;* that he did not scrue it up to
an higher and more spiritual notion. For 'tis very agreeable to the choycest,
and supremest being; and the Apostle tells us of ἡ θεῖα φύσις[17] [the divine
nature]. So that 'tis time at length to draw the veile from *Natures* face, and
to look upon her beauty.

[26] And first, 'tis the usual language of many, both Philosophers and
others, to put *Nature* for God himself, or at least for the general providence of God; and this in the Schoolmens rough and unpolisht Latin, is
stiled *Natura naturans;*[18] thus *Nature* is took for that constant and Catholick Providence, that spreads its wings over all created beings, and shrouds
them under its warme and happy protection. Thus that elegant Moralist
Plutarch speaks more like to himself then in his former description. Πανταχοῦ γὰρ ἡ φύσις ἀκριβής, καὶ φιλότεχνος, ἀνελλιπὴς καὶ ἀπερίτμητος;[19]
Nature is in all things accurate and punctual, 'tis not defective nor parsi-
monious, nor yet sprouting and luxuriant: and consonant to this is

that sure axiome, *Natura nihil facit frustra*[20] [nature does nothing in vain]. Thus God set up the world as a fair and goodly clock, to strike in time, and to move in an orderly manner, not by its own weights (as *Durand* would have it)[21] but by fresh influence from himself, by that inward and intimate spring of immediate concourse, that should supply it in a most uniform and proportionable manner.

Thus God framed this great Organ of the world, he tuned it, yet not so as that it could play upon it self, or make any musick by vertue of this general composure, (as *Durand* fansies it) but that it might be fitted and prepared for the finger of God himself, and at the presence of his powerful touch might sound forth the praise of its Creatour in a most sweet and harmonious manner.

And thus *Nature* is that regular line,[22] which the wisdome of God himself has drawn in being, τάξις γὰρ ἢ τάξεως ἔργον ἡ φύσις[23] [for nature is order or a work of order], as he speaks, whereas that which they miscall'd Fortune, was nothing but a line fuller of windings and varieties; and as *Nature* was a fixt and ordinary kinde of Providence, so *Fortune* was nothing but a more abstruse, and mysterious, and occult kinde of Providence, and therefore *Fortune* was not blinde, as they falsely painted and represented her; but they themselves were blinde and could not see into her. And in this sense that speech of that grave Moralist *Seneca* is very remarkable, *Providentia, fatum, natura, casus, fortuna sunt ejusdem Dei varia nomina*[24] [providence, fate, nature, chance, fortune are various terms for the same God].

But then secondly, *Nature* as 'tis scattered and distributed in particular beings, so 'tis the very same with essence it self, and therefore spirituals, as they have their essence, so they have their *Nature* too, and if we gloried in names, 'twould be easie to heap up a multitude of testimonies in which these two must needs be ἰσοδυναμοῦντα [synonymous].

And thus *Nature* speaks these two things.

1) It points out *Originem entis* [the origin of being], 'tis the very *Genius* of Entity, 'tis present at the nativity of every being, nay 'tis being it self. There is no moment in which you can imagine a thing to be, and yet to be without its *Nature*.

[27] 2) It speaks *Operationem entis* [the action of being], and 'tis a principle of working in spirituals, as well as *principium motus & quietis* [the

origin of motion and rest] in corporeals. All essence bubbles out, flows forth, and paraphrases upon it self in operations. Hence it is that such workings as are facilitated by custome, are esteemed *natural*. Hence that known speech of *Galen*, Ἐπίκτητοι φύσεις τὰ ἔθη;[25] Customes are frequently adopted and ingraffed into *Nature*. Hence also our usual Idiom calls a good disposition a good nature. Thus the Moralists expresse Vertues or Vices that are deeply rooted, by this terme πεφυσιωμένα[26] [naturalized].

And so some, and *Grotius* amongst the rest, would understand that place of the Apostle, *Does not even Nature it self teach you*, of a general custome:[27] but that word Αὔτη ἡ φύσις [nature itself] does plainly refuse that interpretation; and the learned *Salmasius* does both grant and evince, that it cannot be meant of custome there.[28] And thus having seen what *Nature* is, 'twill be very easie in the next place to tell you what the Law of *Nature* is.

Of the Nature of a Law in General

[28] Before we can represent unto you the *Law* of *Nature,* you must first frame and fashion in your mindes the just notion of a *Law in general.* And *Aquinas* gives us this shadowy representation of it; *Lex est quaedam regula & mensura, secundum quam inducitur aliquis ad agendum, vel ab agendo retrahitur*[1] [law is a certain rule and measure, according to which any agent is led to act, or restrained from acting]. But *Suarez* is offended with the latitude of this definition, and esteems it too spreading and comprehensive, as that which extends to all *Naturals,* I, and to Artificials too; for they have *regulas & mensuras operationum* [rules and measures of their operations]; Thus God has set a Law to the waves, and a Law to the windes; nay, thus clocks have their lawes, and Lutes have their Lawes, and whatsoever has the least appearance of motion, has some rule proportionable to it. Whereas these workings were always reckoned to be at the most but *inclinationes, & pondera* [tendencies and gravitations], and not the fruits of a legislative power. But yet the Apostle *Paul,* to staine the pride of them that gloried in the Law, calls such things by the name of Law as were most odious and anomalous. Thus he tells us of Νόμος θανάτου, & Νόμος ἁμαρτίας[2] [the law of death and the law of sin], though sin be properly ἀνομία [lawless]: Thus he mentions *Legem membrorum*[3] [the law of members], the same which the Schoolmen call *Legem fomitis*[4] [the law of passion].

And yet this is sure, that a rational creature is only capable of a Law, which is a moral restraint, and so cannot reach to those things that are necessitated to act *ad extremum virium*[5] [to the limit of their powers].

And therefore *Suarez* does give us a more refined description, when he

tells us that *Lex est mensura quaedam actuum moralium, ita ut per confor-
mitatem ad illam, Rectitudinem moralem habeant, & si ab illa discordent,
obliqui sint*[6] [law is a certain measure of moral acts, such that by conformity to it, they are judged morally right, by disagreement with it, morally
wrong]. A Law is such a just and regular tuning of Actions, as that by vertue of this they may conspire into a moral musick, and become very pleasant and harmonious. Thus *Plato* speaks much of that Εὐρυθμία &
συμφωνία [melody and harmony] that is in Lawes, and in his second book
De Leg.[7] he does altogether discourse of harmony, and does infinitely prefer mental and intellectual musick, those powerful and prac[29]tical strains
of goodnesse, that spring from a well-composed spirit, before those delicious blandishments, those soft and transient touches that comply with
sense, and salute it in a more flattering manner; and he tells you of a spiritual dancing that is answerable to so sweet a musick, to these τὰ θείοτατα
αὐλήματα[8] [most divine flutings]. Whilest the Lawes play in consort, there
is a Chorus of well ordered affections that are raised and elevated by them.

And thus as *Aristotle* well observes, some Lawes were wont to be put in
verse, and to be sung like so many pleasant odes, that might even charme
the people into obedience.

'Tis true, that learned Philosopher gives this reason of it, they were put
into verse, ὅπως μὴ ἐπιλάθωνται,[9] that they might remember them the
better: but why may not this reason also share with it, that they might
come with a greater grace and allurement, that they might hear them as
pleasantly as they would do the voice of a Viall or an Harp, that has Rhe-
torick enough to still and quiet the evil spirit? But yet this does not sufficiently paint out the being of a Law, to say that 'tis only *regula & mensura*
[rule and measure]; and *Suarez* himself is so ingenuous as to tell us that he
cannot rest satisfied with this description, which he drew but with a coale
as a rudiment rather then a full portraiture; and therefore we'll give him
some time to perfect it, and to put it into more orient colours.

And in the meane time we'll look upon that speculative Law-giver,
Plato I mean, who was alwayes new modelling of Lawes, and rolling Political Ideas in his minde.

Now you may see him gradually ascending and climbing up to the description of a law, by these four several steps, & yet he does not reach the

top & ἀκμὴ of it neither. First, he tells us that Lawes are τὰ Νομιζόμενα,[10] such things as are esteemed fitting; but because this might extend to all kinde of customes too, his second thoughts limit and contract it more, and tell us that a Law is Δόγμα πόλεως, *Decretum civitatis* [the decree of a state], yet because the masse and bulk of people, the rude heap and undigested lump of the multitude may seek to establish τὸ Δόγμα πονηρὸν [a wicked decree], as he calls it; therefore he bethinks himself how to clarifie a Law, how to purge out the drosse from it, and tells us in the next place, that it is τοῦ ὄντος ἐξεύρεσις, *inventio ejus quod vere est* [the discovery of what truly is], where it is very remarkable what this Philosopher means by τὸ ὂν [being], by which he is wont usually to point out a Deity, which is stiled by *Aristotle* ὂν ὄντων[11] [the Being of beings], but it is not capable of this sense here, for thus Lawes are not τοῦ ὄντος ἐξευρήσεις [discoveries of the Deity], but rather τοῦ ὄντος εὑρήματα [discoveries by the Deity]. *Lex est inventio, vel donum Dei* [law is the discovery or gift of God], as the Oratour speaks.[12] Τὸ ὂν [being] therefore in this place speaks these two particulars. (1) Τὸ ὀρθόν [right], for all rectitude has a being, and flows from [30] the fountain of being, whereas obliquities and irregularities are meere privations, and non-entities; and 'tis a notable speech of *Plato,* τὸ μὲν ὀρθὸν νόμος ἐστὶ Βασιλικὸς[13] [the right is a royal law], the very same expression which the Apostle gives to the Law of God, when he calls it the royal Law.[14] (2) Τὸ ὂν [being] implyes τὸ χρηστὸν [the useful], every thing that is profitable has a being in it, but you can gather no fruit from a privation; there is no sweetnesse in an obliquity, and therefore a Law is an wholsome mixture of that that is just and profitable, and this is τέλος τοῦ νόμου [the end of a law], as *Plutarch* speaks.[15] Whereas *turpe praeceptum non est lex, sed iniquitas*[16] [a wicked rule is not a law, but an injustice], for obligation that's the very forme and essence of a Law; Now every Law *obligat in Nomine Dei* [binds in the name of God];[17] but so glorious a name did never binde to any thing that was wicked and unequal. πᾶν δίκαιον ἡδὺ, & πᾶν δίκαιον ὠφέλιμον[18] [all justice is sweet, all justice is beneficial], and that only is countenanc'd from heaven. The golden chain of Lawes, 'tis tied to the chair of *Jupiter,*[19] and a command is only vigorous as it issues out, either immediately or remotely, from the great Sovereigne of the world. So that τὸ ὂν [being] is the sure bottome and foundation of every

Law. But then because he had not yet exprest who were the competent searchers out of this τὸ ὂν [being], therefore he tells you in the last place that Laws are πολιτικὰ συγγράμματα²⁰ [political ordinances], which he clears by other things; for ἰατρικὰ συγγράματα [medical ordinances], are ἰατρικοὶ νόμοι [medical laws], & γεωμετρικὰ συγγράμματα [geometrical ordinances] are γεωμετρικοὶ νόμοι [geometrical laws]. And he resolves it into this, that in all true kinds of government there is some supreme power derived from God himself, and fit to contrive Laws and Constitutions agreeable to the welfare and happinesse of those that are to be subject to them; and οἱ κρείττονες²¹ [the better men] (as he speaks) are the fittest makers of Lawes.

Yet you must take notice here of these two things. (1) That he did not lay stresse enough upon that binding vertue, which is the very sinew, nay the life and soul of a Law. (2) That these three descriptions τὰ νομιζόμενα, δόγμα πόλεως, πολιτικὰ συγγράμματα [things esteemed fitting, a decree of the state, political ordinances] intend only humane Lawes, and so are not boild up to the purer notion of a Law in general.

And though that same other branch τοῦ ὄντος ἐξεύρεσις [the discovery of what truly is] may seem to reach farther yet, 'tis too obscure, too much in the clouds to give a cleer manifestation of the nature of a Law. And yet *Aristotle* does not in this supply *Platoes* defects, but seems rather to paraphrase upon these descriptions of humane Lawes, and tells in more enlarged language, that ὁ νόμος ἐστὶν ὁ λόγος ὡρισμένος καθ' ὁμολογίαν κοιὴν πόλεως, μηνύων πῶς δεῖ πράττειν ἕκαστα²² [law is a decree determined by the agreement of the state, [31] indicating in what way each thing ought to be done]. Where yet he cannot possibly mean that every *individuum* should give his suffrage, but certainly the representative consent of the whole will content him.

But I see these ancient Philosophers are not so well furnisht, but that we must return to the Schoolmen again, who by this time have lickt their former descriptions into a more comely forme. We will look upon *Aquinas* his first.

Lex (saies he) *est ordinatio rationis ad bonum commune ab eo qui curam habet Communitatis, Promulgata.*²³ It is a rational Ordinance for the advancing of publike good, made known by that power, which has care and tuition of the publike.

And *Suarez* his picture of a Law, now that 'tis fully drawn, hath much the same aspect. *Lex est commune praeceptum, justum ac stabile, sufficienter promulgatum.*[24] A Law is a publike command, a just and immovable command, lifting up its voice like a trumpet, and in respect of the Law-giver, though it do *praesupponere actum intellectus* [presuppose an act of the intellect], as all acts of the will do; yet it does formally consist *in actu voluntatis* [in an act of the will]; not the understanding, but the will of a Law-giver makes a Law.[25] But in respect of him that is subject to the Law it does consist *in actu rationis* [in a rational act], 'tis required only that he should know it, not *in actu voluntatis* [in an act of the will], it does not depend upon his obedience. The want of his will is not enough to enervate and invalidate a Law when 'tis made; all Lawes then would be abrogated every moment. His will indeed is required to the execution and fulfilling of the Law, not to the validity and existence of the Law: and thus all the lawes of God do not at all depend upon the will of man, but upon the power and will of the Law-giver. Now in the framing of every Law there is to be

1. *Intentio boni communis*[26] [an aiming at the common good], and thus that speech of *Carneades, Utilitas justi prope mater, & aequi*[27] [utility is, in one sense, the mother of what is just and fair], if it be took in this sense, is very commendable; whereas in that other sense (in which 'tis thought he meant it) it is not so much as tolerable. Law-givers should send out lawes with Olive-branches in their mouths, they should be fruitful and peaceable; they should drop sweetnesse and fatnesse upon a land. Let not then *Brambles* make lawes for *Trees*, lest they scratch them and tear them, and write their lawes in blood.[28] But Law-givers are to send out lawes, as the Sun shoots forth his beams, *with healing under their wings:*[29] and thus that elegant Moralist *Plutarch* speaks, God (saies he) is angry with them that counterfeit his thunder and lightning, οὐ σκῆπτρον, οὐ κεραυνὸν, οὐ τρίαιναν;[30] his Scepter, and his Thunderbolt, and his Trident, he will not let them meddle with these. He does not love they should imitate him in his absolute dominion and sovereignty; but loves to see them darting out those warme, and amiable, and cherishing ἀκτινοβολίαι,[31] those [32] beam-

ings out of Justice, and goodnesse, and clemency. And as for Lawes, they should be like so many green and pleasant pastures, into which these πο-ιμένες λαῶν³² [shepherds of nations] are to lead their flocks, where they may feed sweetly and securely by those refreshing streams of justice, that runnes down like water, *and righteousnesse like a mighty torrent.*³³ And this consideration would sweep down many cobweb-lawes, that argue only the venome and subtilty of them that spin them; this would sweep down many an *Achitophels* web and many an *Hamans* web, many an *Herods* web;³⁴ every spiders web that spreads lawes only for the catching and en-tangling of weaker ones; such Law-givers are fit to be *Domitians* play-fellows, that made it his Royal sport and pastime to catch flies, and insult over them when he had done.³⁵ Whereas a Law should be a staffe for a Common-wealth to lean on, and not a Reed to pierce it through. Laws should be cords of love, not nets and snares. Hence it is that those laws are most radical and fundamental, that principally tend to the conservation of the vitals and essentials of a Kingdome; and those come neerest the Law of God himself, and are participations of that eternal Law, which is the spring and original of all inferiour and derivative lawes. τοῦ ἀρίστου ἕνεκα πάντα τὰ νόμιμα³⁶ [all laws exist for the sake of the good], as *Plato* speaks; and there is no such publick benefit, as that which comes by lawes; for all have an equal interest in them, and priviledge by them. And therefore as *Aristotle* speaks most excellently, Νόμος ἐστὶ νοῦς ἄνευ ὀρέξεως.³⁷ A Law is a pure intellect, not only without a sensitive appetite, but without a will. 'Tis pure judgement without affections, a Law is impartial and makes no factions; and a Law cannot be bribed though a Judge may. And that great Philosopher does very well prosecute this; If you were to take physick (saies he) then indeed 'tis ill being determined by a book, 'tis dangerous taking a printed *recipe,* you had better leave it to the breast of the Physi-cian, to his skill and advice, who mindes your health and welfare, as being most for his gain and credit.³⁸ But in point of justice the case is very dif-ferent; you had better here depend upon a Rule, then to leave it to the arbitrary power of a Judge, who is usually to decide a controversie between two; and if left to himself, were apt to be swayed and biassed by several interests & engagements, which might encline him to one more then an-other. Nay now that there is a fixt rule, an immovable law, yet there is too much partiality in the application of it; how much more would there be, if there were no rule at all?

But the truth is, the Judge should only follow the *ultimum & practicum dictamen legis* [last and practical dictate of the law]; his will like a *caeca potentia* [blind power] is to follow the *novissimum lumen intellectus* [most recent intellectual light] of this *Νοῦς* [mind] that is to rule and guide him, and therefore justice was painted blinde, though *ipsa lex* [the law itself] be *oculata* [sighted], [33] for *Νοῦς ὁρᾷ, Νοῦς ἀκούει*[39] [the mind sees, the mind hears], and the will is to follow the *ultimum nutum capitis* [the last assent of the mind], the meaning of the Law in all circumstances.

2. In a Law-giver, there is to be *judicium & prudentia Architectonica ad ferendas leges*[40] [judgment and constructive discretion for making laws]; the Aegyptian Hieroglyphick for legislative power, was *Oculus in sceptro*[41] [an eye in a sceptre]; and it had need be such an eye that can see both *πρόσσω καὶ ὀπίσσω*[42] [before and behind]. It had need have a full and open prospect into publike affairs, and to put all advantages into one scale, and all inconveniences into another.

To be sure the Lawes of God, they flow from a fountain of wisdome, and the lawes of men are to be lighted at this *Candle of the Lord,* which he has set up in them, and those lawes are most potent and prevalent that are founded in light, *ἡ τοῦ λογισμοῦ ἀγωγὴ χρυσῆ καὶ ἱερά*[43] [the guidance of reason is golden and divine]. Other laws are *σκληροὶ, καὶ σιδήρεοι,* they may have an iron and adamantine necessity, but the others have a soft and downy perswasion going along with them, and therefore as he goes on *τοῦ λογισμοῦ καλοῦ μὲν ὄντος, πράου δὲ καὶ οὐ βιαίου. Reason* is so beautiful, as that it wins and allures, and thus constrains to obedience.

3. There is to be *sigillum Legis* [a seal of law], I meane *Electio & Determinatio Legis* [the selection and determination of a law], after a sincere aime at publick good, and a clear discovery of the best means to promote it, there comes then a fixt and sacred resolution; *Volumus & statuimus* [we will and decree], this speaks the will of the Law-giver, and breaths life into the Law, it adds vigour and efficacy to it.[44] But yet notwithstanding,

4. There must be *vox tubae* [the voice of the trumpet], that is, *promulgatio & insinuatio Legis*[45] [the promulgation and recommendation of the law]; The Law 'tis for a publick good, and is to be made known in a pub-

lick manner; for as none can desire an unknown good, so none can obey an unknown Law; and therefore invincible ignorance does excuse; for else men should be bound to absolute impossibilities. But whether it be required to the publishing of a Law that it should be in way of writing, which is more fixt and durable, or whether the manifestation of it in a Vocal and Oral manner will suffice, (which yet is more transient and uncertain) I leave the Lawyers and Schoolmen to dispute it. This I am sure, that all the Lawes of God are proclaimed in a most sufficient and emphatical manner.

Of the Eternal Law

[34] Having thus lookt upon the being of a Law in general, we now come to the spring and original of all Lawes, to the eternal Law, that fountain of Law, out of which you may see the Law of *Nature* bubbling and flowing forth to the sons of men. For, as *Aquinas* does very well tell us, the Law of *Nature* is nothing but *participatio Legis aeternae in Rationali creatura,*[1] the copying out of the eternal Law, and the imprinting of it upon the breast of a Rational being, that eternal Law was in a manner incarnated in the Law of *Nature.*

Now this eternal Law it is not really distinguished from God himself. For *Nil est ab aeterno nisi ipse Deus*[2] [nothing exists eternally except God himself], so that 'tis much of the same nature with those decrees of his, and that Providence which was awake from everlasting. For as God from all eternity by the hand of infinite wisdom did draw the several faces and lineaments of being, which he meant to shew in time: So he did then also contrive their several frames with such limits and compasse as he meant to set them; and said to every thing, *Hither shalt thou go, and no farther.*[3]

This the Platonists[4] would call ἰδέαν τῶν νόμων [the ideal of laws], and would willingly heap such honourable titles as these upon it, ὁ νόμος ἀρχηγὸς, πρωτουργὸς, αὐτοδίκαιος, αὐτόκαλος, αὐτοάγαθος, ὁ ὄντως νόμος, ὁ νόμος σπερματικός [the archetypal law, primary, intrinsically just, beautiful and good, the essential law, the seminal law]. And the greatest happinesse the other Lawes can arrive unto, is this, that they be Νόμοι δουλεύοντες, καὶ ὑπηρετοῦντες, ministring and subservient Lawes; waiting upon this their Royal Law. Σκιαὶ νόμων; Or as they would choose to stile them, Νομοειδεῖς, some shadows & appearances of this bright and glorious Law, or at the best, they would be esteemed by them but Νόμοι ἔκγονοι, the noble off-spring and progeny of Lawes; blessing this womb that bare them, and this breast that gave them suck.[5]

And thus the Law of *Nature* would have a double portion as being *Lex primogenita,* the first-born of this eternal Law, and the beginning of its strength.[6] Now as God himself shews somewhat of his face in the glasse of creatures, so the beauty of this Law gives some representations of it self in those pure derivations of inferiour Lawes that stream from it. And as we ascend to the first and [35] supreme being, by the steps of second causes; so we may climb up to a sight of this eternal Law, by those fruitful branches of secondary Lawes, which seem to have their root in earth, when as indeed it is in heaven; and that I may vary a little that of the Apostle to the Romanes, *The invisible Law of God long before the creation of the world, is now clearly seen being understood by those Lawes which do appear;*[7] so that τὸ γνωστὸν τοῦ νόμου [the knowledge of the law] is manifested in them, God having shown it to them. Thus, as the Schoolmen say very well, *Omnis lex participata supponit legem per essentiam*[8] [every derivative law supposes a self-existent law], every impression supposes a seal from whence it came; every ray of light puts you in minde of a Sun from which it shines. Wisdome and power, these are the chief ingredients into a Law; now where does Wisdome dwell, but in the head of a Deity? and where does power triumph, but in the arme of Omnipotency?

A Law is borne *ex cerebro Jovis* [from the brain of Jove], and it is not *brachium seculare* [a worldly arm], but *Coeleste* [a heavenly one] that must maintain it, even humane Lawes have their vertue *radicaliter, & remote* [fundamentally and ultimately] (as the Schooles speak) from this eternal Law. Thus that famous and most renowned Orator and Patriot (*Tully* I mean) does most admirably express the lineage and descent of Lawes in this golden manner. *Hanc video sapientissimorum fuisse sententiam, Legem neque hominum ingeniis excogitatam, neque scitum aliquod esse Populorum, sed aeternum quiddam quod universum mundum regeret, imperandi prohibendique sapientia. Ita principem illam Legem & ultimam mentem dicebant omnia ratione aut cogentis, aut vetantis Dei.*[9] Which I shall thus render, Wise men did ever look upon a Law, not as on a spark struck from humane intellectuals, not blown up or kindled with popular breath, but they thought it an eternal light shining from God himself irradiating, guiding and ruling the whole Universe; most sweetly and powerfully discovering what wayes were to be chosen, and what to be refused. And the minde of God himself is the centre of Lawes, from which they were drawn, and into which they must return.

Thus also that florid Moralist *Plutarch* resolves all Law and Justice into that Primitive and eternal Law, even God himself, for even thus he tells us. Justice (saies he) does not only sit like a Queen at the right hand of *Jupiter* when he is upon his throne, but she is alwayes in his bosome, and one with himself; and he closes it up with this, that God himself is τῶν νόμων πρεσβύτατος, καὶ τελειότατος.[10] As he is the most ancient of dayes,[11] so also is he the most ancient of lawes; as he is the perfection of beings, so is he also the rule of operations.

Nor must I let slip that passage of *Plato*, where he calls a law Ζῆνος σκῆπτρον,[12] the golden Scepter by which God himself rules and commands; [36] for as all true Government has a bright stamp of divine Sovereignty, so every true Law has a plain superscription of his Justice. Lawes are anoynted by God himself, and most precious oile drops down upon them to the skirts of a Nation; and the Law of *Nature* had the oile of gladnesse poured out upon it above its fellowes.[13]

So then, that there is such a prime and supreme Law is clear, and unquestionable; but who is worthy to unseal and open this Law? and who can sufficiently display the glory of it? we had need of a *Moses* that could ascend up into the Mount, and converse with God himself, and yet when he came down he would be faine to put a veile upon his face, and upon his expressions too, lest otherwise he might too much dazzle inferiour understandings;[14] but if the Schoolmen will satisfie you, (and you know some of them are stiled Angelical, and Seraphical)[15] you shall hear, if you will, what they'l say to it.

Now this Law according to them is *Aeterna quaedam ratio practica totius dispositionis, & gubernationis Universi*.[16] 'Tis an eternal Ordinance made in the depth of Gods infinite wisdome and councel for regulating and governing of the whole world, which yet had not its binding vertue in respect of God himself, who has alwayes the full and unrestrained liberty of his own essence,[17] which is so infinite, as that it cannot binde it self, and which needs no Law, all goodness and perfection being so intrinsecal and essential to it: but it was a binding determination in reference to the creature, which yet in respect of all irrational beings, did only *fortiter inclinare* [strongly incline], but in respect of Rationals, it does *formaliter obligare*[18] [formally bind].

By this great and glorious Law every good action was commanded, and all evill was discountenanc'd, and forbidden from everlasting. According to this righteous Law all rewards and punishments were distributed in the eternal thoughts of God. At the command of this Law all created beings took their several ranks and stations, and put themselves in such operations as were best agreeable and conformable to their beings. By this Law all essences were ordained to their ends by most happy and convenient means. The life and vigour of this Law sprang from the will of God himself; from the voluntary decree of that eternal Law-giver, minding the publike welfare of being; who when there were heaps of varieties and possibilities in his own most glorious thoughts, when he could have made such or such worlds in this or that manner, in this or that time, with such & such species, that should have had more or fewer individuals, as he pleased, with such operations as he would allow unto them; he did then select and pitch upon this way and method in which we see things now constituted; and did binde all things according to their several capacities to an exact and accurate observation of it.

So that by this you see how those eternal *ideas* in the minde of God, and this [37] eternal Law do differ. I speak now of *Ideas* not in a Platonical sence, but in a Scholastical, (unlesse they both agree, as some would have them.) For *Idea est possibilium, Lex tantum futurorum* [an idea relates to the possible, a law only to the future], God had before him the picture of every possibility, yet he did not intend to binde a possibility, but only a futurity. Besides, *Ideas* they were situated only in the *understanding* of God; whereas a Law has force and efficacy from his *will;* according to that much commended saying, *In Coelesti & Angelica curia voluntas Dei Lex est*[19] [in the heavenly and angelic court the will of God is law]. And then an *Idea* does *magis respicere artificem* [relate more to the author], it stayes there where first it was; but a Law does *potius respicere subditum* [relate more to an inferior], it calls for the obedience of another, as *Suarez* does very well difference them.[20]

Neither yet is this eternal Law the same with the providence of God, though that be eternal also. But as *Aquinas* speaks, *Lex se habet ad providentiam, sicut principium generale ad particulares conclusiones* [the law has the same relation to providence, as a general principle to particular conclusions]; or, if you will, *Sicut principia prima practica ad prudentiam*[21] [as practical first principles to prudence]; his meaning is this, that Providence is a more punctual and particular application of this binding rule, and is not the Law it self but the superintending power, which looks to the execution and accomplishment of it; or as the most acute *Suarez* has it, *Lex dicit jus in communi constitutum, providentia dicit curam quae de singulis actibus haberi debet*[22] [law refers to a rule of right established in common, providence to the care which should be exercised about individual acts].

Besides, a Law in its strict and peculiar notion, does only reach to rational beings; whereas Providence does extend and spread it self over all. But that which vexes the Schoolmen most, is this, that they having required promulgation as a necessary condition to the existence of a Law, yet they cannot very easily shew how this eternal Law, should be publisht from everlasting.[23] But the most satisfactory account that can be given to that, is this, that other Law-givers being very voluble and mutable before their minde and will be fully and openly declared, they may have a purpose indeed, but it cannot be esteem'd a Law. But in God there being no variablenes nor shadow of turning,[24] this his Law has a binding vertue as soon as it has a being, yet so as that it does not actually and formally oblige a creature till it be made known unto it: either by some revelation from God himself which is possible only, and extraordinary; or else by the mediation of some other Law, of the Law of *Nature*, which is the usual and constant way that God takes for the promulgation of this his eternal Law. For that νόμος γραπτὸς,[25] that sacred Manuscript, which is writ by the finger of God himself in the heart of man, is a plain transcript of this original Law, so far [38] as it concerns mans welfare. And this you see does most directly bring me to search out the *Law of Nature*.

❧ CHAPTER 6 ❧

Of the Law of Nature in General,
Its Subject and Nature

[39] *The Law of Nature* is that Law which is intrinsecal and essential to a rational creature; and such a Law is as necessary as such a creature, for such a creature as a creature has a superiour to whose Providence and disposing it must be subject, and then as an intellectual creature 'tis capable of a moral government, so that 'tis very suitable and connatural to it to be regulated by a Law; to be guided and commanded by one that is infinitely more wise and intelligent then it self is; and that mindes its welfare more then it self can. Insomuch that the most bright and eminent creatures, even angelical beings, and glorified souls are subject to a Law, though with such an happy priviledge, as that they cannot violate and transgresse it; whereas the very dregs of entity, the most ignoble beings are most incapable of a Law; for you know inanimate beings are carried on only with the vehemency and necessity of natural inclinations; nay, sensitive beings cannot reach or aspire to so great a perfection as to be wrought upon in such an illuminative way as a Law is; they are not drawn with these cords of men, with these moral ingagements, but in a more impulsive manner driven and spurred on with such impetuous propensions as are founded in matter; which yet are directed by the wise and vigilant eye, and by the powerful hand of a Providence to a more beautiful and amiable end, then they themselves were acquainted with. But yet the Lawyers, the Civilians would faine enlarge the Law of *Nature,* and would willingly perswade us that all sensitive creatures must be brought within the compasse of it; for this they tell us, *Jus naturale est quod natura omnia animalia docuit, nam jus illud non solum Humani Generis est proprium, sed omnium animalium*

40

quae in terra marique nascuntur, avium quoque commune est[1] [the natural law is that which nature has taught all animals, for that law is not confined to the human race, but is common to all animals that are begotten on land or in the sea, and also to birds]. Nay, they are so confident of it, as that they instance in several particulars, *Maris & foeminae conjunctio, Liberorum procreatio, educatio, conservatio, Plurima in tutelam propriam facta, Apium respub. Columbarum conjugia*[2] [the union of male and female, the procreation, rearing and preservation of offspring, the great number of things done for self-protection, the common-wealth of bees, the marriages of doves]. But not only the Criticks, but the [40] Schoolmen also do sufficiently correct the Lawyers for this their vanity; for certainly these men mean to bring beasts, birds and fishes into their Courts, and to have some fees out of them. Perhaps they expect also that the Doves should take Licences before they marry: it may be they require of the beasts some penitential, or (which will suffice them) some pecuniary satisfaction for all their adulteries; or it may be the *Pope* will be so favourable, as to give his fellow-*Beasts* some dispensation for all their irregular and incongruous mixtures.

But yet notwithstanding, they prosecute this their notion, and go on to frame this difference between νομιμὸν ἐθικὸν, & νομιμὸν φυσικὸν: *Jus Gentium*, & *Jus Naturale*. The Law of *Nature* (say they) is that which is common with men to irrational Creatures also; but the Law of Nations is only between men:[3] but this distinction is built upon a very sandy bottome; what the true difference is we shall see hereafter. Now all that can be pleaded in the behalf of the Lawyers, is this, that they erre more in the word then in the reality. They cannot sufficiently clear this *Title* of a Law; for that there are some clear and visible stamps and impressions of *Nature* upon sensitive beings, will be easily granted them by all, and those instances which they bring, are so many ocular demonstrations of it; but that there should a formal obligation lie upon Brutes; that they should be bound to the performance of natural commands in a legal manner; that there should be a Νόμος γραπτὸς[4] [written law] upon them, ὥστε εἶναι ἀναπολογήτους,[5] so as that they should be left without excuse, and lie under palpable guilt, and be obnoxious to punishment for the violation of it, this they cannot possibly finde out, unlesse they could set up this *Candle of the Lord* in sensitive creatures also; whereas there are in them only some μιμήματα τῆς ἀνθρωπίνης ζωῆς[6] as the Philosopher calls them, which the Oratour renders, *virtutum simulacra,*[7] some apish imitations of reason, some shadows of morality, some counterfeit Ethicks, some wilde Oeconomicks, some faint representations of Politicks amongst some of them. Yet all this while they are as farre distant from the truth of a Law, as they are from the strength of Reason. There you may see some sparks of the divine power and goodnesse, but you cannot see *the Candle of the Lord.* Now these men might have considered if they had pleased, that as for the prints and foot-steps of *Nature,* some of them may be seen in every being. For *Nature* has stampt all entity with the same seal, some softer beings took the impression very kindly and clearly; some harder ones took it more obscurely.

Nature plaid so harmoniously and melodiously upon her Harp, as that her musick prov'd not only like that of *Orpheus,* which set only the sensitive creatures on dancing; but like that of *Amphion,* inanimate beings were elevated by it, even the very stones did knit and unite themselves to the building of the Universe.

[41] Shew me any being, if you can, that does not love its own welfare, that does not seek its own rest, its centre, its happinesse, that does not desire its own good οὗ πάντα ἐφίεται[8] [which all things desire], as he speaks; pick out an entity, if you can tell where, that does not long for the continuation and amplification, for the diffusion and spreading of its own being. Yet surely the Lawyers themselves cannot imagine that there is a Law given to all inanimate beings, or that they are accountable for the violation.

Let them also demurre awhile upon that argument which *Suarez* urges against them,[9] that these sensitive creatures are totally defective in the most principal branches of the Law of *Nature;* as in the acknowledging of a Deity, in the adoring of a Deity, where is there the least adumbration of divine worship, in sensitive beings? What do they more then the heavens, which declare the glory of God; or the firmament, which shewes his handy work?[10] Unlesse perhaps the Lawyers can finde not only a Commonwealth, but a Church also among the Bees; some Canonical obedience, some laudable ceremonies,[11] some decency and conformity amongst them.

We'll only set some of the Poets to laugh the Lawyers out of this opinion; Old *Hesiod* tells them his minde very freely.

> Τὸν δὲ γὰρ ἀνθρώποισι νόμον διέταξε κρονίων,
> Ἰχθύσι γὰρ καὶ θηρσὶ καὶ οἰωνοῖς πετεηνοῖς
> Ἔσθεμεν ἀλλήλους, ἐπεὶ οὐ δίκη ἐστὶ μετ' αὐτῶν,
> Ἀνθρώποισι δ' ἔδωκε δίκην, ἣ πολλὸν ἀρίστη.¹²

[*For the son of Chronos has decreed this law for men, that fish and beasts and winged birds should devour each other, for justice is not in them; but he gave justice to men, which is by far the best.*]

What are those Lawes that are observed by a rending and tearing Lion, by a devouring Leviathan? does the Wolf oppresse the Lamb by a Law? Can birds of prey shew any Commission for their plundering and violence? thus also that amorous Poet shews that these sensitive creatures, in respect of lust, are absolute *Antinomians*. For thus he brings in a wanton pleading.

> *Coeunt animalia nullo*
> *Caetera delicto, nec habetur turpe juvencae*
> *Ferre patrem tergo; fit equo sua filia conjux:*
> *Quasque creavit init pecudes caper; ipsaque cujus*
> *Semine concepta est, ex illo concipit ales.*¹³

[42] [*Other animals mate innocently, nor is it held base for a heifer to bear her sire; nor for his filly to be a horse's mate; the goat enters in among the herd which he has sired, and the birds themselves conceive from those from whom they were conceived.*]

And what though you meet with some ἅπαξ λεγόμενα [exceptions], some rare patterns of sensitive temperance? a few scattered and uncertain stories will never evince that the whole heap and generality of brutes act according to a Law. You have heard it may be of a chaste Turtle, and did you never hear of a wanton Sparrow? It may be you have read some story of a modest Elephant, but what say you in the meane time to whole flocks of lascivious Goats? Yet grant that the several multitudes, all the species of these irrational creatures were all without spot and blemish in respect of their sensitive conversation, can any therefore fancy that they dresse themselves by the glasse of a Law? Is it not rather a faithfulnesse to their own natural inclinations? which yet may very justly condemne some of the sons of men, who though they have *the Candle of the Lord,* and the Lamp of his Law, yet they degenerate more then these inferiour beings, which have only some general dictates of *Nature.*

This is that motive with which the Satyrist quicken'd and awaken'd some of his time;

> *Sensum e coelesti demissum traximus arce,*
> *Cujus egent prona & terram spectantia; Mundi*
> *Principio indulsit communis Conditor illis*
> *Tantum animas, nobis animum quoque.*[14]

> [*We have drawn down from its heavenly seat that intelligence which grovelling and earth-gazing creatures lack; the Creator of both, at the beginning of time, gave to them life alone, to us a soul as well.*]

A Law 'tis founded in intellectuals, in נשמה [reason] not in נפש[15] [sense], it supposes a Noble and free-borne creature, for where there is no Liberty, there's no Law, a Law being nothing else but a Rational restraint and limitation of absolute Liberty. Now all Liberty is *Radicaliter in Intellectu* [rooted in the intellect]; and such Creatures as have no light, have no choice, no Moral variety.

The first and supreme being has so full and infinite a liberty as cannot be bounded by a Law; and these low and slavish beings have not so much liberty as to make them capable of being bound. *Inter Bruta silent leges*[16] [among brutes laws are silent]. There is no *Turpe* [base] nor *Honestum* [honourable] amongst them: no duty nor obedience to be expected from them, no praise or dispraise due to them, no punishment nor reward to be distributed amongst them.

[43] But as the learned *Grotius* does very well observe; *Quoniam in bestias proprie delictum non cadit, ubi bestia occiditur ut in lege Mosis ob concubitum cum homine, non ea vere poena est, sed usus dominii humani in bes-*

tiam[17] [since, to be precise, evil is not to be attributed to beasts, when a beast is killed according to the law of Moses as a consequence of cohabitation with a man, this is not a true punishment, but the exercise of human dominion over the beast]. For punishment in its formal notion is ἁμαρτήματος ἐκδίκησις[18] [the avenging of a crime] (as the Greek Lawyers speak) or as the fore-mentioned Author describes it; 'Tis *malum Passionis quod infligitur ob malum actionis*[19] [an evil of suffering which is inflicted because of the evil of action]. In all punishment there is to be some ἀντάλλαγμα & ἀμοιβὴ[20] [exchange and requital], so that every *Damnum* or *Incommodum* [injury or inconvenience] is not to be esteem'd a punishment, unlesse it be *in vindictam culpae*[21] [a satisfaction for guilt]. So as for those Lawes given to the Jewes, where sometimes the Beast also was to be put to death: the most renowned *Selden* gives a very full and satisfactory accompt of it out of the Jewish writings, and does clearly evidence that the meaning was not this, that the Beast was guilty of a crime, and had violated a Law, and therefore was to be condemned and put to death; but it was in order to the happinesse and welfare of men; for *Bestia cum homine concumbens*[22] [the beast cohabiting with man] was to be ston'd: partly because it was the occasion of so foule a fact, and so fatal punishment unto man; and partly that the sight and presence of the object might not repeate so prodigious a crime in the thoughts of men, nor renew the memory of it, nor continue the disgrace of him that died for it. But there was another different reason *in Bove cornupeta* [in the case of the butting ox], for there, as *Maimonides* tells us, in his *Moreh Nebachim,* 'twas *ad poenam exigendam a Domino:* the putting of that to death was a punishment to the owner, for not looking to it better;[23] for I cannot at all consent to the fancy of the Jewes, which *Josephus* mentions; μηδ᾽ εἰς τροφὴν εὔχρηστος εἶναι κατηξιωμένος[24] [that it was not considered useful for food]. Although the fore-named Critick give a better sense of it, then 'tis likely the Author ever intended: *non in alimentum sumi debuit unde scilicet in Domini commodum cederet* [the ox should not be taken for food since then it would yield a profit for the owner]: but how such an interpretation can be extracted out of εὔχρηστος εἰς τροφὴν [useful for food] is not easily to be imagined; for those words of *Josephus* plainly imply, that the Jewes thought such an Oxe could not yield wholesome nourishment; or at the best, they look't upon it as an unclean Beast, which was not to be eaten, which indeed was a fond and weak conceit of them, but they had many such, which yet the learned Author loves to excuse, out of his great favour and indulgence to them. Yet, which is very remarkable, if the Oxe had kill'd a Gentile, they did not put it to death. It seems it would yield wholesom nourishment for all that. But this we [44] are sure of, that as God does not take care for Oxen[25] (which the acute *Suarez* does very well understand of *Cura Legislativa*[26] [legislative care], for otherwise God hath a Providential care even of them) so neither does he take care for the punishment of Oxen, but 'tis written for his *Israels* sake, to whom he has subjected these creatures, and put them under their feet.

Neither yet can the proper end of a punishment agree to sensitive creatures; for all punishment is ἕνεκα τοῦ ἀγαθοῦ [for the sake of the good], as *Plato* speakes; οὐκ ἕνεκα τοῦ κακουργῆσαι, οὐ γὰρ τὸ γεγονὸς ἀγένητον ἔσται ποτέ[27] [it exists not for the sake of the evil deed, for what has once been done cannot be undone]. 'Tis not in the power of punishment to recal what is past, but to prevent what's possible. And that wise Moralist *Seneca* does almost translate *Plato verbatim; Nemo prudens punit quia peccatum est, sed ne peccetur: Revocari enim praeterita non possunt, futura prohibentur*[28] [No wise man punishes because a sin has been committed, but so that it may not be committed; for past evil cannot be recalled, but future evil may be prevented].

So that the end of all punishment is either *in compensationem*[29] [compensation], which is κακοῦ ἀνταπόδοσις εἰς τὸ τοῦ τιμωροῦντος συμφέρον ἀναφερομένη[30] [a retribution for evil which benefits the avenger], 'Tis *in utilitatem ejus contra quem peccatum est* [for the advantage of the injured party]; or else 'tis *in emendationem* [for correction], and so *in utilitatem peccantis* [for the advantage of the transgressor]; in respect of which that elegant Moralist *Plutarch* stiles punishment ἰατρείαν Ψυχῆς[31] [medical treatment of the soul], and *Hierocles* calls it ἰατρικὴν πονηρίας[32] [medicine for wickedness]: or else it is *in exemplum, in utilitatem aliorum; ἵνα ἄλλοι πρόνοιαν ποιῶνται καὶ φοβῶνται*[33] [for the sake of example, for the advantage of others; so that others may exercise foresight and be afraid], as the Greek Oratour speaks; the same which God speaks by *Moses, that Israel may hear and fear:*[34] and thus punishment does παραδειγματίζειν[35] [serve as an example].

But now none of these ends are applyable to sensitive creatures, for there is no more *satisfaction* to justice in inflicting an evill upon them, then there is in the ruining of inanimate beings, in demolishing of Cities or Temples for Idolatry; which is only for the good of them that can take notice of it; for otherwise as that grave Moralist *Seneca* has it, *Quam stultum est his irasci, quae iram nostram nec meruerunt, nec sentiunt*[36] [how stupid it is to be angry with those inanimate objects which neither have deserved, nor feel, our anger]: No satisfaction to be had from such things as are not apprehensive of punishment. And therefore Annihilation, though a great evil, yet wants this sting and aggravation of a punishment, for a creature is not sensible of it.

Much lesse can you think that a punishment has any power to *mend* or meliorate sensitive beings, or to give *example* to others amongst them.

[45] By all this you see that amongst all irrational beings there is no ἀ-νομία [lawlessness], and therefore no ἁμαρτία [guilt], and therefore no πιμωρία [punishment]: from whence it also flows that the Law of *Nature* is built upon Reason.

There is some good so proportionable and nutrimental to the being of man, and some evil so venemous and destructive to his nature, as that the God of *Nature* does sufficiently antidote and fortifie him against the one, and does maintain and sweeten his essence with the other. There is so much harmony in some actions, as that the soul must needs dance at them, and there is such an harsh discord and jarring in others, as that the soul cannot endure them.

Therefore the learned *Grotius* does thus describe the Law of *Nature; Jus naturale est dictatum Rectae Rationis, indicans, actui alicui, ex ejus convenientia vel disconvenientia cum ipsa natura Rationali, inesse Moralem turpitudinem, aut necessitatem Moralem; & consequenter ab Authore Naturae ipso Deo, talem actum aut vetari aut praecipi.*[37] Which I shall thus render; The Law of *Nature* is a streaming out of Light from *the Candle of the Lord,* powerfully discovering such a deformity in some evil, as that an intellectual eye must needs abhor it; and such a commanding beauty in some good, as that a rational being must needs be enamoured with it; and so plainly shewing that God stampt and seal'd the one with his command, and branded the other with his disliking.

Chrysostome makes mention of this Νόμος φυσικὸς [natural law], and does very rhetorically enlarge himself upon it in his twelfth and thirteenth Orations περὶ Ἀνδριάντων [*Of Statues*]; where he tells us, that it is αὐτο-δίδακτος ἡ γνῶσις τῶν καλῶν, καὶ τῶν οὐ τοιούτων[38] [an instinctive knowledge of good and of its opposite], a Radical and fundamental knowledge, planted in the being of man, budding and blossoming in first principles, flourishing and bringing forth fruit, spreading it self into all the faire and goodly branches of Morality, under the shadow of which the soul may sit with much complacency and delight. And as he poures out himself very fluently; οὐ χρεία τῶν λόγων, οὐ τῶν διδασκάλων, οὐ τῶν πόνων, οὐ καμάτων:[39] There's no need of Oratory to allure men to it, you need not heap up arguments to convince them of it: No need of an Interpreter to acquaint them with it: No need of the minds spinning, or toyling, or sweating for the attaining of it; it grows spontaneously, it bubbles up freely, it shines out cheerfully and pleasantly; it was so visible as that the most infant-age of the world could spell it out, and read it without a Teacher: οὐ Μωυσῆς, οὐ προφῆται, οὐ δικασταί[40] [without Moses, or the prophets, or the judges], as he goes on, 'twas long extant before *Moses* was born, long before *Aaron* rung his golden Bells, before there was a Prophet or a Judge in *Israel.* Men knew it οἴκοθεν παρὰ τοῦ συνειδότος διδαχθέντες[41] [being taught inwardly by conscience]. They had a Bible of Gods own printing, they had this [46] Scripture of God within them. By this *Candle of the Lord, Adam* and *Eve* discovered their own folly and nakednesse; this *Candle* flamed in *Cains* conscience, and this Law was proclaimed in his heart with as much terror as 'twas publisht from Mount *Sinai,* which fill'd him with those furious reflections for his unnatural murder. *Enoch* when he walkt with God,[42] walkt by this light, by this rule. *Noah* the Preacher of righteousnesse[43] took this Law for his text. Nay, you may see some print of this Law upon the hard heart of a *Pharoah,* when he cries out, *the Lord is righteous, but I and my people have sinned.*[44] Hence it was that God when he gave his Law afresh, gave it in such a compendious Brachygraphy; he wrote it as 'twere in Characters, οὐ φονεύσεις, οὐ μοιχεύσεις, οὐ κλέψεις[45] [thou shalt not kill, thou shalt not commit adultery, thou shalt not steal] without any explication, or amplification at all. He only enjoyned it with an Imperatorious brevity, he knows there was enough in the breasts of men to convince them of it, and to comment upon it, only in the second Command there is added an enforcement, because his people were excessively prone to the violation of it; and in that of the Sabbath there is given an exposition of it, because in all its circumstances it was not founded in Natural Light. So that in *Plutarchs* language the Decalogue would be call'd νόμος σφυρήλατος[46] [roughly hammered law], Gold in the lump, whereas other Law-givers use to beat it thinner. Of this Law as 'tis printed by *Nature*, *Philo* speaks very excellently; Νόμος δ' ἀψευδὴς ὁ ὀρθὸς λόγος, οὐκ ὑπὸ τοῦ δεῖνος ἢ τοῦ δεῖνος θνητοῦ φθαρτὸς ἐν χαρτιδίοις ἢ στήλαις ἀψύχοις, ἀλλ' ὑπ' ἀθανάτου φύσεως ἄφθαρτος ἐν ἀθανάτῳ διανοίᾳ τυπωθείς.[47] Right Reason (saies he) is that fixt and unshaken Law, not writ in perishing paper by the hand or pen of a creature, nor graven like a dead letter upon livelesse and decaying Pillars, but written with the point of a Diamond, nay with the finger of God himself in the heart of man; a Deity gave it an *Imprimatur;* and an eternal Spirit grav'd it in an immortal minde. So as that I may borrow the expression of the Apostle, the minde of man is στύλος καὶ ἑδραίωμα τῆς ἀληθείας ταύτης[48] [the pillar and ground of this truth]. And I take it in the very same sense as 'tis to be took of the Church: 'Tis a Pillar of this Truth not to support it, but to hold it forth. Neither must I let slip a passage in *Plutarch* which is very neer of kin to this of *Philo*, ὁ Νόμος οὐκ ἐν βιβλίοις ἔξω γεγραμμένος, οὐδέ τισι ξύλοις, ἀλλ' ἔμψυχος ὢν ἑαυτῷ λόγος ἀεὶ συνοικῶν καὶ παραφυλάττων καὶ μηδέποτε τὴν ψυχὴν ἐῶν ἔρημον ἡγεμονίας.[49] You may take it thus: This Royal Law of *Nature* was never shut up in a paper-prison, was never confin'd or limited to any outward surface; but it was bravely situated in the Centre of a Rational Being, alwayes keeping the Soul company, guarding it, and guiding it; Ruling all its Subjects, (every obedient *Action*) with a Scepter of Gold, and crushing in pieces all its enemies (breaking every rebellious *Action*) with a Rod of Iron. You may [47] hear the Lyrick singing out the praises of this Law in a very lofty straine; Νόμος ὁ πάντων βασιλεὺς θνατῶν τε καὶ ἀθανάτων, οὗτος ἄγει βιαίως τὸ δικαιώτατον ὑπερτάτᾳ χειρί;[50] This Law which is the Queen of Angelical and humane Beings does so rule and dispose of them, as to bring about Justice, with a most high and powerful, and yet with a most soft and delicate hand.

You may hear *Plato* excellently discoursing of it, whilest he brings in a Sophister disputing against *Socrates*, and such a one as would needs un-

dertake to maintain this Principle, Ταῦτα ἐναντία ἀλλήλοις ἐστὶν ἥτε φύσις καὶ ὁ νόμος:[51] That there was an untunable antipathy between *Nature*
and *Law;* that Lawes were nothing but *hominum infirmiorum commenta*
[the fabrications of weaker men]; that this was Τὸ λαμπρότατον τῆς φύσεως δίκαιον, the most bright and eminent Justice of *Nature,* for men to
rule according to Power, and according to no other Law: that ὁ ἰσχυρό-
τερος [the stronger] was ὁ κρείττων [the superior], and ὁ βελτίων [the bet-
ter]; that all other Lawes were παρὰ φύσιν ἅπαντες [all contrary to nature]:
Nay, he calls them cheatings and bewitchings, οὐκ ᾠδαὶ ἀλλ᾽ ἐπῳδαί, they
come (saies he) like pleasant songs, when as they are meer charmes and
incantations. But *Socrates* after he had stung this same *Callicles* with a few
quick Interrogations, pours out presently a great deale of honey and sweetnesse, and plentifully shewes that most pleasant and conspiring harmony
that is between *Nature* and *Law.* That there's nothing more κατὰ φύσιν
[natural] then a Law, that Law is founded in *Nature,* that it is for the maintaining and ennobling and perfecting of *Nature.* Nay, as *Plato* tells us elsewhere, There's no way for men to happinesse, unless they follow Τὰ ἴχνη
τῶν λόγων;[52] these steps of Reason, these foot-steps of *Nature.* This same
Law *Aristotle* does more then once acknowledge, when he tells us of Νόμος
Ἴδιος [private law] and Νόμος κοινὸς [public law]; a Positive Law with
him is a more private Law, καθ᾽ ὃν γεγραμμένον πολιτεύονται [according
to the written form of which men govern themselves in society]; but Natures Law is a more publike and Catholike Law, ὅσα ἄγραφα παρὰ πᾶσιν
ὁμολογεῖσθαι δοκεῖ[53] [the unwritten laws which seem to be recognized by
all], which he proves to be a very Sovereign and commanding Law, for
thus he saies, ὁ νόμος ἀναγκαστικὴν ἔχει δύναμιν, λόγος ὢν ὑπό τινος
φρονήσεως καὶ νοῦ.[54] The Law that is most filled with Reason must needs
be most victorious and triumphant.

The same Philosopher in his tenth Book *De Rep.* has another distinction of Lawes; one branch whereof does plainly reach to the Law of *Nature.*

There are, saies he, Νόμοι κατὰ γράμματα [written laws], which are the
same with those which he call'd Νόμοι ἴδιοι [private laws] before, and then
there are Νόμοι κατὰ τὰ ἔθη [moral laws], which are all one with that he
stil'd before Νόμος κοινός[55] [public law]. Now, as he speaks, these Νόμοι

κατὰ τὰ ἔθη [moral laws] are κυρίωτεροι[56] [more authoritative]; Lawes of the first [48] magnitude, of a Nobler Sphere, of a vaster and purer influence. Where you see also that he calls the Law of *Nature,* the Moral Law; and the same which the Apostle calls Νόμος γραπτὸς [the written law], he with the rest of the Heathen calls it Ἄγραφα νόμιμα[57] [unwritten laws], couching the same sense in a seeming contradiction.

The Oratour has it expressely; *Non scripta, sed nata lex*[58] [a law not written, but innate].

And amongst all the Heathen, I can meet with none that draws such a lively pourtraiture of the law of *Nature* as that Noble Oratour does.

You may hear him thus pleading for it: *Nec si regnanta Tarquinio nulla erat scripta lex de stupris, &c.*[59] Grant, (saies he) that *Rome* were not for the present furnisht with a Positive Law able to check the lust and violence of a *Tarquin;* yet there was a Virgin-law of *Nature,* which he had also ravisht and deflour'd: there was the beaming out of an eternal Law, enough to revive a modest *Lucretia,* and to strike terror into the heart of so licentious a Prince: for as he goes on, *Est quidem vera lex Recta Ratio, Naturae congruens, diffusa in omnes, constans, sempiterna; quae vocet ad officium jubendo, vetando a fraude deterreat; quae tamen Probos, neque frustra, jubet aut vetat, nec improbos jubendo aut vetando movet. Hinc Legi nec Propagari fas est, neque derogari ex hac aliquid licet. Neque tota abrogari potest. Nec vero aut per Senatum, aut per Populum solvi hac Lege possumus. Neque est quaerendus explanator, aut interpres ejus alius. Non erat alia Romae, alia Athenis: Alia nunc, alia posthac: sed & omnes gentes, omnitempore, Una Lex, & sempiterna & immutabilis continebit, unusque erit quasi communis magister & Legislator omnium Deus: Ille Legis hujus Inventor, Disceptator, Lator; Cui qui non parebit ipse se fugiet, & Naturam hominis aspernabitur; Hoc ipso licet maximas poenas, etiamsi caetera, quae putantur, effugerit.*[60]

His meaning is not much different from this:

Right Reason is a beautiful Law; a Law of a pure complexion, of a natural colour, of a vast extent and diffusion; its colour never fades, never dies. It encourages men in obedience with a smile, it chides them and frowns them out of wickednesse. Good men heare the least whispering of its pleasant voice, they observe the least glance of its lovely eye; but wicked men sometimes will not heare it though it come to them in thunder; nor take the least notice of it, though it should flash out in lightning. None must inlarge the Phylacteries of this law, nor must any dare to prune off the least branch of it. Nay the malice of man cannot totally deface so indelible a beauty. No Pope, nor Prince, nor Parliament, nor People, nor Angel, nor Creature can absolve you from it. This Law never paints its face, it never changes its colour, it does not put on one Aspect at *Athens* and another face at *Rome,* but looks upon all Nations & persons with an impartial eye, it shines upon all ages and times, and conditions, with a perpetual [49] light, *it is yesterday and today, the same for ever.*[61] There is but one Law-giver, one Lord and supreme Judge of this Law, *God blessed for evermore.*[62] He was the contriver of it, the commander of it, the publisher of it, and none can be exempted from it, unless he will be banisht from his own essence, and be excommunicated from humane Nature.

This punishment would have sting enough, if he should avoid a thousand more that are due to so foul a transgression.

Thus you see that the Heathen, not only had this Νόμος γραπτὸς[63] [written law] upon them; but also they themselves took special notice of it, and the more refined sort amongst them could discourse very admirably about it, which must needs leave them the more inexcusable for the violation of it. We come now to see where the strength of the Law of Nature lies, where its nerves are, whence it has such an efficacious influence, such a binding vertue.

And I finde *Vasquez* somewhat singular, and withal erroneous in his opinion, whilest he goes about to shew that the formality of this Law consists only in that harmony and proportion, or else that discord and disconvenience, which such and such an object, and such and such an action has with a Rational Nature; for, saies he, every Essence is *Mensura Boni &* *Mali*[64] [a measure of good and evil] in respect of it self.

Which, as he thinks, is plainly manifested and discovered also in corporal beings, which use to flie only from such things as are destructive to their own formes, and to embrace all such neighbourly and friendly beings as will close and comply with them. But he might easily have known that as these material beings were never yet so honoured, as to be judg'd capable of a Law; so neither can any naked Essence, though never so pure and noble, lay a Moral engagement upon it self, or binde its own being: for this would make the very same being superior to it self, as it gives a Law, and inferiour to it self, as it must obey it.

So that the most high and Sovereigne being even God himself, does not subject himself to any Law; though there be some Actions also most agreeable to his Nature, and others plainly inconsistent with it, yet they cannot amount to such a power, as to lay any obligation upon him, which should in the least Notion differ from the liberty of his own essence.

Thus also in the Common-wealth of humane Nature, that proportion which Actions bear to Reason, is indeed a sufficient foundation for a Law to build upon; but it is not the Law it self, nor a formal obligation.

Yet some of the School-men are extreme bold and vaine in their suppositions; so bold, as that I am ready to question whether it be best to repeate them; yet thus they say,

Si Deus non esset, vel si non uteretur Ratione, vel si non recte judicaret de Rebus, si tamen in homine idem esset dictamen Rectae rationis, quod nunc est, haberet etiam [50] *eandem Rationem Legis quam nunc habet*[65] [if there were no God, or if He did not make use of reason, or if He did not judge rightly concerning things, if, nevertheless, there were in man the same direction of right reason which now exists, he would still have the same system of law which he now has].

But what are the goodly spoyles that these men expect, if they could break through such a croud of Repugnancies and impossibilities? the whole result and product of it will prove but a meer Cipher, for Reason as 'tis now does not binde in its own name, but in the name of its supreme Lord and Sovereigne, by whom Reason lives, and moves, and has its being.[66]

For if only a creature should binde it self to the observation of this Law, it must also inflict upon it self such a punishment as is answerable to the violation of it: but no such being would be willing or able to punish it self in so high a measure as such a transgression would meritoriously require; so that it must be accountable to some other Legislative power, which will vindicate its own commands, and will by this means ingage a Creature to be more mindeful of its own happinesse, then otherwise it would be.

For though some of the Gallanter Heathen can brave it out sometimes in an expression; that the very turpitude of such an action is punishment enough, and the very beauty of goodnesse is an abundant reward and compensation; yet we see that all this, and more then this, did not efficaciously prevaile with them for their due conformity and full obedience to Natures Law; such a single cord as this, will be easily broken.

Yet there is some truth in what they say, for thus much is visible and apparent, that there is such a Magnetical power in some good, as must needs allure and attract a Rational Being; there is such a native fairnesse, such an intrinsecal lovelinesse in some objects as does not depend upon an external command, but by its own worth must needs win upon the Soul: and there is such an inseparable deformity and malignity in some evill, as that Reason must needs loath it and abominate it.

Insomuch as that if there were no Law or Command, yet a Rational being of its own accord, out of meere love would espouse it self to such an amiable good, 'twould claspe and twine about such a precious object, and if there were not the least check or prohibition, yet in order to its own welfare, 'twould abhor and flie from some black evils, that spit out so much venome against its Nature.

This is that which the School-men meane, when they tell us, *Quaedam sunt mala, quia prohibentur; sed alia prohibentur, quia sunt mala:*[67] that is, in Positive Lawes, whether Divine, or Humane; Acts are to be esteem'd evill upon this account, because they are forbidden; but in the Law of Nature such an evill was intimately and inevitably an evil, though it should not be forbidden.

Now that there are such *Bona per se,* and *Mala per se,* (as the Schools speak) [51] I shall thus demonstrate: *Quod non est Malum per se potuit non prohiberi,*[68] for there is no reason imaginable why there should not be a possibility of not prohibiting that which is not absolutely evil, which is in its own nature indifferent.

But now there are some evils so excessively evil, so intolerably bad, as that they cannot but be forbidden; I shall only name this one; *Odium Dei,*[69] for a Being to hate the Creatour and cause of its being, if it were possible for this not to be forbidden, it were possible for it to be lawful; for *Ubi nulla Lex, ibi nulla praevaricatio:*[70] Where there's no Law, there's no Ἀνομία; where there's no Rule, there's no Anomaly; if there were no prohibition of this, 'twould not be sin to do it. But that to hate God should not be sin, does involve a whole heap of contradictions; so that this evill is so full of evill, as that it cannot but be forbidden; and therefore is an evil in order of Nature before the Prohibition of it. Besides, as the Philosophers love to speak, *Essentiae rerum sunt immutabiles,*[71] Essences neither ebbe nor flow, but have in themselves a perpetual Unity and Identity: and all such properties as flow and bubble up from Beings, are constant and unvariable, but if they could be stopt in their motion, yet that state would be violent, and not at all connatural to such a subject.

So that grant only the being of man, and you cannot but grant this also, that there is such a constant conveniency and Analogy, which some objects have with its Essence, as that it cannot but encline to them, and that there is such an irreconcileable Disconvenience, such an Eternal Antipathy between it and other objects, as that it must cease to be what it is before it can come neer them.

This *Suarez* termes a Natural Obligation, and a just foundation for a Law;[72] but now before all this can rise up to the height and perfection of a Law: there must come a Command from some Superiour Powers, from whence will spring a Moral obligation also, and make up the formality of a Law.

Therefore God himself, for the brightning of his own Glory, for the better regulating and tuning of the world; for the maintaining of such a choyce peece of his workmanship as man is, has publisht this his Royal command, and proclaim'd it by that Principle of Reason, which he has planted in the being of man: which does fully convince him of the righteousnesse, and goodnesse, and necessity of this Law, for the materials of it; and of the validity and authority of this Law, as it comes from the minde and will of his Creatour. Neither is it any eclipse or diminution of the Liberty of that first being to say that there is some evill so foul and ill-favour'd, as that it cannot but be forbidden by him; and that there is some good so fair and eminent, as that he cannot but command it.

For, as the Schoolmen observe, *Divina voluntas, licet simpliciter libera sit ad extra, ex suppositione tamen unius Actus liberi, potest necessitari ad alium.*[73]

Though the will of God be compleatly free in respect of all his looks and glances towards the Creature, yet notwithstanding upon the voluntary and free [52] precedency of one Act, we may justly conceive him necessitated to another, by vertue of that indissoluble connexion and concatenation between these two Acts, which does in a manner knit and unite them into one.

Thus God has an absolute liberty and choyce, whether he will make a promise or no, but if he has made it, he cannot but fulfil it. Thus he is perfectly free, whether he will reveal his minde or no, but if he will reveal it, he cannot but speak truth, and manifest it as it is.

God had the very same liberty whether he would create a world or no, but if he will create it, and keep it in its comelinesse and proportion, he must then have a vigilant and providential eye over it; and if he will provide for it, he cannot but have a perfect and indefective Providence agreeable to his own wisdome, and goodnesse, and being, so that if he will create such a being as Man; such a Rational Creature furnisht with sufficient knowledge to discern between some good and evill; and if he will supply it with a proportionable concourse in its operations, he cannot then but prohibit such acts as are intrinsecally prejudicial and detrimental to the being of it; neither can he but command such acts as are necessary to its preservation and welfare.

God therefore when from all eternity in his own glorious Thoughts he contriv'd the being of man, he did also with his piercing eye see into all conveniences and disconveniences, which would be in reference to such a being; and by his eternal Law did restrain and determine it to such acts as should be advantageous to it, which in his wise Oeconomy and dispensation, he publisht to man by the voyce of Reason, by the Mediation of this Natural Law.

Whence it is that every violation of this Law, is not only an injury to mans being, but *ultra nativam rei malitiam*[74] [beyond the intrinsic evil of the thing], (as the Schools speak) 'tis also a vertual and interpretative contempt of that supreme Law-giver, who out of so much wisdome, love, and goodnesse did thus binde man to his own happinesse.

So much then as man does start aside and Apostatize from this Law, to so much misery and punishment does he expose himself.

Though it be not necessary that the *Candle* of nature should discover the full extent and measure of that punishment which is due to the breakers of this Law, for to the Nature of punishment, *non requiritur ut prae-*

cognita sit poena, sed ut fiat actus Dignus tali poena[75] [it is not necessary that the punishment should be foreknown, but that an act should be committed worthy of such punishment]. The Lawyers and the Schoolmen both will acknowledge this Principle.

For as *Suarez* has it, *Sequitur reatus ex intrinseca conditione culpae, Ita ut licet poena per Legem non sit determinata, Arbitrio tamen competentis judicis puniri possit*[76] [responsibility follows from the intrinsic condition of guilt, so that even if the punishment were not determined by law, yet a crime could be punished in [53] accordance with the decision of a competent judge]. Yet the Light of Nature will reveal and disclose thus much: That a being totally dependent upon another, essentially subordinate and subject to it, must also be accountable to it for every provocation and rebellion: And for the violation of so good a Law, which he has set it, and for the sinning against such admirable Providence and justice as shines out upon it, must be liable to such a punishment, as that glorious Law-giver shall judge fit for such an offence; who is so full of justice, as that he cannot, and so great in goodnesse, as that he will not punish a Creature above its desert.

CHAPTER 7

The Extent of the Law of Nature

[54] There are stampt and printed upon the being of man, some cleare and undelible Principles, some first and Alphabetical Notions; by putting together of which it can spell out the Law of Nature.

There's scatter'd in the Soul of Man some seeds of light, which fill it with a vigorous pregnancy, with a multiplying fruitfulnesse, so that it brings forth a numerous and sparkling posterity of secondary Notions, which make for the crowning and encompassing of the Soul with happinesse.

All the fresh springs of Common and Fountain-Notions are in the Soul of Man, for the watering of his Essence, for the refreshing of this heavenly Plant, this *Arbor inversa*[1] [inverted tree], this enclosed being, this Garden of God.

And though the wickednesse of man may stop the pleasant motion, the clear and Crystalline progresse of the Fountain, yet they cannot hinder the first risings, the bubling endeavours of it. They may pull off Natures leaves, and pluck off her fruit, and chop off her branches, but yet the root of it is eternal, the foundation of it is inviolable.

Now these first and Radical Principles are wound up in some such short bottomes as these: *Bonum est appetendum, malum est fugiendum; Beatitudo est quaerenda; Quod tibi fieri non vis, alteri ne feceris*[2] [good is to be sought, evil avoided; happiness is to be striven for; do not do to others, what you do not wish to have done to yourself]. And Reason thus ᾠοτόκησε τὸν νόμον, *incubando super haec ova*, by warming and brooding upon these first and oval Principles of her own laying, it being it self quicken'd with an heavenly vigour, does thus hatch the Law of Nature.

For you must not, nor cannot think that Natures Law is confin'd and contracted within the compasse of two or three common Notions, but Reason as with one foot it fixes a Centre, so with the other it measures and spreads out a circumference, it drawes several conclusions, which do all meet and croud into these first, and Central Principles. As in those Noble Mathematical Sciences there are, not only some first αἰτήματα [postulates], which are granted as soone as they are askt, if not before, but there are also whole heaps of firme and immovable Demonstrations, that are built upon them. In the very same manner, Nature has some *Postulata,* some προλήψεις [preconceptions], (which *Seneca* [55] renders *praesumptiones,* which others call *Anticipationes Animi,*)[3] which she knows a Rational being will presently and willingly yeeld unto; and therefore by vertue of these it does engage and oblige it, to all such commands as shall by just result, by genuine production, by kindly and evident derivation flow from these.

For men must not only look upon the capital letters of this Νόμος γραπτὸς[4] [written law], but they must reade the whole context, and coherence of it; they must look to every jot and Apex of it, for heaven and earth shall sooner passe away, then one jot or title of this Law shall vanish.[5]

They must not only gaze upon two or three Principles of the first Magnitude, but they must take notice of the lesser Celestial *Sporades,*[6] for these also have their light and influence.

They must not only skim off the Creame of first Principles, but whatsoever sweetnesse comes streaming from the Dugge of Nature, they must feed upon it, they may be nourisht with it.

Reason does not only crop off the tops of first Notions,[7] but does so gather all the flowers in Natures Garden, as that it can binde them together in a pleasant posie, for the refreshment of it self and others.

Thus as a noble Author of our own does well observe, *Tota fere Ethica est Notitia communis:*[8] All Morality is nothing but a collection and bundling up of natural Precepts. The Moralists did but πλατύνειν φυλακτήρια [make broad their phylacteries], enlarge the fringes of Natures garment;[9] they are so many Commentators and Expositors upon Natures Law. This was his meaning that stil'd Moral Philosophy, ἡ περὶ τὰ ἀνθρώπινα φιλοσοφία,[10] that Philosophy which is for the maintaining and edifying of humane nature. Thus Natures Law is frequently call'd the Moral Law. But the School-men in their rougher language make these several ranks and distributions of natural Precepts, *Τὰ πρῶτα κατὰ φύσιν*.[11] First, there come in the front *Principia Generalia,* (as some call them) *per se Nota; ut Honestum est faciendum; Pravum vitandum* [general principles known naturally as, we must do good, and avoid evil]. Then follow next *Principia Particularia, & magis determinata; ut justitia est servanda; Deus est colendus; vivendum est Temperate*[12] [particular and more defined principles; as, we must maintain justice, we must worship God, we must live temperately]. At length come up in the reare, *conclusiones evidenter illatae, quae tamen cognosci nequeunt nisi per discursum; ut Mendacium, furtum, & similia prava esse*[13] [conclusions clearly inferences which, however, cannot be known without intellectual effort; as that lying, theft and the like are wicked].

These, though they may seeme somewhat more remote, yet being fetcht from clear and unquestionable premisses, they have *Natures* Seal upon them; and are thus farre sacred, so as to have the usual priviledge of a Conclusion, to be untoucht and undeniable.

[56] For though that learned Author, whom I mention'd not long before, do justly take notice of this,[14] that discourse is the usual in-let to Errour, and too often gives an open admission, and courteous entertainment to such falsities as come disguis'd in a Syllogistical forme, which by their Sequacious windings and Gradual insinuations, twine about some weak understandings: yet in the nature of the thing it self, 'tis as impossible to collect an Errour out of a Truth, as 'tis to gather the blackest night out of the fairest Sun-shine, or the foulest wickednesse out of the purest goodnesse. A Conclusion therefore that's built upon the Sand, you may very well expect its fall, but that which is built upon the Rock is impregnable and immovable; for if the Law of *Nature* should not extend it self so farre, as to oblige men to an accurate observation of that, which is a remoov or two distant from first Principles, 'twould then prove extremely defective in some such Precepts as do most intimately and intensely conduce to the welfare and advantage of an Intellectual being.

And these first Notions would be most barren inefficacious speculations, unless they did thus encrease and multiply, and bring forth fruit with the blessing of heaven upon them.

So that there is a necessary connexion, and concatenation between first Principles, and such Conclusions. For as *Suarez* has it, *Veritas Principii continetur in conclusione*[15] [the truth of the principle is contained in the conclusion]: so that he that questions the Conclusion, must needs also strike at the Principle. Nay, if we look to the notion of a Law, there is more of that to be seen in these more particular determinations, then in those more Universal notions; for *Lex est proxima Regula operationum* [law is the proximate rule of operation]. But now particulars are neerer to existence and operation then universals: and in this respect do more immediately steere and direct the motions of such a being. The one is the bending of the bowe, but the other is the shooting of the Arrow.

Suarez does fully determine this in such words as these, *Haec omnia Praecepta* (he means both Principles and Conclusions) *prodeunt a Deo Auctore Naturae, & tendunt ad eundem finem, nimirum ad debitam conservationem, & Naturalem perfectionem, seu foelicitatem Humanae Naturae* [All these precepts proceed from God the Author of nature, and tend to the same end, which is clearly the due preservation and natural perfection, or happiness of human nature].

This Law of *Nature* as it is thus brancht forth, does binde *in foro Conscientiae*[16] [in the court of conscience]; for as that noble Author, (whom I more then once commended before) speaks very well in this; Natural Conscience 'tis *Centrum Notitiarum Communium* [the centre of general knowledge], and 'tis a kinde of *Sensus Communis* [common sense] in respect of the inward faculties, as that other is in respect of the outward Senses.[17] 'Tis a competent Judge of this Law of *Nature:* 'tis the Natural Pulse of the Soul, by the beating and motion of which [57] the state and temper of men is discernable. The Apostle *Paul* thus felt the Heathens pulse, and found their consciences sometimes accusing them, sometimes making Apology for them. Yet there's a great deale of difference between Natural Conscience, and the Law of *Nature;* for (as the School-men speak) Conscience, 'tis *Dictamen Practicum in Particulari*[18] [a practical dictate about particulars]; 'tis a prosecution and application of this Natural Law, as Providence is of that Eternal Law.

Nay, Conscience sometimes does embrace only the shadow of a Law, and does engage men though erroneously to the observation of that which was never dictated by any just Legislative power. Nor is it content to glance only at what's to come, but *Janus*-like it has a double aspect, and so looks back to what's past, as to call men to a strict accompt for every violation of this Law.

Which Law is so accurate as to oblige men not only *Ad Actum* [to the act], but *ad modum* [to the mode] also:[19] it looks as well to the inward forme and manner, as to the materiality and bulk of outward actions: for every being owes thus much kindnesse and courtesie to it self, not only to put forth such acts as are essential and intrinsecal to its own welfare; but also to delight in them, and to fulfil them with all possible freenesse and alacrity, with the greatest intensnesse and complacency. Self-love alone might easily constraine men to this natural obedience. Humane Lawes indeed rest satisfi'd with a visible and external obedience; but Natures Law darts it self into the most intimate Essentials, and looks for entertainment there.

You know that amongst the Moralists only such acts are esteem'd *Actus Humani* [human acts] that are *Actus Voluntarii* [voluntary acts]. When *Nature* has tuned a Rational Being, she expects that every string, every faculty should spontaneously and cheerfully sound forth his praise.

And the God of *Nature,* that has not chain'd, nor fetter'd, nor enslav'd such a Creature, but has given it a competent liberty and enlargement; the free diffusion and amplification of its own Essence; he looks withal that it should willingly consent to its own happinesse, and to all such means as are necessary for the accomplishment of its choicest end: and that it should totally abhorre whatsoever is destructive and prejudicial to its own being; which if it do, 'twill presently embrace the Law of *Nature,* if it either love its God or it self; the command of its God, or the welfare of it self.

Nay, the precepts of this natural Law are so potent and triumphant, as that some acts which rebel against it, become not only *Illiciti* [illegal], but *Irriti*[20] [ineffectual], as both the Schoolmen and the Lawyers observe: they are not only irregularities, but meere nullities: and that either *ob defectum Potestatis & Incapacitatem Materiae*[21] [from lack of power and physical impossibility], as if one should go about to give the same thing to two several Persons, the second [58] Donation is a Moral Non-entity: or else *Propter Perpetuam rei indecentiam, & Turpitudinem Durantem*[22] [because of the perpetual indecency and lasting infamy of the thing], as in some Anomalous and incestuous marriages. And this Law of *Nature* is so exact, as that 'tis not capable of an Ἐπιείκεία [mitigation], which the Lawyers call *Emendatio Legis*[23] [the emendation of the law]: but there is no mending of Essences, nor of Essential Lawes, both which consist *in Puncto, in indivisibili* [in an indivisible atom], and so cannot *Recipere magis & minus* [admit more or less]: nor is there any need of it, for in this Law there's no rigour at all, 'tis pure equity, and so nothing is to be abated of it. Neither does it depend only *a mente Legis-latoris* [on the intention of the legislator], which is the usual Rise of Mitigation; but 'tis conversant about such acts as are *Per se tales* [in themselves such], most intrinsecally and inseparably.[24]

Yet notwithstanding this Law does not refuse an Interpretation, but *Nature* her self does glosse upon her own Law, as in what circumstances such an Act is to be esteem'd murder, and when not; and so in many other branches of *Natures* Law, if there be any appearance of Intricacy, any seeming knot and difficulty, *Nature* has given edge enough to cut it asunder.

There is another Law bordering upon this Law of *Nature, Jus Gentium, Juri Naturali Propinquum & consanguineum* [the law of nations, bordering on and related to the law of nature]; and 'tis *Medium quoddam, inter Jus Naturale & Jus Civile*[25] [as it were, a mean between natural and civil law]. Now this *Jus Gentium* [the law of nations] is either *per similitudinem & concomitantiam* [through similarity and agreement], when several Nations in their distinct conditions have yet some of the same positive Lawes: or else (which indeed is most properly Νομιμὸν ἐθνικὸν [the law of nations]) *Per communicationem & Societatem,*[26] which, as the learned *Grotius* describes, *Ab omnium, vel multarum gentium voluntate vim obligandi accepit:*[27] that is, when all or many of the most refined Nations bunching and clustering together, do binde themselves by general compact, to the observation of such Lawes, as they judge to be for the good of them all. As the honourable entertainment of an Embassadour, or such like.

So that 'tis *Jus humanum, non scriptum*[28] [human law, unwritten]. 'Tis εὕρημα βίου, καὶ χρόνου[29] [a discovery of life and time]. For as *Justinian* tells us, *Usu exigente, & Humanis necessitatibus, Gentes humanae quaedam sibi jura constituerunt*[30] [As a result of necessary practice and human needs, the nations of men have established certain laws for themselves]. Whereas

other humane Lawes have a narrower sphere and compasse, and are limited to such a state, which the Oratour stiles, *Leges populares*[31] [laws of the
people], the Hebrews call their positive Lawes חקים [statutes], sometimes
משפטים [judgments], though the one do more properly point at Ceremo-
nials, the other at Judicials;[32] The *Septuagint* render them ἐντολαὶ [com-
mandments], some others call them [59] τὰ τῆς δευτερώσεως[33] [secondary
laws], as they call natural Lawes מצות[34] [commandments], which the Hellenists render δικαιώματα[35] [ordinances]. But according to the Greek Idiom, these are tearmed τὰ ἐν φύσει [natural], and the others τὰ ἐν τάξει[36]
[ordered].

Now, though the formality of humane Lawes do flow immediately
from the power of some particular men; yet the strength and sinew of
these Lawes is founded in the Law of *Nature:* for *Nature* does permissively
give them leave to make such Lawes as are for their greater convenience;
and when they are made, and whilest they are in their force and vigour, it
does oblige and command them not to break or violate them: for they are
to esteem their own consent as a Sacred thing; they are not to contradict
their own Acts, nor to oppose such commands, as *ex Pacto* [by agreement]
were fram'd and constituted by themselves.

Thus much for the Law of *Nature* in general. We must look in the next
place, to that *Lumen Naturae* [light of nature], that *Candle of the Lord* by
which this Law of *Nature* is manifested and discovered.

How the Law of Nature Is Discovered?
Not by Tradition

[60] GOD having contrived such an admirable and harmonious Law for
the guiding and governing of his Creature, you cannot doubt but that he
will also provide sufficient means for the discovery and publishing of it;
Promulgation being pre-requir'd as a necessary condition before a Law can
be valid and vigorous. To this end therefore he has set up an Intellectual
Lamp in the soul, by the light of which it can read this νόμος γραπτὸς[1]
[written law], and can follow the commands of its Creatour.

The *Schoolmen* with full and general consent understand that place of
the Psalmist of this *Lumen Naturale*[2] [natural light], and many other Authors follow them in this too securely. Nay, some *Critical* writers[3] quote
them, and yet never chide them for it. The words are these, עלינו אור פניד
נסה *Eleva super nos lumen vultus tui*[4] [lift thou up the light of thy countenance upon us]: but yet they, very ignorantly, though very confidently render them, *Signatum est super nos lumen vultus tui*[5] [the light of thy countenance is imprinted upon us]: and they do as erroneously interpret it of
the light of Reason, which (say they) is *Signaculum quoddam, & impressio
increatae lucis in Anima*[6] [a certain seal and stamp of uncreated light in the
soul]. So much indeed is true, but it is far from being an Exposition of this
place. Yet perhaps the *Septuagint* misled them, who thus translate it; Ἐση-
μειώθη ἐφ᾽ ἡμᾶς τὸ φῶς τοῦ προσώπου σοῦ [the light of thy countenance
is marked upon us]; but *Aquila,* that had a quicker eye here, renders it
Ἔπαρον [lift up], and *Symmachus* ἐπίσημον ποίησον[7] [mark].

The words are plainly put up in the forme of a Petition to heaven, for
some smiles of love, for some propitious and favourable glances, for Gods

gracious presence and acceptance. And they amount to this sense; *If one Sun do but shine upon me, I shall have more joy, then worldlings have, when all their Stars appear.*[8]

But to let these passe with the Errours of their vulgar Latin; I meet with one more remarkable and of larger influence; I mean that of the Jewes, who (as that worthy Author of our own in his learned book *De Jure Naturali secundum Hebraeos* makes the report) do imagine and suppose that the light of *Nature* shines only upon themselves originally and principally, and upon the Gentiles only by way of Participation and dependance upon them: They all must light [61] their candles at the Jewish Lamp. Thus they strive as much as they can to engrosse and monopolize this natural light to themselves; only it may be sometimes out of their great liberality they will distribute some broken beams of it to the Gentiles. As if these מצוה בני נוח these *Praecepta Noachidarum*[9] [precepts of the children of Noah] had been lockt up and cabinetted in *Noahs* Ark, and afterwards kept from the prophane touch of a Gentile: as if they had been part of that bread, which our Saviour said was not to be cast unto dogs; and therefore they would make them be glad to eate of the crumbs that fall from their masters table. As if they only enjoyed a *Goshen* of Natural light, and all the rest of the world were benighted in most palpable and unavoidable darknesse; as if this Sun shin'd only upon *Canaan;* as if *Canaan* onely flow'd with this milk and honey; as if no drops of heaven could fall upon a Wildernesse, unlesse an Israelite be there; As if they had the whole impression of Natures Law; as if God had not dealt thus with every Nation; as if the Heathen also had not the knowledge of this Law. 'Tis true, they had the first beauty of the rising Sun, the first peepings out of the day, the first dawnings of natural light; for there were no other that it could then shine upon: but do they mean to check the Sun in its motion, to stop this Giant in his race, to hinder him from scattering rayes of light in the world? Do they think that Natures Fountain is enclos'd, that her Well is seal'd up, that a Jew must only drink of it, and a Gentile must die for thirst? O but they tell you they are עם מגלה *Λάος περιούσιος*, a Darling, and peculiar Nation.[10]

We shall fully acknowledge with the Hebrew of Hebrews, *Πολὺ τὸ περισσὸν τοῦ Ἰουδαίου*[11] [the advantage of the Jew is great], though not in respect of natural light, which doubtlesse is planted by *Nature* in the heart

both of Jew and Gentile, and shines upon both with an equal and impartial beam. And yet this must not be denied, that the Jewes had even these Natural notions much clarified & refin'd from those clouds and mists which יצר הרע[12] Original sin had brought upon them, and this by means of that pure and powerful beam of heavenly truth which shined more peculiarly upon them; those Lawes which *Nature* had engraven ἐν δέλτοις φρενῶν upon the tables of their hearts,[13] sin like a moth had eaten and defaced (as in all other men it had done) but in them those fugitive letters were call'd home again, and those many *Lacunae* were supplyed and made good again by comparing it with that other Copy (of Gods own writing too) which *Moses* received in the Mount; and besides, they had a great number of revealed truths discovered to them, which were engraffed indeed upon the stock of *Nature,* but would never have grown out of it: so that this second Edition was *Auctior* [expanded] also, as well as *Emendatior* [corrected]; but yet for all this they have no greater a portion *of the light of Nature* then all men have. Thus Christians also are עם מנלה[14] [a peculiar
[62] people], and yet in respect of their natural condition, have no more then others.

Now if the Jewes have so many priviledges, why are not they content, why do not they rest satisfied with them? Why will they thus be claiming and arrogating more then their due?

Are they the first-born, and have they a double portion, and do they envy their younger brethren, their birth and being? Have they a bright and eminent Sun-shine, and do they envy a Gentile *the Candle of the Lord?*

No (as that learned Author tells us) they will grant that the Gentiles had their Candle, and their Torch, but it was lighted at the Jewes Sun. They may have some bottles of water to quench their thirst, but they must be fill'd at their streams, ἐκ τῶν Ἑβραικῶν ναμάτων, *ex fluentis Hebraicis*[15] [from the streams of the Hebrews].

But truly, if they were at their disposing, there be some that will question, whether they would let them sip at their fountain or no; whether they would let them light a Candle with them or no. Yes (may some say) *Pythagoras* lighted his Candle there, and *Plato* lighted his Candle at theirs.[16]

But what did they borrow common Notions of them? did they borrow any Copies of Natures Law from them? was this Νόμος γραπτὸς[17] [written law], only some Jewish Manu-script, which they translated into Greek? Can *Pythagoras* know nothing, unlesse by a present μετεμψύχωσις [metempsychosis] a Jews soul come and enforme him? That *Pythagoras* should be circumcis'd by the perswasion of the Jews is not impossible; but that he could not know how to forbid Blasphemy, without the Jews teachings, deserves a good argument to prove it.

If they will but attend to *Pythagoras* himself, they shall hear him resolving these first Notions of his and others, into *Natures* bounty, and not into the Jews courtesie; for thus he sings;— Θεῖον γένος ἐστὶ βροτοῖσι, οἷς ἱερὰ προφέρουσα φύσις δείκνυσιν ἕκαστα[18] [the race of man is divine; for him nature brings forth and reveals every sacred thing]. And *Hierocles* in his Comment (which is as golden as *Pythagoras* his Verses) does thus paraphrase upon his meaning, Πάντες ἀφορμὰς ἔχοντες ἐν συμφύτοις πρὸς ἐπίγνωσιν τῆς ἑαυτῶν οὐσίας [all men have among their innate principles the resources for knowing their own natures]. And these Principles which he does call here τὰ σύμφυτα [innate], he does not long after stile τὰς φυσικὰς ἐννοίας[19] [natural notions].

Then as for *Plato,* to be sure he'll tell them, that he has connate *Species* of his own, for which he was never beholding to the Jews. He'll tell them, that he has many Spermatical Notions, that were never of their sowing; Many vigilant sparks that were never of their striking or kindling. He'll but set his Reminiscence awork, and will visit his old acquaintance, recal many ancient truths, that are now slipt out of his memory, and have been too long absent.

[63] And surely *Aristotle* never thought that his *Rasa Tabula,* could have nothing printed upon it, till a Jew gave it an *Imprimatur,* he little imagin'd that the Motion of his Soul depended upon these Oriental Intelligences.

Therefore if they please they may spare that pretty story of theirs, which that learned Author, whom I have so often commended, does acquaint us with, but yet withall esteems it fabulous of *Simeon* the just, the High Priest reading of Lectures to *Aristotle* a little before his death, of the immortality of the soul, and the reward and punishment which are reserved for another life: and that so powerfully, as that he convinced him, and converted him.[20]

But certainly that brave Philosopher could easily spy out immortality stampt upon his own soul, though such a Monitor had been absent, and did know long before that time by the improvement of his own intellectuals, that he must give an account of his being and operations to his ʾΟν ὄντων[21] [Being of beings].

What means then that voice of the Oracle;

Μοῦνοι χαλδαῖοι σοφίαν λάχον, ἠδ᾽ ἄρ᾽ Ἑβραῖοι
Αὐτογένεθλον ἄνακτα σεβαζόμενοι θεὸν ἀγνῶς[22]

[*The Chaldeans alone have obtained wisdom, together with the Hebrews, who reverence a self-existent king as their sacred God.*]

Truly the Oracle here is not so obscure, but that you may easily perceive that by Σοφία [wisdom], it did not mean *Intelligentia,* which is ἡ γνῶσις τῶν πρώτων στοιχείων [the knowledge of first principles], but only *Sapientia,* which is ἡ γνῶσις τῶν τιμιωτάτων [the knowledge of what is most valuable]. Now why they had more of this, the Apostle will give you the best account of it; ὅτι ἐπιστεύθησαν τὰ λόγια τοῦ θεοῦ[23] [because that unto them were committed the oracles of God], because they had a better Oracle to consult withal, then this was.

Yet surely neither Jew nor Gentile need go to an Oracle to enquire of common Notions. But in respect of these that *Anonymous* Author of the life of *Pythagoras* speaks an unquestionable truth; οὐκ ἐπείσακτος, ὡς εἰπεῖν, ἡ παιδεία ἐν ταῖς Ἀθήναις, ἀλλ᾽ ἐκ φύσεως ὑπάρχουσα;[24] that is the Athenians had not an Adventitious and Precarious kinde of knowledge; but that *Nature* which gave them a Being, gave them Education also; As her womb bare them, so her breasts gave them suck; As they were Αὐτόχθονες [born by nature], so likewise Αὐτοδίδακτοι[25] [taught by nature].

But you shall hear a bragging and doting Egyptian telling you, Ἕλληνας ἀεὶ παῖδας εἶναι.[26] The Greeks were alwayes boys in knowledge. Grant that they were children; yet cannot they suck at *Natures* dug? Cannot they read *Natures* Alphabet, unlesse a Jew come with his fescue and teach them?

[64] Howere, the Egyptian has little Reason to triumph, for to be sure, if there be any light in *Egypt* more then this of *Nature,* they may thank Israelites for it: if there be any corne in *Egypt,* they may thank a *Joseph* for

providing of it. These, if any, lighted their Candles at the Israelites, and receiv'd more precious jewels from them, then ever they were robb'd of by them.

This indeed must be granted that the whole generality of the Heathen went a gleaning in the Jewish fields. They had some of their grapes, some eares of corne that dropt from them. *Pythagoras* and *Plato* especially were such notable gleaners, as that they stole out of the very sheaves, out of those truths that are bound up in the sacred volume. Yet all this while they nere stole first Principles, nor demonstrations; but they had them οἴκο-θεν[27] [at home], and needed not to take such a long journey for them.

Give then unto the Jew the things of the Jews, and to the Gentile, the things that are the Gentiles, and that which God has made common, call not thou peculiar. The Apostle *Pauls* question is here very seasonable, ἦ Ἰουδαίων ὁ θεὸς μόνον; οὐχὶ δὲ καὶ ἐθνῶν; ναὶ καὶ ἐθνῶν[28] [Is He the God of the Jews only? Is He not also of the Gentiles? Yes, of the Gentiles also].

There was never any partition-wall between the Essence of Jew and Gentile. Now the Law of *Nature* 'tis founded in Essentials. And that which is disconvenient to that Rational *Nature* which is in a Jew, is as opposite and disagreeable to the same *Nature* in a Gentile; as that good which is suitable and proportionable to a Jew in his Rational being, is every way as intrinsecal to the welfare of a Gentile, that does not differ essentially from him. So likewise for the Promulgation of this Law, being it does equally concerne them both, and equally oblige them both; it is also by *Nature* equally publisht and manifested to them both. So that what the Apostle speaks in respect of the freenesse of Evangelical light, we may say the very same in respect of the commonnesse of natural light: οὐκ ἔνι Ἕλλην καὶ Ἰουδαῖος, περιτομὴ καὶ ἀκροβυστία, βάρβαρος, Σκύθης, δοῦλος, ἐλεύ-θερος[29] [where there is neither Greek nor Jew, circumcision nor uncircum-cision, Barbarian, Scythian, bound nor free], but all these are one in re-spect of *Nature,* and natures Law, and natures Light.

CHAPTER 9

The Light of Reason

[65] This law of Nature having a firme and unshaken foundation in the necessity and conveniency of its materials, becomes formally valid and vigorous by the minde and command of the Supreme Law-giver; So as that
all the strength and nerves, and binding virtue of this Law are rooted and
fasten'd partly in the excellency and equity of the commands themselves,
but they principally depend upon the Sovereignty and Authority of God
himself: thus contriving and commanding the welfare of his Creature, and
advancing a Rational Nature to the just perfection of its being. This is the
rise and original of all that obligation which is in the Law of Nature. But
the publishing and manifestation of this Law which must give notice of all
this, does flow from that heavenly beame which God has darted into the
soul of man; from *the Candle of the Lord,* which God has lighted up for
the discovery of his owne Lawes; from that intellectual eye which God has
fram'd and made exactly proportionable to this Light.

Therefore we shall easily grant that the obligation of this Law does not
come from this *Candle of the Lord;* and others I suppose will not deny that
the *Manifestation* of this Law does come from this *Candle of the Lord,* that
the *Promulgation* of this Law is made by the voice of *Reason.*

In order of *Nature,* this Law, as all others, must be made, before it can
be made known, Entity being the just Root and bottome of Intelligibility.
So that *Reason* does not *facere* [make] or *ferre legem* [produce the law], but
only *invenire* [discover it], as a Candle does not produce an object, but
only present it to the eye, and make it visible. All verity 'tis but the glosse
of Entity, there's a loving Union and Communion between them, as soone
as being is it may be known.

So that *Reason* is the Pen by which *Nature* writes this Law of her own composing; This Law 'tis publisht by Authority from heaven, and Reason is the Printer: This eye of the soul 'tis to spy out all dangers and all advantages, all conveniences and disconveniences in reference to such a being, and to warne the soul in the name of its Creator, to fly from such irregularities as have an intrinsecal and implacable malice in them, and are prejudicial and destructive to its *Nature,* but to comply with, and embrace all such acts and objects as have a native comelinesse and amiablenesse, and are for the heightning and ennobling of its being.

[66] *Hierocles* does most excellently set forth this, whilest he brings that golden Verse of *Pythagoras* to the Touch-stone; Μηδ᾿ ἀλογίστως σαυτὸν ἔχειν περὶ μηδὲν ἐθίζου[1] [never accustom yourself to acting irrationally], and does thus brighten it, and display it in its full glory, ὡς γὰρ πρὸς κανόνα τὴν οὐσίαν ἡμῶν ἀποβλέποντες, τὸ δέον ἐν πᾶσιν εὑρίσκομεν, κατὰ τὸν ὀρθὸν λόγον, συμφώνως τῇ ἑαυτῶν οὐσία διαζῶντες;[2] his meaning's this: There is a kinde of Canon-Law in the essences of men, and a Rational tuning all their faculties according to those lessons which *Nature* has set; it does ζῆν συμφώνως [live harmoniously], with a most grateful and harmonious life, pleases both it self and others. So whilest he weighs that other golden verse in the Ballance, he speaks very high. Βουλεύου δὲ πρὸ ἔργου ὅπως μή μῶρα πέληται[3] [think before you act, lest stupidities result]; he gives us this learned accompt of it; Λόγῳ δ᾿ ὀρθῷ πείθεσθαι, καὶ θεῷ ταὐτόν ἐστι. τὸ γὰρ λογικὸν γένος εὐμοίρησαν τῆς οἰκείας ἐλλάμψεως, ταῦτα βούλεται ἃ ὁ θεῖος ὁρίζει νόμας, καὶ γίνεται σύμψηφος θεῷ ἡ κατὰ θεὸν διακειμένη ψυχὴ, καὶ πρὸς τὸ θεῖον, καὶ τὸ λαμπρὸν ἀποβλέπουσα πράττει ἃ ἂν πράττῃ. ἥδε ἐναντίως διακειμένη πρὸς τὸ ἄθεον, καὶ σκοτεινὸν, εἰκῆ καὶ ὡς ἔτυχε φερομένη, ἅτε τῆς μόνης τῶν καλῶν στάθμης, νοῦ καὶ θεοῦ ἀποπεσοῦσα;[4] which I may thus render; To obey right Reason, 'tis to be perswaded by God himself; who has furnisht and adorn'd a Rational Nature with this intrinsecal and essential Lamp, that shines upon it, and guides it in the wayes of God, so as that the soul and its Creator become perfect Unisons, and being blest with the light of his countenance, it steeres all its motions and actions with much security and happinesse. But if this Lamp of Reason be darken'd and obscured, the soul presently embraces a Cloud, and courts a Shadow; the blackest and most

palpable Atheisme and wickednesse must needs cover the face of that soul, that starts back and apostatizes from its God and its Reason. Where you cannot but take notice that he calls the light of Reason Οἰκεία ἔλλαμψις [a natural illumination], which is an expression very parallel to this of *Solomon, the Candle of the Lord.*

That wise Heathen *Socrates* was of the very same minde, in whose mouth that speech was so frequent and usual, οὐδενὶ χρὴ πείθεσθαι πλὴν τῷ ὀρθῷ λόγῳ;[5] 'Tis in vaine to trust anything but that which Reason tells you has the Seal of God upon it. Thus that Heathen Oratour very fully and emphatically; *Nos Legem bonam a Mala nulla alia nisi Naturali norma dividere possumus; Nec solum Jus & Injuria a Natura dijudicantur, sed omnino omnia honesta & Turpia. Nam & communis Intelligentia nobis Res notas efficit, ea quae in animis nostris inchoavit, ut Honesta in virtute ponuntur, in vitiis Turpia;*[6] That is, Nature has distinguisht good from evil, by these indelible stamps and impressions which she has graven upon both; and has set Reason as a competent Judge to decide all Moral controversies, which by her first seeds of light plainly discovers an [67] honourable beauty in goodnesse, and an inseparable Blot in wickedness: hence these three ζῆν κατὰ φύσιν, ζῆν κατὰ λόγον, ζῆν κατὰ θεὸν [to live according to nature, to live according to reason, to live according to God] are esteem'd equivalencies by that Emperour and Philosopher *Marcus Antoninus.*[7] But yet the Jews will by no means yeeld that there is light enough in the dictates of Reason to display common notions, for they look upon it as a various and unsatisfactory light mixt with much shadow and darknesse, labouring with perpetual inconstancy and uncertainty. What, are first Principles become so mutable and treacherous? Are Demonstrations such fortuitous and contingent things? had I met with this in a fluctuating Academick, in a Rowling Sceptique, in a *Sextus Empiricus,*[8] in some famous Professor of doubts, I should then have lookt upon it as a tolerable expression of their trembling and shivering opinion. But how come I to finde it among those Divers into the depths of knowledge, who grant a certainty, and yet will not grant it to *Reason?* I would they would tell us then, where we might hope to finde it; Surely not in an Oriental Tradition, in a Rabinical dream, in a dusty Manuscript, in a Remnant of Antiquity, in a Bundle of Testimonies; and yet this is all you are like to get of them, for they tell you this story, that these Natural precepts, *tum in ipsis rerum initiis, tum in ea quae fuit post diluvium instauratione, Humano generi, ipsa sanctissima Numinis voce fuisse imperata, atque ad Posteros per Traditionem solum inde manasse;*[9] that is, that these commands were proclaim'd by the voice of God himself, first to *Adam* in the first setting out of the world; and then they were repeated to *Noah* when there was to be a reprinting, and new Edition of the world after the Deluge; and thus were in way of Tradition to be propagated to all posterity. O rare and admirable foundation of Plerophory![10] O incomparable method and contrivance to finde out certainty, to rase out first Principles, to pluck down Demonstrations, to demolish the whole structure and fabrick of *Reason,* and to build upon the word of two or three Hebrew Doctors, that tell you of a voice, and that as confidently, as if they had heard it, and they are entrusted with this voice, they must report and spread it unto others, though they do it like unfaithful Ecchos with false and imperfect rebounds.

This is to tell you that men have no *Candle of the Lord* within them, but only there must be *Traditio Lampadis,*[11] a General and Publique light, that must go from one hand to another.

This is to blot out the Νόμος γραπτὸς[12] [written law], to leave out Canonical Scripture, and to give you *Apochrypha* in the room of it. 'Tis to set a Jew in the chaire dictating the Law of Nature, with the very same infallibility, that the Pope promises himself in determining all points of Religion. Therefore some it may be will have recourse to such an *Intellectus Agens*[13] [active intellect] as must clear up all things. Now this is another Oriental Invention, for those Arabian [68] writers *Averroes* and *Avicen,* did not look upon the spirit of a man as *the Candle of the Lord,* but must needs have an Angel to hold the Candle to enlighten men in their choicest operations. Nay, *Averroes* will allow but one Angel to superintend and prompt the whole *Species* of mankinde; yet *Zabarel* questions whether his bounty will not extend to two, the one for an *Intellectus Agens,* the other for an *Intellectus Patiens*[14] [passive intellect]. To be sure *Averroes* fanci'd man as the most imperfect and contemptible being that could be, totally dependant upon an Angel in his most essential workings; the whole sphere of his being was to be mov'd by an Intelligence.

He fanci'd him a Ship steer'd only by an Angel; he fanci'd him a Lute that made no musick but by the touch of an Angel. It had been well if his *Genius* would have tun'd him a little better. It had been well if his Pilot would have kept him from making shipwrack of *Reason*. If his Intelligence would but have mov'd his Head a little more harmoniously. But by this, if he had pleas'd he might have perceiv'd that there were pluralities and differences of understandings, because there were so few of his minde. Yet *Plotinus* and *Themistius* that were his Seniors, had more then a tincture of this Errour; and lookt upon this Νοῦς ποιητικὸς [active intellect], as if it had been *Sol quidam incorporeus nulli oriens aut occidens, sed semper & ubique omnibus praesens*[15] [a sort of spiritual sun, neither rising nor setting, but always and everywhere present in all].

Which notion *Cardan* prosecutes so far, as that he falls into this most Prodigious conceit, that this *Intellectus Agens* does offer its light and assistance to sensitive beings also, but that the churlishnesse of the matter will not wellcome and entertain such pure irradiations, for thus he speaks; *Eundem Intellectum etiam belluis imminere, easque ambire: At ipsi non patere Aditum, propter materiae ineptitudinem. Igitur hominem intus irradiare, circum belluas extrinsecus collucere. Neque alia re Hominis Intellectum, ab Intellectu differre belluarum. Idcirco belluas ea omnia habere inchoata, quae in homine perfecta sunt*[16] [That the very same Intellect hangs over beasts, and surrounds them, but cannot gain access, because of the unsuitableness of the matter. Therefore it shines within man, but outside and around beasts. And the intellect of man does not differ from that of beasts in any other way; therefore beasts possess all the crude elements which are brought to perfection in man.] But *Scaliger* has sufficiently corrected him for this brutish Tenent; so that I shall need only to adde this; *Cardans Intellectus Agens,* was so familiar, as that some question whether he were a good Angel or no. Nay, some tell us that he was left him for an inheritance, shut up in a Ring, enclos'd in a golden circle, a goodly sphere for an Intelligence to move in. But there were many others also enamour'd with this opinion of an *Intellectus Agens;* the *Platonists* were excessively enclinable to it, and were alwayes so much conversant with spirits, which made their Philosophy ever question'd for a touch of [69] Magick. Nay, *Scaliger*

tells us of some others, that will have this *Intellectus Agens* to be *caput &*
Author consiliorum omnium, the contriver of the rarest and wittiest inventions; the Author of Guns, of Clocks, of Printing, of the *Pyxis nautica: Ma-*
terialem vero Intellectum esse quasi Usufructuarium, & beneficiarium illius[17]
[the compass; and that the material intellect is a sort of usufructary and
beneficiary of it].

The Jews especially admire and adore the Influence of an *Intellectus*
Agens, and not forgetful of their Primogeniture and priviledges, but being
alwayes a conceited and a bragging generation, they would fain perswade
us that God himself is their *Intellectus Agens,* but to the Gentiles he sends
only an Angel to illuminate them.[18]

The Jews indeed sometimes call every faculty an Angel, as one of the
best amongst them, *Maimonides* tells us,[19] but yet here they properly mean
an Angelical being, distinct and separate from the soul, and just according
to *Averroes* Determination, the lowest Intelligence, *Ultimus Motor Coeles-*
tium[20] [the final mover of heavenly beings]. Their own *Intellectus Agens*
they call שבינה & רוח הקדש,[21] the presence and power of God dwelling in
the understanding, the influence of it they tearme שפע,[22] as the forementioned *Maimonides* observes, that is, a copious and abundant supply of
light shining upon the Minde. According to which they understand that
place of the Psalmist באורך נדאו אור *in lumine tuo videbimus lumen*[23] [in
thy light shall we see light]; which the Schoolmen more truly expound of
the *Lumen Gloriae* [the light of glory] in the Beatifical vision, though it
may reach also to that joy and delight which Saints have in communion
with God here.

Amongst fresher and more moderne writers, *Zabarel* is very intense and
zealous for this, that God himself is the *Intellectus Agens* of the soul: but
being a most humble and devoted servant of *Aristotle,* he can by no means
quiet and content himself unlesse he can shew the world that his Master
was of the same judgement.[24]

This makes him to suborne two or three Testimonies, or at least to tam-
per with a place or two; and then bravely to conclude that without doubt
'twas the minde of the Philosopher, which is not only against the whole
stream of other Interpreters, but against the known & Orthodox Principles of him that was wiser then to countenance such a vanity.

It should seeme by that eminent writer of our own, that *Fryer Bacon* was of the same mind too, for whose words these are quoted amongst many others, out of an *Oxford*-Manuscript; *Deus respectu animae est sicut Sol respectu Oculi Temporalis,* & *Angeli sicut stellae*[25] [God, in the view of the soul, is like the sun to the physical eye, and angels are like stars]. Now what angels they were that this *Roger Bacon* fixt his eye upon, whether they were not fallen Stars, let others [70] examine. I should think that *Cardans Intellectus Agens* and his were both much of the same colour.

But this you may perceive in him and the rest of the great Pleaders for an *Intellectus Agens,* that they found all their Arguments in a pretty similitude of an eye, and light, and colours, as if this were some inconquerable Demonstration. Whereas that great Master of subtleties, whom I have more then once nam'd before, has made it appear, that the whole Notion of an *Intellectus Agens* is a meere fancy and superfluity.[26]

Yet this may be granted to all the foremention'd Authors, and this is the only spark of Truth, that lies almost buried in that heap of Errours; That God himself as he does supply every being, the Motion of every Creature with an intimate and immediate concourse every way answerable to the measure and degree of its Entity; so he does in the same manner constantly assist the Understanding with a proportionable Co-operation. But then as for any such Irradiations upon the soul in which that shall be meerly patient: God indeed if he be pleas'd to reveal himself in a special and extraordinary manner, he may thus shine out upon it, either immediately by his own light, or else drop Angelical influence upon it: but that this should be the natural and ordinary way, necessarily required to Intellectual workings, is extremely prejudicial to such a noble Being as the soul of Man is; to which God gave such bright participations of himself, and stampt his Image upon it, and left it to its own workings, as much as any other created being whatsoever. Nay, as *Scaliger* does most confidently object it to *Cardan,* you will not have one Argument left, by which you can evince the Immortality of the soul, if ye shall resolve all the excellency of its being and operations into an *Intellectus Agens* really distinct from it.

But then to make this Νοῦς ποιητικὸς [active intellect], and παθητικὸς [passive], only the various aspects and different relations of the same soul, is but a weak and needlesse device, and if 'twere *Aristotles,* to be sure 'twas none of his Master-pieces;[27] for 'tis built upon I know not what Phantasms and false Appearances.

Whereas those *Species* and colours, those pictures and representations of being that are set before an Intellectual eye, carry such a light and beauty in themselvs as may justly engratiate them with the understanding. And though some tell us that they have too much drosse & impurity, that they are too muddy and feculent, not proportionable to the purity of a reasonable soul, yet let them but think of those many strainers they have gone through: those double refinings and clarifyings, that they have had from so many percolations: and withall they may know that the understanding can drink in the most pure and flowring part of the *Species,* and can leave the dregges at the bottome. Have you not thus often seen a seal stamping it self upon the waxe, and yet not communicating the [71] least particle of matter, but only leaving a form and impression upon it?

However, there is as much proportion between these *Species* and an *Intellectus Patiens,* as between these and an *Intellectus Agens.*[28] Nay, there is more proportion between these *Species* and the understanding, then between the soul and body, which yet are joyn'd and married together in a most loving and conjugal union.

Of the Consent of Nations

[72] Though Natures law be principally proclaim'd by the voyce of *Reason;* though it be sufficiently discover'd by *the Candle of the Lord;* yet there is also a secondary and additional way, which contributes no small light to the manifestation of it: I mean the harmony & joynt consent of Nations, who though there be no κοινωνία nor συνθήκη,[1] no communion, nor commerce, nor compact between them, yet they do tacitly and spontaneously conspire in a dutiful observation of the most radical and fundamental Lawes of *Nature.*

So that by this pleasant consort of theirs you may know that the same *Nature* did tune them all. When you see the same prints and impressions upon so many several Nations, you easily perceive that they were stampt *eodem communi Sigillo,* with the same publique Seal. When you see the very same seeds thrown in such different soyles, yet all encreasing and multiplying, budding and blossoming, branching out and enlarging themselves into some fruitful expressions; you know then that 'twas Natures hand, her bountiful & successful hand that scatter'd such Seminal Principles amongst them; you presently know that 'tis no enclosed way, 'tis a *Via Regia* [king's highway], in which you meet with so many Travellers, such a concourse and confluence of People.

Amongst many others, the learned *Grotius* is ful and expresse for searching out the Law of *Nature* in this manner.

You shal hear his own words which he speaks in that excellent work of his, *De jure Belli & Pacis: Esse aliquid juris Naturalis probari solet tum ab eo quod Prius est, tum ab eo quod Posterius; quarum probandi Rationum illa subtilior est, haec popularior. A Priori, si ostendatur Rei alicujus convenientia*

*aut disconvenientia Necessaria cum Natura Rationali ac Sociali. A posteriori
vero, si non certissima fide, certe probabiliter admodum juris Naturalis esse
colligitur id, quod apud gentes omnes, aut moraliores omnes tale esse creditur*
[It is usual to prove that something is according to the law of nature either
a priori or *a posteriori;* of these methods of proof the former is more subtle,
the latter more popular. The proof is *a priori* if it is shown that anything
necessarily agrees or disagrees with a rational and social nature; it is *a posteriori* if it is concluded, not with absolute certainty, but very probably,
that that accords with natural law which all nations, or at least the more
civilized nations, believe accords with it]. And he does annex this [73] reason of it; *Universalis effectus, Universalem requirit causam*[2] [a universal effect requires a universal cause]. When you see such fresh springs and
streams of Justice watering several Kingdoms and Nations, you know that
they are participations of some rich Fountain, of a vast Ocean. When you
see so many Rayes of the same light, shooting themselves into the several
corners of the world, you presently look up to the Sun; as the glorious
original of them all.

Let me then a little vary that place in the *Acts* of the Apostles:[3] you may
hear every man in his own Language, in his own Dialect, and Idiom speaking the same works of *Nature;* Parthians, and Medes, and Elamites, and
the dwellers in *Mesopotamia,* and in *Judea,* and *Cappadocia;* in *Pontus,* in
Asia, Phrygia, and *Pamphylia,* in *Egypt,* and in the parts of *Libya* about
Cyrene, and strangers of *Rome,* Jewes and Proselytes, Cretes and Arabians,
you may hear them speak in their Tongues the wonderful works of God
and *Nature.*

For whatsoever is Natural and Essential is also universal in order to such
a *Species.* The Philosopher speaks to this very pertinently; Τὸ μὲν φύσει
ἀκίνητον, καὶ πανταχοῦ τὴν αὐτὴν ἔχει δύναμιν, ὥσπερ τὸ πῦρ καὶ ἐνθάδε
καὶ ἐν Πέρσαις καίει;[4] That is, whatsoever is Natural is immovable, and
in the same manner perpetually energetical; as fire does not put on one
colour amongst the Grecians, and paint its face otherwise amongst the
Persians: but it has alwayes the same ruddinesse and purity, the same zeal
and vehemency.

As *Nature* shews choice variety and Needle-work in this, in that she
works every *Individuum* with several flourishes, with some singular and

distinguishing notes: So likewise she plainly aspires to concord and unity, whilst she knits altogether in a common and specifical identity. Not only in the faces of men, but in their beings also, there is much of Identity, and yet much of variety.

You do not doubt, but that in all Nations there is an exact likenesse and agreement in the fabrick and composure of mens bodies in respect of integrals, excepting a few Monsters and Heteroclites in *Nature;* nor can you doubt but that there is the very same frame and constitution of mens spirits in respect of Intrinsecals, unlesse in some prodigious ones, that in the Philosophers language are Ἁμαρτήματα τῆς φύσεως[5] [sports of nature]. As face answers face, so does the heart of one man the heart of another, even the heart of an Athenian, the heart of an Indian.

Wherefore the Votes and Suffrages of *Nature* are no contemptible things. Φήμη δ᾽ οὔ τις πάμπαν ἀπόλλυται ἥν τινα λαοὶ πολλοὶ φημίζουσι[6] [no tradition which many nations spread is ever wholly destroyed]; as the Poet sings. This was the minde of that grave Moralist *Seneca,* as appears by that speech of his; *Apud nos veritatis argumentum est aliquid omnibus videri*[7] [among us the fact that something seems so to all is evidence for its truth]. But the Oratour is [74] higher and fuller in his expression; *Omni autem in re, Consensio omnium Gentium Lex Naturae putanda est*[8] [but in all things the consensus of all nations ought to be considered evidence of a law of nature]. And that other Oratour *Quintilian* does not much differ from him in this; *Pro certis habemus ea, in quae communi opinione concessum est*[9] [we regard as certain those things about which common opinion has agreed]. Or if the judgement of a Philosopher be more potent and prevalent with you, you may hear *Aristotle* telling you, Κράτιστον πάντας Ἀνθρώπους φαίνεσθαι συνομολογοῦντας τοῖς ῥηθησομένοις[10] [it is best that all men should appear unanimous about what shall be said]. You may hear *Heraclitus* determining that ὁ λόγος ξυνὸς [general opinion] is an excellent κριτήριον [criterion] of Truth; and therefore he was wont to lay down this for a Maxime, τὰ κοινῇ φαινόμενα πιστὰ[11] [common beliefs are trustworthy], which may be rendred *Vox Populi, Vox Dei* [the voice of the people is the voice of God]; yet upon this condition, that it be took with its due restraints and limitations: If you would have a sacred Author set his seal to all this, *Tertullian* has done it; *Quod apud multos unum invenitur, non est erratum sed traditum*[12] [that which is found agreed upon by many is not an error but the inherited truth].

Surely that must needs be a clear convincing light that can command respect and adoration from all beholders; it must be an orient Pearl indeed, if none will trample upon it.[13] It must be a conquering and triumphant truth, that can stop the mouths of gain-sayers, and passe the world without contradiction. Surely that's pure gold that has been examin'd by so many several Touch-stones, and has had approbation from them all; certainly 'tis some transcendent beauty that so many Nations are enamour'd withall. 'Tis some powerful musick that sets the whole world a dancing. 'Tis some pure and delicious relish, that can content and satisfie every palate. 'Tis some accurate piece that passes so many Criticks without any Animadversions, without any *Variae lectiones* [variant readings]. 'Tis an Elegant Picture, that neither the eye of an Artist, nor yet a Popular eye can finde fault withall. Think but upon the several tempers and dispositions of men; how curious are some? how censorious are others? how envious and malicious are some? how various and mutable are others? how do some love to be singular? others to be contentious? how doubtful and wavering is one? how jealous and suspicious is another? and then tell me whether it must not be some Authentical and unquestionable Truth, that can at all times have a Certificate and *Commendamus* from them all?

Then look upon the diversities of Nations & there you will see a rough and barbarous Scythian, a wild American, an unpolisht Indian, a superstitious Egyptian, a subtile Ethiopian, a cunning Arabian, a luxurious Persian, a treacherous Carthaginian, a lying Cretian, an elegant Athenian, a wanton Corinthian, a desperate Italian, a fighting German, & many other heaps of [75] Nations, whose titles I shall now spare, and tell me whether it must not be some admirable and efficacious Truth, that shall so overpower them all, as to passe currant amongst them, and be own'd and acknowledg'd by them.

Yet notwithstanding, as we told you before, that the obligation of *Natures* Law did not spring from Reason, so much lesse does it arise from the consent of Nations. That Law indeed which is peculiarly term'd Νόμιμον ἐθνικὸν, *Jus Gentium* [the law of nations], has its vigor and validity from those mutual and reciprocal compacts, which they have made amongst themselves: but the meeting of several Nations in the observation of *Natures* Law, has no binding or engaging virtue in it any otherwise then in an exemplary way; but yet it has a confirming and evidencing power, that shews that they were all obliged to this by some supreme Authority, which had such an ample influence upon them all. Thus you know the sweetnesse of Honey, both by your own taste, and by the consent of Palates too: yet neither the one, nor the other does drop any sweetnesse or lusciousnesse into the Honey-comb.[14] Thus you see the beauty and glory of light, and you may call most men in the world to be eye-witnesses of it, yet those several eyes adde no glosse or lustre to it, but only take notice of it.

Man being ζῶον πολιτικὸν and ζῶον ἥμερον as the Philosopher styles him,[15] a sociable and peaceable Creature; Ἀγελαστικὸν καὶ συγγνώμον ζῶον, as that sacred Oratour[16] termes him, a congregating Creature that loves to keep company, he must needs take much delight and complacency in that, in which he sees the whole Tribe and *Species* of mankinde agreeing with him.

Why then do the Jews look upon the גוים[17] [heathen peoples] with such a disdaining and scornful eye, as if all the Nations in comparison of them, were no more then what the Prophet saies, they are in respect of God, *as the drop of a bucket, as the dust of the Ballance,*[18] that cannot encline them one way or other.

Do but hear a while how that learned and much honoured Author of our own, does represent their minde unto you. *Gentium* (saies he) *sive omnium, sive complurium opiniones, mores, constitutiones, mensurae apud Hebraeos, in eo decernendo quod jus esse velint Naturale, seu universale, locum habent nullum* [the opinions, customs, constitutions and measures of all, or at least many other nations carry no weight with the Hebrews in their decisions about the nature of natural or universal law]. These are the Contents of that Chapter which he begins thus; *Quemadmodum ex aliorum animantium actibus aut usu, jus aliquod naturale disci, aut designari nolunt Ebraei; ita neque ex aliarum, sive omnium sive plurimarum Gentium usu ac moribus de Jure Naturali, seu hominum universali decerni volunt*[19] [as the Hebrews do not believe that any natural law is exemplified or designated by the acts or custom of other animated beings, so they will not consider, in determining the natural or universal law of man, the practice and habits of either all or most other nations]. It seems the Jews look upon the Gentiles, as if [76] they differ'd specifically from them: as they do not search for the Law of Nature amongst Sensitive Beings, so neither amongst other Nations.

But I had thought that the Jewish Writers had promis'd the Heathens an Angel, an Intelligence, to irradiate & illuminate them, and does he shine upon them no clearer? does he performe his office no better? The Jews told us that they themselves were to enforme them and instruct them, and have they taught them their lessons no better? they mention'd a voice that came to *Adam* and to *Noah,* and have they whisper'd it only in one anothers eare? Why have they not proclaim'd it to the rest of the world?

How sad were the condition of the Gentiles, if they were to live upon the Jews courtesie and benevolence, that would strip them of Nature, plunder them of their essences, rob them of their first Principals and Common Notions? But God has not left them like Orphans to such unmerciful Guardians. He himself has took care of them, and has made better provision for them.

Now these several Nations are to be consider'd either in the common bulk and heap of them, or else in the major part of them, or in the noblest & most refined sort amongst them, either οἱ πάντες and οἱ πολλοὶ or οἱ εὐγενέστεροι and φρονιμώτεροι.

If we take them in the fullest universality of them, then that worthy Author of our own saies truly, *Nec olim, nec hactenus, aut qualesnam, aut quot sint, fuerintve, est ab aliquo satis exploratum*[20] [the nature and number of these have not been satisfactorily established by anyone either in ancient times or recently]. Nor indeed is it at all material in respect of this, whether we know them or no; but having the formal consent of so many, and knowing that there is *Par Ratio Reliquorum* [the same faculty of reason in the rest], being that they have the same natural engagements and obligations upon them, we cannot justly distrust, but that if there should new Nations, nay if there should new worlds appear, that every Rational *Nature* amongst them, would comply with and embrace the several Branches of this Law: and as they would not differ in those things that are so intrinsecal to Sense; so neither in those that are essential to the Understanding. As their corporal eye would be able to distinguish between beauty and deformity, so their Intellectual eye would as easily discerne some goodnesse from some kinde of wickednesse.

But are there not many Nations of them that live in the perpetual violation of Natures Law? If you speak of the more capital letters of this Νόμος γραπτός²¹ [written law], you finde no Nation so barbarous but that it can read them and observe them. I never heard of a Nation apostatizing from common Notions, from these first Principles. But if you mean the whole context and coherence of Natures Law, if you speak of those Demonstrations that may be built upon these fundamental Principles, of those kindly derivations and conclusions that flow [77] from these fountain-Notions: then this indeed must be granted, that 'tis the condemning sin of the Heathen, That so many of them imprison this natural light, and extinguish this *Candle of the Lord.*

There are many wilde and Anomalous *Individuums* amongst them οἱ πόρρω βάρβαροι, θηριώδεις, ἀλόγιστοι [remote barbarians, savage and irrational], as *Aristotle* calls them;²² οἱ διεφθαρμένοι [ruined men], as others terme them; but are there not such also even amongst Jews? nay amongst such as call themselvs Christians, that are lapst and fallen below themselves? many natural precepts are violated even amongst them; have you weeds, & bryers, & thornes in a garden? no wonder then that you meet with more in a wildernesse. Are there some prodigies in *Europe?* you may very well look for more Monsters in *Africa.* Do Christians blur and blot the Law of *Nature?* no wonder then that an American seeks quite to rase it out. Does an Israelite put Truth sometimes in Prison? no wonder then that an Egyptian puts it in a Dungeon. Yet notwithstanding amongst all those that have had so much Culture and Morality as to knit, and embody, and compact themselves into a Common-wealth; to become τοῖς νόμοις ὑποκείμενοι, to be regulated by a legal government, you will scarce finde any Nation that did generally and expressely and for long continuance, either violate or countenance the violation of any precept clearly Natural.

This is that in which the learned *Grotius* satisfies himself, that *Omnes Gentes Moraliores & Illustriores*²³ [all the more civilized and illustrious nations], gave due obedience and conformity to Natures Law, so that all Testimonies fetcht from them, are to have an high price and esteem put upon them.

But the famous *Salmasius* in his late Tractate *De Coma* goes a far different way; and tells us that he had rather search for Natures Law in a naked Indian, then in a spruce Athenian, in a rude American, rather then in a gallant Roman; in a meer Pagan, rather then in a Jew or Christian. His words are these, *Quanto magis Barbari, tanto felicius, faciliusque Naturam Ducem sequi putantur: Eam detorquent, aut ab ea magis recedunt politiores gentes*[24] [the more barbarous nations are, the more happily and easily they are to be thought to follow nature's guidance; the more cultivated nations distort her or recede from her].

Those Nations that have more of Art and emprovement amongst them, have so painted Natures face, have hung so many Jewels in her eare; have put so many Bracelets upon her hand; they have cloth'd her in such soft and silken rayment, as that you cannot guesse at her so well, as you might have done, if she had nothing but her own simple and neglected beauty: you cannot taste the Wine so well, because they have put Sugar into it, and have brib'd your palate.

So that the learned *Salmasius* will scarce go about to fetch the Law of Nature from the Jews principally; you see he chooses to fetch it rather from a Scythian, from a Barbarian; there he shall see it without any glosses, without any Super-[78]structures, without any carving and gilding, a Νόμος γραπτὸς[25] [written law] plainly written, without any flourishes & amplifications. Yet the Author, whom I but now commended, (*Salmasius* I mean) neither could nor would go about to vindicate all those Nations from some Notorious Rebellions against Natures Law, but he would rather choose, (as much as he could) to abstract their Intellectuals from their Practicals, and would look to their opinions and Lawes, rather then to their life and conversation.

Indeed *Aristotle* tells us, πόλλα τῶν ἐθνῶν πρὸς τὸ κτείνειν καὶ ἀνθρωποφαγίαν εὐχερῶς ἔχει[26] [many nations have a tendency to murder and cannibalism]. That same phrase εὐχερῶς ἔχει [to have a tendency], does only speak a propensity and inclination in their vile affections to such wickednesses as these were; which sometimes also they acted in a most violent and impetuous manner. Though to be sure they could not be long a Nation if they did thus kill and eat up and devoure one another.

But let us suppose that they dealt thus with their enemies, yet can it be shewn us that they establisht Anthropophagy by a Law? that their Natural Conscience did not check them for it? or if their reason did connive at them; yet how comes it to passe that their Angel did not jog them all this while, that their *Intellectus Agens* did not restraine them?

But out of what Antiquity doth it appear that any Nation did favour Atheisme by a Law? that any Kingdome did licence Blasphemy by a statute, or countenance Murder by a Law? Out of what Author can they shew us a Nation that ever did allow the breaches of solemne compacts, the dishonouring of Parents, that ever made a Law for this, that there should be no Law or Justice amongst them?

Till all this can appear, let the Testimonies of Gentiles be esteem'd somewhat more then the barking of dogs. Me thinks if they were meere Cyphers, yet the Jews going before them, they might amount to somewhat. Let the prints of Nature in them be accounted sacred: a Pearle in the head of a Heathen, some Jewels hid in the rubbish of Nations, let them be esteem'd precious. Whatsoever remains of Gods image upon them, let it be lov'd and acknowledg'd. Their darknesse and misery is great enough, let not us aggravate it, and make it more. To mix the light of their Candle, with that light which comes shining from the Candle of an Heathen, is no disparagement to Jew nor Christian.

CHAPTER II

The Light of Reason Is a Derivative Light

[79] Now the Spirit of man *is the Candle of the Lord.*

First, as *Lumen derivatum, φῶς ἐκ φωτός*[1] [a derivative light, a light from a light]. Surely there's none can think that light is primitively and originally in the Candle; but they must look upon that only as a weak participation of something that is more bright and glorious. All created excellency shines with borrowed beames, so that reason is but *Scintilla divinae lucis*[2] [a spark of the divine light], 'tis but *Divinae particula aurae*[3] [a breath of the divine breeze]. This was the very end why God framed intellectual creatures, that he might communicate more of himself to them, then he could to other more drossie and inferiour beings, and that they might in a more compleat and circular manner *redire in principium suum* (as the Schoolmen speak) that they might return into the bosom of the first and supreme cause by such operations as should in some measure imitate and represent the working of God himself, who being a most free and intellectual Agent, would have some creature also that should not only take notice of these his perfections, so as to adore and admire them, but should also partake of them, and should follow the Creator in his dispensations and workings, though still at an infinite distance and disproportion.

This moved him to stamp upon some creatures understanding and will, which in themselves make up one simple and entire print and signature of Reason, though we break the seal for the better opening of them, and part them into two several notions. To this end he fill'd the highest part of the world with those Stars of the first magnitude, I mean those Orient and Angelical beings, that dwell so neere the fountain of light, and continually drink in the beams of glory; that are exactly conformable to their Creatour in all his motions, for the same end he furnished and beautified this lower part of the world with intellectual lamps, that should shine forth to the praise and honour of his name, which totally have their dependance upon him, both for their being, and for their perpetual continuation of them in their being. 'Twas he that lighted up these lamps at first; 'tis he that drops הוהב the golden oile into them. Look then a while but upon the parentage and original of the soul & of Reason, & you'll presently perceive that it was *the Candle of the Lord*. And if you have a minde to believe *Plato,* he'll tell you such a feigned story as this, That there were a goodly [80] company of Lamps, a multitude of Candles, a set number of souls lighted up altogether, and afterwards sent into bodies, as into so many dark Lanthorns. This stock and treasure of souls was reserved, and cabinetted in I know not what Starres, perhaps that they might the better calculate their own incarnation, the time when they were to descend into bodies, and when they came there they presently sunk into ὕλη [matter]; they slipt into λήθη [forgetfulness], which he tearms ἐπιστήμης ἀποβολὴ,[4] the putting off of knowledge for a while, the clouding and burying of many sparkling and twinkling notions, till by a waking reminiscence as by a joyful resurrection, they rise out of their graves again. *Plato* it seems lookt upon the body as the blot of nature, invented for the defacing of this νόμος γραπτὸς[5] [written law], or at the best as an impertinent tedious parenthesis, that checkt and interrupted the soul in her former notions; that eclipsed and obscured her ancient glory, which sprung from his ignorance of the resurrection, for had he but known what a glory the body was capable of, he would have entertained more honourable thoughts of it.

Yet *Origen* was much taken with this Platonical notion, it being indeed a pretty piece of Philosophy for him to pick allegories out of. And though he do a little vary from *Plato* in a circumstance or two, yet in recompence of that he gives you this addition, and enlargment, that according to the carriage & behavior of these naked spirits before they were embodied, there were prepared answerable mansions for them. That such a soul as had walkt with God acceptably was put into a fairer prison, was clothed with an amiable and elegant body; But that soul which had displeased and provoked its Creator, was put into a darker dungeon, into a more obscure and uncomely body. That Candle which had shined clearly, was honoured with a golden Candlestick; that which had soiled its light, was condemned to a dark Lanthorne: one would think by this, that *Origen* had scarce read *Genesis,* he doth in this so contradict the Sacred History of the Creation. Nor is this the just product of *Plato's* opinion, but 'tis pregnant with much more folly, he returns him his own with usury, gives him this as the just Τόκος [interest] and improvement of it.[6]

Aquinas doth clash in pieces all these Platonical fictions in his two books *Contra Gentiles;*[7] yet upon this sinking and putrid foundation was built the tottering superstructure of connate *Species.* For when *Plato* had laid down this Error for a maxime: Πρὶν γενέσθαι ἡμᾶς ἦν ἡμῶν ἡ ψυχή, that the souls of men were long extant before they were born, then that other phansie did presently step in ἠπιστάμεθα καὶ πρὶν γενέσθαι,[8] that the soul was very speculative and contemplative before it was immerst in the body, which made way for the next conceit, that the soul brought many of its old notions along with it into the body, many faithful attendants that would bear the soul company in her most withering condition, when other more volatile and fugitive notions took wing to [81] themselves and flew away; many a precious pearl sunk to the bottome of *Lethe,* but some reliques of notions floated upon the top of the waters, and in the general Deluge of notions there was an Ark prepared for some select principles, some *praecepta Noachidarum*[9] [precepts of the children of Noah], which were to increase and multiply and supply the wants of an intellectual world.

This makes the Platonists look upon the spirit of man as *the Candle of the Lord* for illuminating and irradiating of objects, and darting more light upon them then it receives from them. But *Plato* as he failed in corporeal vision whilest he thought that it was *per extramissionem radiorum* [by the emission of rays]; So he did not *ab errore suo recedere*[10] [relinquish his error] in his intellectual opticks: but in the very same manner tells us that spiritual vision also is *per emissionem radiorum* [by the emission of rays]. And truly he might as well phansie such implanted *Ideas,* such seeds of light in his external eye, as such seminal principles in the eye of the minde. Therefore *Aristotle* (who did better clarifie both these kindes of visions) pluckt these motes out of the sensitive eye, and those beames out of the intellectual. He did not antedate his own knowledge, nor remember the several postures of his soul, and the famous exploits of his minde before he was born; but plainly profest that his understanding came naked into the world. He shews you an ἄγραφον γραμματεῖον,[11] an *abrasa tabula* [blank tablet], a virgin-soul espousing it self to the body, in a most entire, affectionate, and conjugal union, and by the blessing of heaven upon this loving paire, he did not doubt of a Notional off-spring & posterity; this makes him set open the windows of sense to welcome and entertain the first dawnings, the early glimmerings of morning-light. *Clarum mane fenestras intrat & Angustas extendit lumine rimas*[12] [it enters the windows bright in the morning, and extends its light in the narrow crevices]. Many sparks and appearances fly from variety of objects to the understanding; The minde, that catches them all, and cherishes them, and blows them; and thus the Candle of knowledge is lighted. As he could perceive no connate colours, no pictures or portraictures in his external eye: so neither could he finde any signatures in his minde till some outward objects had made some impression upon his νοῦς ἐν δυνάμει,[13] his soft and plyable understanding impartially prepared for every seal. That this is the true method of knowledge he doth appeal to their own eyes, to their own understandings; do but analyse your own thoughts, do but consult with your own breasts, tell us whence it was that the light first sprang in upon you. Had you such notions as these when you first peept into being? at the first opening of the souls eye? in the first *exordium* of infancy? had you these connate *Species* in the cradle? and were they rockt asleep with you? or did you then meditate upon these principles? *Totum est majus partae, & Nihil potest esse & non esse simul*[14] [the whole is greater than the part, nothing can be and not be at the same time]. Ne're tell us that you wanted [82] organical dispositions, for you plainly have recourse to the sensitive powers, and must needs subscribe to this, that al knowledg comes flourishing in at these lattices. Why else should not your Candle enlighten you before? who was it that chained up, and fettered your common notions? Who was it that restrained and imprisoned your connate *Ideas?* Me thinks the working of a Platonists soul should not at all depend on ὕλη [matter]; and why had you no connate demonstrations, as well as connate principles? Let's but see a catalogue of all these truths you brought with you into the world.

If you speak of the principles of the Laws of Nature, you shall hear the
Schoolmen determining: *Infans pro illo statu non obligatur lege naturali,
quia non habet usum Rationis & libertatis*[15] [an infant, because of its condition, is not obligated by the law of nature, because it does not have the
use of reason and free will]. And a more sacred Author saies as much, *Lex
Naturae est lex intelligentiae quam tamen ignorat pueritia, nescit infantia*
[the law of nature is the law of reason, of which, however, youth is ignorant and infants unaware]. There's some time to be allowed for the promulgation of Natures Law by the voice of Reason. They must have some
time to spell the Νόμος γραπτός[16] [written law] that was of Reasons writing. The minde having such gradual and climbing accomplishments, doth
strongly evince that the true rise of knowledge is from the observing and
comparing of objects, and from thence extracting the quintessence of
some such principles as are worthy of all acceptation; that have so much
of certainty in them, that they are neer to a Tautology and Identity, for
this first principles are.

These are the true and genuine κοιναὶ ἔννοιαι [common notions]; these
are the λόγοι σπερματικοὶ[17] [seminal principles]; these are the props of
Reasons contriving, upon which you may see her leaning, about which
you may see her turning and spreading and enlarging her self. That
learned Knight, in his discourse concerning the soul, doth at large shew
the manner how the minde thus goes a gathering of knowledge;[18] How
like a Bee it goes from flower to flower, from one entity to another, how it
sucks the purest and sweetest of all, how it refuses all that is distasteful to
it, and makes a pleasant composition of the rest, and thus prepares honey-
combs for it self to feed on.

But if it were at all to be granted that the soul had any stamps and characters upon it; that it had any implanted and ingraffed *Species;* 'twere
chiefly to be granted that it hath the connate notion of a Deity, that pure
and infinitely refined entity, abstracted from all appearance of matter. But
mark how the great Doctor of the Gentiles convinces them of the Τὸ
γνωστὸν τοῦ θεοῦ[19] [the knowledge of God], he doth not set them a
searching their connate *Species,* but bids them look into the glasse of the
creatures; O but (might some Platinist say) why, he is all spirit and an invisible being, what shall we finde of him amongst material objects? yes

(saies the Apostle) τὰ ἀόρατα τοῦ θεοῦ,[20] the invisible [83] things of God are made known by the things that do appear; for a being indowed with such a soul as man is, can easily in a discoursive way, by such eminent steps of second causes ascend to some knowledge of a prime and supreme being; which doth fully explain that he means by his νόμος γραπτὸς[21] [written law], those clear dictates of Reason fetched from the several workings of the understanding, that have sealed and printed such a truth upon the soul; so that no other innate light, but only the power and principle of knowing and reasoning is *the Candle of the Lord.*

Yet there is a noble Author of our own, that hath both his *truth* and his *errour,* (as he hath also writ about both) who pleads much for his *instinctus naturales*[22] [natural instincts], so as that at the first dash you would think him in a Platonical strain; but if you attend more to what he sayes, you will soon perceive that he prosecutes a farre different notion much to be preferred before the other phansy.

For he doth not make these instincts any connate *Ideas* and representations of things, but tels us that they are powers and faculties of the soul, the first-born faculties and beginning of the souls strength, that are presently espoused to their Virgin-objects closing and complying with them, long before discourse can reach them; nay, with such objects as discourse cannot reach at all in such a measure and perfection: these instincts he styles *Naturae dotes, & providentiae Divinae universalis idea, & typus optimus*[23] [gifts of nature, and a universal representation and superlative reflection of divine providence]. Some of these are to be found in the lowest inanimate beings, which yet have no connate *Species* among them; though they have powers and propension to their own welfare, a blinde tendency and inclination to their own security; for thus he speaks—*Instinctus ille Naturalis in quovis inarticulato licet & incauto elemento, sapiens est ad conservationem propriam*[24] [that natural instinct, in whatever indistinct and unconscious form, tends towards self-preservation]; and such a noble being as man is, must needs have it in a more sublime and eminent manner.

Therefore he tearms these instincts in man *facultates noeticae, & facultates Deo analogae* [intellectual powers and powers resembling God]; whereas those other inferiour faculties are esteem'd *facultates analogae mundo*[25] [powers resembling the world]; his words being somewhat cloudy, I shall thus paraphrase upon them: The soul 'tis made with a through light, with a double window, at one window it looks upon corporeals, at the other it hath a fair prospect upon spirituals. When it takes notice of the material world, it looks out at the window of sense, and views the *putamina & cortices rerum,* the outward husks and shells of being, but not at all pleas'd or contented with them, those higher powers, those purer faculties of the soul unclasp and disclose themselves, and extend themselves for receiving some delight more precious and satisfactory, being made in as harmonious proportion suitable to spiritual objects, as [84] the eye is to colours, or the eare to sounds. And as you know, a corporeal eye is so fashioned and organiz'd, that though it have no connate *Species* of the Sunne, yet tis pleasant to behold it; so the eye of the soul doth willingly open it self to look upon God *per modum objecti* [as an object], and has all *per receptionem* [by reception] from him, fixing its eye upon so transcendent and beautiful an object, and viewing all those streamings out of light, those beamings out of eternal and universal notions, that flow from him as the fountain of lights, where they have dwelt from everlasting, which now appear to it in time with a most powerful and enamouring ray, to direct the soul to that happinesse it longed for, and to guide and conduct it in all its operations. If you ask when these highest faculties did first open and display themselves, he tells you 'tis then when they were stimulated and excited by outward objects, and it may be upon this account, that when the soul can finde nothing there worthy one glance, one cast of its eye, impatient of such empty and shadowy sights, it opens it self to the τὰ ἄνω[26] [things above], and warmes it self in those everlasting Sun-beams; but when it comes down from the mount, it puts on the veile of sense, and so converses with material objects.

Yet I do not here positively lay down this for a truth in all the branches of it, but only represent the minde of the forementioned Author, who himself doth acknowledge that the rise of these first principles is very Cryptical and mysterious. His words are these. *Vos interea non morari debet quod quomodo eliciantur istae notitiae communes nesciatis. Satis superque diximus vos nescire quomodo fiat gustus, odoratus, tactus, &c.*[27] [the fact of your not knowing how these common ideas are drawn forth ought not to prove an obstacle; we have told you sufficiently before, that you are ignorant how taste, smell, touch etc. begin to operate]. By which you cannot but perceive that he makes the conformity of such a faculty with such an object, the spring and original of common notions. Yet this then had deserved a little clearing, whence the difficulty of understanding spirituals *pro hoc statu* [as such] does arise, if there be such a present, and exact analogy between them; whereas the intuitive knowledge of God, and viewing those goodly notions that are steept in his essence uses to be reserved as a priviledge of a glorified creature. Yet this I suppose may be said that herein is the souls imperfection, that it cannot sufficiently attend both to spirituals and corporeals; and therefore sense being so busie and importunate for the prosecution of her objects; no wonder that these noetical faculties do faint and languish. So that if there be any whom the former discursive way will not suffice, it seems better for them to have recourse to an innate power of the soul that is fitted and fashioned for the receiving of spirituals, *quatenus* [as] spirituals, then to flie to I know not what connate *Species,* of I know not how long duration before the soul was acquainted with the body. Yet that other noble Author of our own, that [85] has the same title of truth not without a competent mixture of error too, doth choose to resolve all into a Platonical remembrance, which yet that acute answerer of him doth shew to be a meer vanity;[28] for as for matters of fact, to be sure they have no implanted Ideas: And if historical knowledge may be acquired without them, why then should discursive knowledge have such a dependence upon them? And I wish that the Platonists would but once determine whether a blinde man be a competent judge of colours by vertue of his connate *Species,* and whether by supply of these Ideas a deaf man may have the true notion of musick and harmony? if not, then they must ingenuously confesse, that the soul for the present wants so much of light as it wants of the window of sense. But if they tell us that some outward objects must jogge and waken these drowsie and slumbring notions, they then lay the foundation in sensitives; and withal let them shew us, why the generality of men in their intellectuals are not equally improved, whereas they have the same objects to quicken and enflame them? in the mean time we will look upon the understanding as *speculum non coloratum,* a glasse not prejudic'd nor prepossest with any connate tinctures, but nakedly receiving, and faithfully returning all such colours as fall upon it. Yet the

Platonists in this were commendable, that they lookt upon the spirit of a man as *the Candle of the Lord,* though they were deceived in the time when 'twas lighted.

Nor is this Candle lighted out of the Essence of God himself, 'twere a farre more tolerable errour to make the light of a Candle a piece of the Sun's essence then to think that this intellectual lamp is a particle of the divine nature. There is but one ἀπαύγασμα τῆς δόζης & χαρακτὴρ τῆς ὑποστάσεως αὐτοῦ[29] [brightness of his glory, and express image of his person], I mean the wonderful ὁ λόγος [Word], not a Candle, but a Sun that shined from everlasting. But I finde the Stoicks challeng'd for this errour, that they thought there was a real emanation, and traduction of the soul out of God, *Ex ipsa Dei substantia* [from the very substance of God], and the Gnosticks, the Manichees and Priscillianists are lookt upon as their successors in this folly.[30]

Now as for the Stoicks you'll scarce finde evidence enough to prove them guilty of this opinion. They have indeed some doting and venturing expressions, when they amplifie and dignifie the nobility of the soul; and will needs have some of the royal blood to run in every veine and faculty of it, nor are the Platonists defective in this, but lift up the soul to as high a pitch of perfection as the Stoicks ever did; yet surely both of them but as a limited and dependant being infinitely remote from the fulnesse of a Deity. Yet *Simplicius* in his Comment upon the grand Stoick *Epictetus* tells us that that Sect of Philosophers were wont to call the soul μέρος ἢ μέλος τοῦ θεοῦ,[31] *pars vel membrum Dei* [a part or a limb of God], which is a grosse and corporeal conceit, not at all agreeable to the indivisibility of spirituals, nor suitable with the souls immateriality, much lesse [86] consistent with the transcendent purity of God himself. But the learned *Salmasius* in his Animadversions on both the forementioned Authors,[32] though he spend paper enough in clearing some passages of the Academicks, Peripateticks, and Stoicks, concerning the nature of the soul; yet doth not in the least measure take notice of any such heterodox tenent among the Stoicks, yet if there had been any such, they had very well deserved Animadversions; but he doth thus represent their Philosophy to you; That whereas the soul is usually lookt upon as τριμερὴς [tripartite], being brancht out into the Vegetative, Sensitive and Rational; the Stoicks they chose to make it ὀκταμερῆς³³ [of eight parts], and would have *septem partes ancillantes, Imperatricem unicam* [seven parts serving, one commanding]; which they reckoned thus: τὰ αἰσθητικὰ [the perceptive faculties] they were five; then τὸ φωνητικὸν, τὸ σπερματικὸν, τὸ ἡγεμονικὸν [the vocal faculty, the generative faculty, the commanding faculty], which was all one with τὸ λογικὸν, or τὸ διανοητικὸν, or τὸ ἐπιστημονικὸν [reason, or the intellect, or knowledge]. Yet as *Plato* and *Aristotle* disposing the soul into three several ranks and distributions, would by no means allow of τριψυχία, a triplicity of souls in one *compositum:* So neither would the Stoicks admit any plurality of souls, but esteemed these τὰ μέρης or τὰ μόρια τῆς ψυχῆς [parts or members of the soul] only as αἱ δυνάμεις, *non membra sed ingenia*³⁴ [powers, not parts but faculties], as *Tertullian* terms them very significantly, stiling the powers and faculties of the soul, the several wits of the soul, so that it was but μία οὐσία πολυδύναμος³⁵ [one essence with many powers], enlarging it self to the capacity and exigency of the body, but in such a manner, as that 'twas *dispensata potius quam concisa*³⁶ [distributed rather than fragmented]. The principal and Hegemonical power of the soul the Stoicks situated in the heart, as *Aristotle* did, though very erroneously, & yet *Plato* had taught him better, for he plac'd it in the brain as the proper tabernacle for reason to dwell in.³⁷ But amongst the Stoicks there are some expressions that seem to depresse & degrade the soul, as much as others seem to advance and exalt it, for though some call it τὸ μέρος τοῦ θεοῦ [a part of God], yet others, and among the rest *Zeno* (the great founder of that Sect,) tearms it σύμφυτον πνεῦμα, & θερμὸν πνεῦμα³⁸ [an innate breath, a hot breath], which that stupid Author of the souls mortality finding somewhere translated into English, catches at, and tells us that the Stoicks hold the soul to be a certain blast hot and fiery, or the vital spirit of the blood;³⁹ whereas at the most, they did only choose that corporeal spirit as *Vehiculum animae* [a vehicle for the soul], a Chariot for a more triumphant spirit to ride in, the principal seate of the soul, which they did so much extol and deifie. 'Tis abundantly clear that their Stoical Philosophy was more refined and clarified, more sublime and extracted from matter, then to resolve the quintessence of a rational nature into I know not what muddy and [87] feculent spirit; this they could not do, if they would be faithful and constant to their own principles. Nay, they were so farre from thus vilifying the soul and detracting from it, as that they were rather excessive and hyperbolical in praising it above the sphere of a creature. Thus that known Stoick *Epictetus* calls the soul of man συγγενὴς θεῷ [akin to God], which *Seneca* renders, *liber animus est Diis cognatus*[40] [a free soul is kinsman to the gods]; and *Arrian* in his Comment upon the forementioned Author doth thus diffuse and amplifie it, Αἰ ψυχαὶ οὕτως εἰσὶν ἐνδεδεμέναι καὶ συναφεῖς τῷ θεῷ, ἅτε αὐτοῦ μόρια οὖσαι, καὶ ἀποσπάσματα.[41] *i.e.* There is connexion and coherence of souls with a Deity, there are mutual touches and embraces between them, they are some delibations, and participations of himself; thus that famous Emperour *M. Antoninus* that had tasted of the Stoical Philosophy, styles the soul ὁ δαίμων ὃν ἑκάστῳ προστάτην, καὶ ἡγεμόνα ὁ ζεὺς ἔδωκεν—, Ἀπόσπασμα ἑαυτοῦ. οὗτος δὲ ἐστὶν ὁ ἑκάστου νοῦς, καὶ λόγος[42] [the genius which Zeus has given to each man as ruler and guide, . . . a fragment of Zeus himself . . . this is the intellect and reason of each man]. Where, at the first one would think he had meant it in an Averroistical sense, but that he himself doth prevent the interpretation, by telling you that he intends nothing else but νοῦς & λόγος [intellect and reason], which therefore he calls ὁ Δαίμων [the genius], because that he knew the soul was separable from the body, and *Pythagoras* long before him had called it by the same name in his golden verses.[43]

But amongst all the rest, *Seneca* is the most high and lofty in magnifying, and very neer deifying of the soul; for thus you may hear him speak; *Quid aliud vocas animum, quam Deum in humano corpore hospitantem?*[44] That is, What lesse title can you give the soul, then that of a God condescending to dwell in an house of clay? which is too neere that of the Apostle θεὸς ἐν σαρκὶ φανερῳ θείς,[45] God manifested in the flesh. Nor yet was this any unwary passage that slipt from *Seneca's* pen on the sudden, but he will stand to it, and repeat it, for thus he saith again. *Ratio nil aliud est quam in corpus humanum pars Divini spiritus mersa,*[46] Reason 'tis somewhat of a Deity steept in a body. From this last speech that learned and eminent writer of our own doth endeavour to evince, that *Seneca* made God the *Intellectus Agens* [active intellect] of the soul,[47] whereas 'tis very evident that this Philosopher only prosecuted that Stoical notion, of the soul being ἀπόσπασμα τοῦ θεοῦ[48] [a shred of God], a branch of a Deity

πεπλασμένον ἐκ Διὸς ἔρνος. Yet notwithstanding, all these strains of Stoical Philosophy do not sufficiently declare that they thought the soul to be
of the very same essence with God himself, but only that they perceived
much similitude between the soul and a Deity; many bright resemblances
of God stampt upon it, which is not only sound Philosophy, but good Divinity too; that the soul was made according to the image of its Creatour.
Thus they made it not [88] only θερμὸν πνεῦμα [a hot breath], but θεῖον
πνεῦμα too, even the breath of a Deity σημειωθὲν καὶ τυπωθὲν σφραγῖδι
τοῦ θεοῦ,[49] stampt with the Seal of God himself, as *Philo* speaks. 'Twas
μετοχὴ τῆς θείας ἐλλάμψεως[50] [a reflector of the divine light], as *Damas-
cen* calls it, very agreeable to this of *Solomon, the Candle of the Lord.* 'Tis
ποίημα θεοῦ λογικὸν,[51] as *Greg. Nyss.* has it, the Poeme of God himself.
That whereas other creatures were as it were writ in Prose, the souls of men
were composed more harmoniously, in more exact number and measure.
No wonder then that the Stoicks spying out such spiritual workmanship,
and embroydery in the soul of man, did esteem it as an inferiour kinde of
Deity, a Bud, and Blossome of Divinity; as they meant by their τὰ μέρη
τῆς ψυχῆς [parts of the soul], nothing but αἱ δυνάμεις [powers], so likewise when they call the soul *Τὸ μέρος τοῦ θεοῦ* [a part of God], they need
intend no more then the Pythagoreans do by their θεῖα δύναμις,[52] that divine vertue and efficacy which the soul has, that makes it look so like its
Creatour. Thus the Pythagoreans were wont to call the higher region of
the soul, τὸ θεῖον [the godlike], and the lower τὸ θηριῶδες[53] [the brutal],
not understanding by the first any particle of a Deity, though it may be by
the last they might understand the soul of a beast, by vertue of their supposed μετεμψύχωσις [metempsychosis]. But I meet with none that doth
so punctually and accurately determine this, as *Trismegistus* does, who
speaks so exactly as if he had spyed out this difficulty and objection, his
words are these. Ὁ νοῦς οὐκ ἔστιν ἀποτετμημένος ἐκ τῆς οὐσιότητος τοῦ
θεοῦ, ἀλλ' ὥσπερ ἡπλωμένος καθάπερ τὸ τοῦ ἡλίου φῶς,[54] The soul, saies
he, was not framed and carv'd out of the essence of a Deity, but it rather
sprung from the dilatation, and diffusion of his power and goodnesse, as
beams do from the Sun, when it spreads forth its quickening and cherishing wings. Yet when you hear the creatures often stiled beams of a Deity,
and drops of a Deity, you must neither imagine that there is the least di-

vision, or diminution, or variation in the most immutable essence of God; nor that the creature does partake the very essence of the Creatour, but that it hath somewhat of his workmanship, obvious and visible in it, and according to the degree of its being, doth give fainter or brighter resemblances of its Creatour. As suppose an accurate Painter should bestow much of his skill in drawing a lively portraicture of himself, you would not think such a picture a piece of his essence, but you would look upon it only as the fruit and product of his skil, and as a witty imitation of himself. Now there is a far greater disproportion between God and any created being, then between the face and the picture of it: So that if you see any heavenly beauty, any divine lineaments sparkling in the soul, you may presently conclude that it was *digitus Dei,* nay the hand of God that drew them there, as the shadowy representations of his own most glorious being. 'Tis the greatest honour that a creature is capable of, to be the picture of its Creatour. You know [89] the very formality of creation doth speak a being raised *ex nihilo;* creation being the production of somthing out of the barren womb of nothing; and if the creature must be *ex nullo praeexistente* [out of nothing pre-existing], then to be sure 'tis not extracted out of the essence of God himself. But the whole generality of the ancient Heathen Philosophers had a vaile upon their face, here they had not a clear and open sight of the creation, but only some obscure and imperfect notions about it, which made them think that all corporeals were made *ex aliqua praejacente materia*⁵⁵ [from some pre-existing material], coexistent with the prime and supreme efficient; and because they could not fetch spirituals out of materials, nor yet conceive that they should be fetcht out of nothing, this made them determine that they sprung out of the essence of God himself, who as a voluntary fountain could bubble them forth when he pleased, who as a father of lights⁵⁶ could sparkle and kindle them when he thought best. But that fiction of *materia ab aeterno* [eternal matter] will do them no service at all; for either 'twas produced by God himself, & then it was created *ex nihilo,* for God himself was a pure immaterial Spirit, and therefore must make matter where none was before; or else it was an Independent eternal being, which makes it another Deity, and that involves a flat repugnancy. Therefore as corporeal and material beings were raised out of nothing by the infinite vigour and power of God himself, so he can with the very same facility produce spiritual beings out of nothing too. Can he not as well light this Lamp out of nothing, as build the goodly fabrick of the world out of nothing? Cannot a creating breath make a soul as well as a creating word make a world? He that can create the shell of corporeals, cannot he as well create the kernel of spirituals? He that created a visible Sun, cannot he as well create an invisible, an intellectual spark? You may hear *Aquinas* disputing against the Gentiles, & most fully and strongly demonstrating, that God could not be either the *materia* or *forma* of any created being,[57] for its not imaginable how the Creator himself should *ingredi essentiam creaturae* [enter into the essence of a creature]. But his causality is by way of efficiency producing & maintaining beings; the best of creatures are but *vasa figuli*[58] [potter's vessels]. Now a vessel, though a vessel of honour, yet it is no piece of the Potters essence, but only the subject of his power and will. One and the same Seal may print all the Wax that's possible, yet there will not be the least mutation in the Seal, but only in the Wax; nor yet doth the Wax at all participate of the seals essence, but only receives a stamp and signature made upon it. So that the Seal was as entire and compleat before it had imprinted the Wax, as it was after-wards; and though all the signatures of the Wax were defaced and obliterated, yet the Seal would be as perfect as before.

Thus God, though he leaves prints of himself upon all the souls in the world, nay upon all the beings in the world, yet these impressions are not particles of [90] himself; nor do they make the least mutation in him, only in the creature; for he was as full and perfect before he had printed any one creature, and if the whole impression of creatures were annihilated, yet his essence were the same, and he could print more when he pleased, and as many as he pleased. Yet all the entity, goodnesse, and reality, that is to be found in the creature, was totally derived from him, and is transcendently treasured up in him, as the print of the wax, though it be really different from the print of the Seal, yet that very stamp and signature had its being from the Seal, 'twas vertually and originally in the Seal; and now gives some resemblance of it. All created goodnesse was *a Deo producta, & a Deo exemplata* [produced by God and patterned on Him], (as the Schools speak) though not very elegantly. 'Tis *a Deo conservata*, & *in Deum ordinata*[59] [conserved by, and ordained for, God], yet all this while 'twas nothing of the essence of a Deity; and indeed it cannot have any of his essence, unlesse it have all of it. He that calls the creature a drop in such a sense, may as well call it a fountain; he that thus termes it a ray of Divinity, may as well call it a Sun, for there are no particles in essentials. All essence 'tis indivisible, how much more the essence of God himself. How fond is the fancy of a semi-Deity; away with the Stoicks τὰ μέρη & ἀποσπάσματα [parts and fragments] here, if this be the meaning of them, who ever heard of fragments in spirituals! Dares therefore any absolutely deifie the soul? or make it coessential or coequal with God himself? Is not the soul a limited and restrained being? short and imperfect in its operations, a dependent and precarious being; and are these things agreeable to a Deity? Is not the soul naturally united to the body for the quickening and enforming of it? and is that a condition fit for a Deity? nay, are not many souls guilty, defiled, miserable beings? and are they all this while spangles of a Deity? They must have very low and dishonourable thoughts of God that make any creature partner or sharer with him in his essence, and they must have high and swelling thoughts of the creature. How proud is that soul that aspires to be a God? Is it not enough for a soul to approach unto his God, to see his face, to enjoy his presence, to be like unto him, to be knit unto him, in love and affection? Happinesse doth advance a creature to his just perfection, but it doth not lift it above the sphere of its being. A glorified being, is still a subservient and finite being. A soul when in its full brightnesse, yet still is but *the Candle of the Lord,* let it come as neer as it can, yet it will be infinitely distant from him. Heaven it doth not mix and blend essences together, but keeps them all in their just beauty and proportions; so that take a creature in what condition you will, and 'tis not the least particle of a Deity. There's another Errour, but it's scarce worth mentioning, of some that would have *the Candle of the Lord* lighted up by Angels, as if they had created the soul; Nay, the Carpocratians[60] thought that all the rest of the world was created by them. But as no secondary being could [91] create it self, so neither can it create any other being. 'Twas no Angelical breath, but the breath of a Deity that gave life to the soul, and 'twas not made after the image of an Angel, but of God himself. Angels and souls both came from the same Almighty Father of spirits, from the same glorious Father of lights,[61] who shewed the greatnesse of his power in raising such goodly beings, not out of himself, but out of nothing.

Whether ever since the first Creation the souls of men be lighted on the same manner immediately by God himself, by that commanding and efficacious word, אור יהי γενηθήτω φῶς, *let there be light*,[62] let there be an intellectual Lamp set up in such a creature; or whether it be lighted by the parents? whether one soul can light another? whether one and the same soul may be lighted by two, as a candle is lighted by two? These are the several branches of that great question, which hath been frequently vext and discussed, but scarce ever quieted and determined. The *Divines* favour the way of creation, the *Physicians* that of traduction;[63] Nay, *Galen* tells in plain termes, that the soul is but κράσις τοῦ σώματος[64] a meere temper or complexion, the right tuning of the body, which is not farre distant from the Fidlers opinion, that *Tully* speaks of, that would needs have the soul to be an harmony. His soul, that plaid him some lessons, and his body danc'd to them. And indeed some of the Physicians are as loath as he was *ab arte sua discedere*[65] [to depart from their art], and therefore they do embody the soul as much as they can, that their skill may extend to the happinesse and welfare of it, as if they could feel the pulse of the soul, and try experiments upon the spirits; as if they could soften and compose the Paroxysme of the minde, and cure all the Languors and distempers of the soul; as if their drugs would work upon immaterial beings; as if they could kill souls as fast as they can kill bodies: as if *the Candle of the Lord* did depend upon these Prolongers; as though the Lamp would go out, unlesse they pour in some of their oile into it. No doubt but there is a mutual communion and intercourse between this friendly and espowsed paire, the soul and body; no doubt but there is a loving sympathy and fellow-feeling of one anothers conditions; but 'tis not so strong and powerful, as that they must both live and die together. Yet I speak not this as though the maintaining of the souls traduction did necessarily prejudice the immortality of it; for I know there are many learned Doctors amongst them (and *Seneca* amongst the rest) that are for the souls beginning in a way of generation, and yet do detest and abominate the least thoughts of its corruption. Nay, some sacred writers contend for the souls traduction, who yet never questioned the perpetuity of it: not only the African father *Tertullian,* but most of the Western Churches also; and the opinion of *Apollinaris* and *Nemesius* that one spiritual being might propagate another, I have not yet found sufficiently disprov'd, though it be generally reprehended.[66] The truth is, the original of all formes, [92] 'tis *in profundo,* 'tis very latent and mysterious; yet the Naturalists must needs acknowledge thus much, that the matter and forme of every thing must have at least an incompleat being before generation; for by that they do not receive any new absolute entity, for then it would be a creation, but the parts are only collected, and disposed, and united by a strict & Gordian knot, by an inward continuity. So that in all such production the *materia oritur ex materia, & forma ex forma generantis* [matter springs from the matter, and the form from the form of the producer], and thus formes are continued according to that degree of being, which they had in the first Creation. Now why there should not be such a *traditio Lampadis*[67] [handing over of the lamp] in the souls of men, will not easily be shewn; the nobility and purity of the soul doth not at all hinder this, for there is a proportionable eminency in the soul, that doth produce it: One soul prints another with the same stamp of immortality, that it self had engraven upon it. But if any question how an immaterial being can be conveighed in such a seminal way, let him but shew us the manner by which 'tis united to the body, and we will as easily tell him how it entered into it. Yet *Hierome* was so zealous against this, that he pronounceth a present *Anathema,* to all such as shall hold the soul to be *ex traduce*[68] [by propagation]. But *Austin* was a great deale more calme and pacate; Nay, indeed he was in this point ἀμφίδοξος καὶ διχογνώμεν, in a kinde of equipoise and neutrality; and therefore with a gentle breath he did labour to fanne and coole the heat of *Hieromes* opinion, and putting on all mildnesse and moderation, plainly confesses, *Se neque legendo, neque orando, neque ratiocinando invenire potuisse quomodo cum Creatione animarum peccatum originale defendatur*[69] [that neither by reading, nor praying, nor contemplating had he been able to discover how the doctrine of original sin could be reconciled with that of the creation of souls]. It seems he could not solve all those difficulties which the Pelagians raised against original sin, unlesse he held the traduction of the soul. He could not perceive how the Candle should be so soyld, if it were lighted only by a pure

Sun-beame fetcht from heaven. Yet that knot (which so skilful and laborious a hand could not unty) some others have easily cut asunder; and indeed there is no such cogency, and prevalency in that argument as can
justly promise it self the victory. For the Schoolmen that are strong asser-
tors of the souls creation, do satisfie all such doubts as these.[70] And the
major part of modern writers do encline to this, that these Lamps are
lighted by God himself, though some indeed do ἐπέχειν [suspend judg-
ment], and will determine nothing, as the acute *Pemble* does among the
rest, in his little Tractate *De Origine Formarum,*[71] and so doth that learned
Knight in his late discourse of the soul, where he doth only drop one brief
passage that countenances the souls traduction, upon which he that pre-
tends to answer him, takes occasion to huddle up no lesse then twenty Arguments against it, which sure he sould by number [93] and not by
weight.[72] But that *Oxford* answerer of that Brutish Pamphlet of *The Souls
Mortality,* doth more solidly and deliberately handle the question, yet being very vehement and intense for the souls Creation, he slips into this
error, that the traduction of the soul, is inconsistent with the immortality
of it.[73] But it may be you had rather hear the votes and suffrages of those
ancient heathen writers, that had nothing to see by but *the Candle of the
Lord;* perhaps you would willingly know what their souls thought of themselves. You'll believe nature, the universal mother, if she tell you who is the
father of spirits. Wee'll begin with *Pythagoras,* and he tells you his minde
freely and fully, whilest he gives you that piece of leafe-gold in one of his
Verses; θάρσει, θεῖον γένος ἐστὶ βροτοῖσι[74] [take courage, the race of man
is divine]. *Aratus* is in the very same streine, and was honoured so farre as
to be quoted by an Apostle for it, τοῦ γάρ καὶ γένος ἐσμέν[75] [for we are
also his offspring]. But if these seeme somewhat more generally, not exactly pointing out at the soul, the *Caldy Oracle* will speak more punctually,
ταῦτα πατὴρ ἐνόησε, βρότος δὲ οἱ ἐψύχωτο,[76] the Father of spirits by his
thought and word, by his commanding breath did kindle this Lamp of the
soul, for the quickening and illuminating of such a noble creature. *Zoro-
aster* pouers it out more at large, and does thus dilate and amplifie it. Χρὴ
δὲ σπεύδειν πρὸς τὸ φάος, καὶ πρὸς πατρὸς αὐγάς. Ἔνθεν ἐπέμφθη σοὶ
ψυχὴ πολὺν ἐσσαμένη νοῦν.[77] O soul (saies he) why do'st thou not aspire,
and mount up to the centre and light of glory, to that fountain of beams

and brightnesse, from whence thou wert derived, and sent down into the world, cloath'd and apparell'd with such rich and sparkling indowments? The consideration of this made the Divine Trismegist[78] break into that pang of admiration, ποία μήτηρ, ποῖος πατὴρ εἰ μὴ θεὸς ἀφανής; what womb (saith he) is fit to bear a soul? who is fit to be the father of the soul? what breast is able to nourish a soul? who can make sufficient provision for a soul, but only that pure and invisible Spirit that shoots them, and darts them into bodies by his own Almighty power? And as the forementioned Author goes on, ὁ δὲ πάντων πατὴρ ὁ νοῦς ὢν ζωὴ καὶ φύσις, ἀπεκύησε τὸν ἄνθρωπον αὐτῷ ἴσον, οὗ ἠράσθη ὡς ἰδίου τόκου, that is, God the Father of being, the Father of life and nature, did frame and fashion man much like himself, and love him as his proper off-spring; for those words of his, τὸν ἄνθρωπον αὐτῷ ἴσον [fashion man much like himself] must be taken in an allayed, and tempered sense, (for they must by no means be understood of an equality, but only of a similitude). In the very same sense he calls God ὁ ζωγράφος, the Painter and trimmer of the soul; thus representing himself to the life; As for the minde of the Platonists and the Stoicks we have before acquainted you with it; one looks so high, as if a Creation would scarce content them, unlesse they may have it *ab aeterno* [from eternity]; and the other seem to plead for a traduction and generation of the soul, not from the parents, [94] but from God himself, which makes *Epictetus* so often mention the affinity and consanguinity of the soul with the Deity; And to use such words as these, ἐὰν ταῦτα ἐστιν ἀληηθῇ, τὰ περὶ τῆς συγγενείας τοῦ θεοῦ καὶ ἀνθρώπων λεγόμενα, ὑπὸ τῶν φιλοσόφων διὰ τί μὴ εἴπῃ τις ἑαυτὸν κόσμιον; διὰ τί μὴ υἱὸν τοῦ θεοῦ[79] [if what is said by the philosophers concerning the kinship of God and man be true, why should man not call himself a world-dweller? why not a son of God]? If the Philosophers (saies he) speak truth, when they tell us how neer a kin the soul is to God; why then doth such a soul streighten and confine it self? why doth it contract and imprison so vast an essence? why does it look upon some spot of ground, with such a partial and peculiar affection? why doth it love the smoke of its earthly countrey, καπνὸν ἐπιθρῴσκοντα;[80] why does it not rather warm it self in the flame of its heavenly original? why does such an one stile himself an Athenian, a Corinthian, a Lacedemonian? why does he not rather think that he hath a whole world within him? why does he not summe up all his happinesse in this great and honourable title, that he is the Son of God? and thus you see ὁ κόσμιος ["world-dweller"] will be the same with *Socrates* his κοσμο-πολίτης[81] ["citizen of the world"]; and the words you see will passe currantly in this sense; But yet (if we may take the liberty of a conjecture) I am ready to think that the first negative particle doth intrude it self too unseasonably, against the drift and meaning of the place, and therefore is to be refused and rejected; so that whereas the words were printed thus, διὰ τὶ μὴ εἴπῃ τὶς ἑαυτὸν κόσμιον [why should man not call himself a world-dweller]; read διὰ τὶ εἴπῃ τὶς ἑαυτὸν κόσμιον [why should man call himself a world-dweller], and then they will run thus, *Quid se mundanum vocat, cur non potius filium Dei?* why doth he think himself a worldling, why doth he measure himself by earth, if he were born of heaven? where yet you may perceive that the Philosopher ascribes that to the first γένεσις [generation] which is due only to the παλιγγενεσία [regeneration] to be called a Son of God. Nay, which indeed is only to the ἀειγενεσία [eternal generation], to the only begotten Son of God.[82] Thus *Philo* the Jew (too Stoical in this) calls souls ἀπαυγάσματα [rays], which is the very same title, that the Apostle applies to God himself;[83] and *Plotinus* gives as much to the soul as the Arrians did to Christ, for he calls it ὁμοούσιον[84] [of the same essence], which Plato stiled ἀθανάτοις ὁμώνυμον[85] [having the same name as the immortals]; but *Epictetus* he goes on to keep τὰ σύμβολα τοῦ θεοῦ[86] [the tokens of God], much in the Language of the Oracle, σύμβολα πατρικὸς νοῦς ἔσπειρε ταῖς ψυχαῖς[87] [the mind of the father scattered tokens in our souls]: by πατρικὸς νοῦς [the mind of the father] it can mean nothing else but God himself, the Father of spirits, and these τὰ σύμβολα [tokens] are such love-tokens as he has left with the sonnes of men to engage their affections to him. These Symbols are the very same which *Moses* calls the image of God;[88] [95] those representations of himself which he has scattered and sown in the being of man; as this word σπείρειν [scatter] does imply, which made the wise Grecian *Thales* conclude ἀδελφοὺς εἶναι ἡμᾶς ὡς τοῦ ἑνὸς θεοῦ, καὶ ἑνὸς διδασκάλου,[89] that all men were brethren born of the same supreme being, that did educate and instruct them; this teaching is the same which the Persian *Magi* call'd a divine inebriation, ὅλη θεόθεν μεμέθυσται,[90] it was replete τῶν θείων καλῶν [with divine beauties], you see then, that the joynt consent of the Chaldeans, Egyptians, Persians, Grecians; was for the creation of the soul; and if you desire more testimonies from them, you may consult with *Eugubin* in his learned work *de perenni Philosophia*,[91] where you shall meet with whole heaps of them. But as for *Aristotles* opinion, you know that his custome was, when he could not beat out a notion into a rational account fairly to passe it by, and not to piece it out with such fabulous inventions, as *Plato* did abound withall; and though it is like he did often dispute this question in his thoughts, yet he makes no solemne entrance upon it in his works, but only toucheth it occasionally, and scatters a passage or two; that seeme very clearly to acknowledge the creation of it: for (not to speak of the place in his morals, where he calls the soul τὸν νοῦν τοῖς θεοῖς συγγενέστατον)[92] [the mind closest to the gods], I shal only commend unto you those ful and pregnant words in his two books *de generatione animalium,* the words are these Λείπεται δὲ τὸν νοῦν μόνον θύραθεν ἐπεισιέναι, καὶ θεῖον εἶναι μόνον[93] [it remains then for the mind alone to enter from without, and alone to be divine], he had but a little before evinced that the sensitive, and vegetative souls were conveighed in a seminal way, like a couple of sparks, they were struck *ex potentia materiae* [from the power of matter]; but (sayes he) but the rational, that came θύραθεν *ex altiori sede*[94] [from without, from a higher realm], as *Seneca* speaks, the window of heaven was open'd, and a present light sprung in, for the compleating of those former rudiments and preparations; the misunderstanding of this ὁ νοῦς θύραθεν [mind from without], did it may be occasion, but it did at least corroborate the phancy of an Angels being an *Intellectus Agens* [active intellect]; yet *Simplicius* that known Interpreter of *Aristotle* does expound it of the souls creation, καὶ γὰρ ἡ ψυχὴ ὑπὸ θεοῦ ἐλλάμπεσθαι λέγεται[95] [for the soul is said to be illuminated by God], as he speaks; and this which *Aristotle* here calls ὁ νοῦς θύραθεν [the mind from without], *Psellus* the Philosopher stiles ὁ νοῦς ἄνωθεν [the mind from above], *Plato* termed it φύτον, οὐκ ἔγγειον, ἀλλ᾽ οὐράνιον [a plant, not of earth but of heaven], the *Sybils* call'd it πύρινον νοῦν [a fiery mind], some others νοερὸν πῦρ καὶ ἀσώματον πῦρ [an intellectual and incorporeal fire], still conspiring with this of *Solomons, the Candle of the Lord;* and *Seneca,* (setting aside his Stoicisme) has very gallant and brave apprehensions of the souls nobility, and tels us that it was *haustus ex divina origine* [a draught from a divine spring], which *Tully,* thus [96] varies, *ex mente divina decerptus*[96] [plucked from the divine mind], souls, like so many flowers, were cropt and gathered out of the garden of God; and were bound up *in fasciculo viventium,*[97] in the bundle of the living: and if you will but attend to the noble Oratour and Philosopher; you shall hear him thus pleading for the souls divinity. *Animorum nulla in terris origo inveniri potest; nihil enim est in animo mixtum atque concretum, aut quod e terra natum; atque fixum esse videatur: nihilque aut humidum quidem, aut stabile, aut igneum, his enim in Naturis nihil inest, quod memoriae vim, mentis, cogitationis habeat; quod & preterita teneat, & futura praevideat, & complecti possit praesentia, quae sola divina sunt, nec evincetur unquam unde ad hominem venire possunt nisi a Deo; singularis igitur quaedam est natura atque vis animi, sejuncta ab his usitatis notisque naturis; ita quicquid est illud quod sentit, quod serpit, quod vult, quod viget, coeleste & divinum est; ob eam rem aeternum sit necesse est;*[98] which I shall thus render. 'Tis in vain to look for the souls parentage upon earth, for there is no mixing and blending of spirituals with corporeals, the earth doth not contribute, for the fixing and consolidating of them; 'tis no aery puff will suffice for the swiftnesse and nimblenesse of their motion; no drops of water will quench their thirst and longings; they have a purer light and heat, then could ever be fetcht from an elementary spark; in those humble and sordid beings, there's nothing fit to represent, much lesse to produce the clasping and retentive power of memory; the masculine and vigorous working of the minde; the refined and comprehensive vertue of those thoughts, that can recall and look back to things past, that can interpret, and comment upon all present objects, and with a Prophetical glance can spy out futurities and possibilities, which are works not unworthy of a Deity; nor can it e're be shewn that such rare priviledges should be communicated to humane nature any other way then by the immediate bounty and indulgence of heaven; there being such singular and inimitable idioms in the minde of man as could never be extracted from those ordinary and vulgar entities. Though a sensitive soul may creep upon the ground, though it may roll and tumble it self in the dust, yet an intellectual being scornes to look lower then heaven it self; and though it be dated in time, yet it means to live as long as eternity. The Poets had veiled and

mufled up the same opinion in their mythology,[99] whiles they tell us that
Prometheus, (which is all one with providence) did work and fashion the
bodies of men out of clay, but he was fain to steal fire from heaven for the
quickening and enlivening them with souls, which made the Prince of Poets sing *Igneus est ollis vigor & Coelestis origo*[100] [these seeds of celestial birth
and fiery energy], and *Ovid* supplies him with a short verse, *Sedibus ae-
thereis Spiritus ille venit*[101] [that spirit comes from a celestial realm]. How
often do you meet with this in *Homer,* that God is the Father of spirits,
πατὴρ ἀνδρῶν τε θεῶντε,[102] the Father of Angelical beings and of the [97]
souls of men; which *Virgil* renders *hominum Sator atque deorum.*[103] Yet all
this while I know not whether you can, I am sure I cannot, sufficiently
perceive that the generality of the Heathen did think that every soul was
immediately created by God himself, but only that at the first there was
bestowed more then ordinary workmanship upon them, which they knew
principally by those generous motions which they found working in their
own souls; and partly by some reliques of Mosaical History, that was scatter'd amongst them. Thus then I have represented unto you, as indiffer-
ently as I can, the state of this great controversie; and though I could easily
tell you which part I do most easily encline to; yet I shall rather refer it to
your own thoughts, with this intimation, that a modest hesitancy may be
very lawful here; for if you will believe *Gregory* the Great, he tells you it's
a question which cannot be determined in this life.[104] However 'tis enough
for us that the spirit of a man either by vertue of its constant creation, or
by vertue of its first creation *is the candle of the Lord.*

As the soul is the shadow of a Deity, so reason also is a weak and faint
resemblance of God himself, whom therefore that learned Emperour *M.
Antoninus* calls λόγος σπερματικὸς[105] [the generative intelligence], 'tis
God that plants reason, 'tis he that waters it, 'tis he that gives it an increase,
ὁ λόγος ἀνθρώπων πέφυκ' ἀπὸ θείου λόγου[106] [the reason of men has
sprung from the reason of God], the title of ὁ λόγος belongs to Christ
himself, *in whom are hid the treasures of wisdome and knowledge.*[107] Reason
first danc'd and triumpht in those eternal Sun-beams, in the thoughts of
God himself, who is the fountain and original of Reason. And as his will
is the rule of goodnesse, so his understanding is the rule of Reason. For
God himself is a most knowing and intellectual being, he is the first mover

of entity, and does *determinate tendere in aliquem finem* [move deliberately
to a certain end], which speaks an intelligent agent; he does propound
most choice designes, and blessed ends to himself, and is not that a work
of Reason? he does contrive, and dispose, and order means for accom-
plishing of them, and doth not that require understanding? He makes all
beings instrumental and subordinate to him, he moves all inferiour wheels
in a regular manner; he moves all the spheres of second causes in a har-
monical way; such blinde entities as want intellectual eyes, he himself
doth lead them, and conduct them; and to others he gives an eye for their
guidance and direction. Now, he that hath fram'd an intellectual eye, shall
not he see?[108] he that hath cloathed the soul with light as with a garment,
shall not he much more be cloathed himself with a fuller and purer brightnesse? In that which we esteem reason amongst men, there are many
clouds and blemishes, many dark spots and wrinkles, that are scattered
and conquered by this more glorious light. The soul 'tis fain to climb up
and ascend to knowledge by several steps and gradations, but his understanding is all at the same height and eminency; Mans reason is fain to
[98] spend time in knitting a proposition, in spinning out a Syllogisme, in
weaving a demonstration; but he is infinitely beyond, and above these
first draughts and rudiments of knowledge; he sees all ἐν ῥιπῇ ὀφθαλ-
μοῦ,[109] at the first opening of his eye from everlasting, with one intellectual
glance, he pierceth into the whole depth of Entity, into all the dimensions
of being. Mans understanding is fain to borrow a *Species* from the object
which presents to the minde the picture and portraicture of it self, and
strikes the intellectual eye with a colour suitable and proportionable to it:
But the divine understanding never receives the least tincture from an
object, no species *ab extra* [from without], but views all things in the pure
Crystal of his own essence, he does not at all see himself in the glasse of
the creatures, as we see him, but he sees creatures in the glasse of his own
being,[110] how else should he see them from everlasting, before they were
extant, before they were visible by any *Species* of their own? God therefore
doth primarily and principally look upon himself, for he is *nobilissimum
intelligibile* [the noblest of intelligible things], he cannot have a more
beautiful and satisfying object to look upon, then his own face, τὸ
γνωστὸν τοῦ θεοῦ [the knowledge of God] is an object fit to enamour

all understanding: for the more any being is abstracted from materiality, the more 'tis refin'd from material conditions, the more graceful and welcome it is to the understanding; for matter does cloud and darken the glosse of being; it doth eclipse an object, and is no friend to intelligibility. So that God being a pure and immaterial spirit must needs be *praestantissimum intelligibile* [the most excellent of intelligible things], and a most adequate object for his own eye to look upon. And this understanding is himself, it being *actio immanens* [an immanent action], always dwelling with him, *Dei scientia est Dei essentia*[112] [the knowledge of God is the essence of God], (as the Schoolmen speak) God is ὅλος ὀφθαλμὸς, ὅλον φῶς, he is both all eye, and all light; as suppose the bright body of the Sun had a visive faculty, so as it could view and surveigh its own light and beams, and could by vertue of them look upon all other things, which its own light does unveil, and discover, 'twould then give some languishing adumbration of a Deity, who is always looking upon his own perfections, and seeing creatures by his own light, by his own uncreated beams. For *Species & similitudo omnium est in Dei essentia*[113] [the species and likeness of all things exist in God's essence]. Thus God looking upon his own omnipotency, knows all possibilities; viewing his own determinations, he sees all futurities; looking upon his own wisdome he beholds all varieties, all degrees and differencies of being, which yet put not the least shadow of difference in him, because the excellencies of all beings are treasured up in him only by way of transcendency, not *per modum compositionis, sed per modum perfectionis*[114] [by composition but by perfection] (as the Schools have it.) So that when God beholds all created beings by vertue of his own essence, yet you must [99] not imagine that the formality of a creature is conteined in an uncreated being, but only that there is enough of being there to give a representation of all being whatsoever. As when a glasse reflects a face, there's not the least mutation in the glasse, much lesse is the face any part of the glasses essence; though the glasse give a sufficient resemblance of it. Yet herein there's this disparity, that the glasse of Gods essence did represent a creature, before any created face could look into it; for God looking upon himself from eternity, did then know *quot modis aliquid assimilari potuit ipsius essentiae*[115] [in how many ways anything could be made to resemble his being], and did know how farre

such a being would imitate his essence, and how farre it would fall short
of it. He saw that this being would come neerer, that that being would
be more distant and remote from him; this picture would be liker him,
that would shew very little of him. Now the actuality and existence of
such an object is not requisite to the understanding of it, for how then
could we conceive of the privation of a not Entity? How can we otherwise
apprehend them, then by framing the notion of something positive in
our mindes, and supposing a total deficiency from it? Thus as they use
to speak, *Rectum est index sui & obliqui, & nobilissimum in unoquoque
genere est mensura, & exemplar reliquorum*[116] [right is the index of itself
and of wrong, and in every kind of thing the most excellent is the
measure and model of the rest], that first and supreme being by the great
example and patern of himself, can judge of all inferiour and imperfect
beings. Nor could he see them *ab aeterno* [eternally] any otherwise then
in himself, there being nothing else eternal, but himself, and in himself
he could clearly see them as we see effects in their cause. All created beings
were eminently contained in the Centre of one indivisible essence, who
by his infinite vertue was to produce them all, who being an intelligent
Centre did see those several lines that might be drawn from him, and
withall, being a free and a voluntary Centre, did know how many lines
he meant to draw from himself. Now you know amongst men, a demonstration *a priori,* is esteemed most certain and scientifical, *Scire est per
causas cognoscere*[117] [to know is to understand causes]. God thus knew
creatures, perfectly knowing himself, who was the first cause of them all;
This doth much speak the immutability of the eternal reason and wisdome
in the minde of God, and doth remove all imperfections from it: For you
see, he did not move in an axiomatical way, *per compositionem & divisi-
onem* [by composition and division]; for he saw things by his own un-
compounded and indivisible essence; much lesse did his knowledge im-
prove it self in a syllogistical way, deducing and collecting one thing out
of another: This is the Schoolmens meaning, when they tell us *cognitio
Dei non est ratiocinativa* [God's knowledge is not sequential], that is, *non
est discursiva*[118] [it is not discursive]. They that will light a candle may
strike such sparks, but the Sunne and Starres want no such light. Angels
are above Syllogismes, how [100] much more is God himself? Nay, even

amongst men, first principles are above disputings, above demonstrations; now all things are more naked in respect of God himself, then common notions are to the sight of men. 'Tis a *motus testudineus* [tortoise-like movement], a tardy and tedious work, a fetching a compasse, to gather one thing out of another; 'Tis the slow pace of a limited understanding. But there's no succession in God, not in the knowledge of God. There's no *prius & posterius* [before and after], no premisses or conclusions; no *transitus ab uno ad aliud* [transition from one thing to another], no *externum medium* [external medium], for he does not *cognoscere per aliud medium a seipso distinctum* [know by any medium distinct from himself], there's a compleat simultaneity in all his knowledge,[119] his essence is altogether, and so is his knowledge; plurality of objects will confound a finite understanding, for they must be presented by different *Species,* and a created eye cannot exactly view such different faces at once, such several pictures at once. The understanding sometimes loses it self in a croud of objects; and when such a multitude comes thronging upon it, it can scarce attend to any of them. But God seeing them all *per unicam speciem, per unicam operationem*[120] [in one species, in one act], takes notice of them all with an infinite delight and facility. For he loves to attend to his own essence, which doth so admirably represent them all; hence his knowledge is always in act, because his essence is a pure act; Humane understandings have much of their knowledge stor'd up in habits, but there are no habits in a Deity, for knowledge is dormant in a habit, but his understanding never slumbers nor sleeps: There's no potentiality in him, but he's always *in ultima perfectione* [in his absolute perfection], he is *semper in actu intelligendi*[121] [alwayes in the act of comprehending], as *Sol* is *semper in actu lucendi* [always in the act of shining]. Humane understandings are faine to unbend themselves sometimes, as if they were faint and weary, but Divinity is always vigorous, and Eternity can never languish. The understanding of God thus being fill'd with light, his Will also must needs be rational, *non caeca, sed oculata notitia* [a knowledge not blind, but clear-sighted]. This makes the Schoolmen very well determine, that though there cannot be *causa divinae voluntatis* [a cause of the divine will]; yet there may be assign'd *ratio divinae voluntatis*[122] [a reason for the divine will]. There can be no cause of his Will, for then there would be a cause of his Essence, his Will being all one with his Essence; but there cannot be *causa prior prima* [a cause prior to the first]. Yet this account may be given of his Will, that *bonum intellectum est fundamentum voliti*[123] [a known good is the basis of volition], so that as God does primarily *intelligere seipsum* [comprehend himself], so he does understand other things, only *per seipsum* [in himself], so likewise he does principally and necessarily *velle seipsum* [will himself], and does will other things secondarily, and out of choice, *propter seipsum*[124] [because of him[101]self]. And as God hath set all other beings a longing after the perfections and conservations of their own beings, and has in a special manner stampt upon a rational nature an intellectual appetite of its own well-fare and happinesse, so as that it cannot but propound an ultimate scope and end to it self, and bend and direct all its desires for the hitting and attaining of it; so he himself also sets up himself, as the most adequate and amiable end of all his workings and motions, and does bend the whole creation, does shoot every being, and order it to his own glory. Now how rational is that Will of his that does chiefly fix it self upon the fairest good, and wills other things only as they are subservient to it, *Deus vult bonitatem suam tanquam finem, & vult omnia alia tanquam media ad finem*[125] [God wills his own goodness as an end, and he wills all other things as means to that end]. Out of the intense and vehement willing of himself, he wills also some prints and resemblances of himself. The beauty of his own face, of his own goodnesse is so great, as that he loves the very picture of it; And because one picture cannot sufficiently expresse it, therefore he gives such various and numerous representations of it. As when men cannot expresse their minde in one word, they are willing to rhetoricate and inlarge themselves into more. God doth give many similitudes of himself, for the greater explication of his own essence. His essence in it self not being capable of augmentation or multiplications, he loves to see some imitations and manifestations of it, to make known his own power & perfection in a way of causality. Now the understanding of God being so vast and infinite, and his will being so commensurate and proportion'd to it, nay all one with it; all those Decrees of his that are the Eternal product and results of his minde and will, must needs be rational also; For in them his understanding and will met together, his truth and goodnesse kissed each other.[126] And though these Decrees of God must be resolved into his absolute supremacy and dominion, yet that very sovereignty of his is founded upon so much reason, and does act so wisely and intelligently, as that no created understanding can justly question it, but is bound obediently to adore it. The prosecution and application of these Decrees, 'tis accompanied with the very same wisdome and reason; for what's Providence but *oculus in sceptro*[127] [an eye in a sceptre], a rational guiding and ruling all affairs in the world, 'tis *ipsa ratio divina in summo principe constituta* [that divine reason established in the supreme ruler]; 'tis *ratio ordinandorum in finem*[128] [the system of ordering things to an end], that which in man is called prudence, in God is called Providence; the right tuning and regulating of all circumstances, and making them to conspire & contribute to his own end & glory. And if man could but rightly interpret and comment upon Providence, what fresh discoveries, what bright displayings of divine reason would they all continually meet withall? what shinings and sparklings of divine wisdome are there in some remarkable provi[102]dential passages? You that are most acquainted with the wayes of God; tell us if you did ever finde any thing unreasonable in them. Enquire still more into his dealings, and you'll see more of reason in them. Could you search deeper into the rich mine of his counsel, you would still meet with more precious veines of wisdome. The depths of his counsels, what are they but the very profoundnesse of his reason? τὰ βάθη τοῦ θεοῦ[129] [the deep things of God] they are τὰ βάθη τοῦ λόγου [the deep things of reason]. And whensoever this secret counsel of his issues out and bubles forth, it is in most rational manifestations. His commands are all rational, his word is the very pith and marrow of reason. His Law is the quickening and wakening of mens reason; his Gospel, 'tis the flowing out of his own reason; 'tis the quintessence of wisdome from above; His spirit is a rational agent; the motions of the holy Ghost are rational breath; the revelations of the holy Ghost, a rational light, as rational as a demonstration: the Apostle calls them so. As when the Spirit of God over-powers the will, it makes a willingnesse there, where there was an absolute nolency,[130] an obstinate refusal before. So when it over-powers the minde, it makes it understand that which it did not, which it could not understand before. Spiritual irradiations stamp new light, create new reason in the soul; Nothing comes to man with the superscription of a Deity, but that which hath upon it some signature of wisdom. God himself is an intelligent worker in his dealing with all beings, how much rather in his dealing with rational beings? By all this you see that God himself is the Eternal spring and head of reason. And that humane wisdome is but a created and an imperfect copy of his most perfect and original wisdom.

Now Philosophy could dictate thus much, Τέλος ἁπάντων ἕπεσθαι τοῖς θεοῖς[131] [the end of all is to follow the gods]. God loves to see such a noble creature as man is, to follow and imitate him in his reason. *Omnia intendunt assimilari Deo*[132] [all things seek to resemble God], as the Schoolmen have it. Now men cannot be more assimilated unto God, then by moving as intelligent agents. Does God himself work according to reason from eternity to eternity? And has he made a creature in time, whose very essence is reason? Why then does it not open its eyes? why does it not use its lamp? and though it cannot discover all, yet let it discern as much as it can. Let it not act in the choicest points of religion, out of blinde and implicit principles, and huddle up its chiefest operations in I know not what confused and obscure and undigested manner. This neither becomes sons of light, nor works of light. The more men exercise reason, the more they resemble God himself, who has but few creatures that can represent him in so bright an excellency as this; only Angels and men; and therefore he expects it the more from them. And the more they exercise their own reason, the more they will admire and adore his; For none can admire reason but they that use some reason themselves. And this may suffice for the [103] first particular, that *The Candle of the Lord* 'tis *lumen derivatum* [a derivative light], it was first lighted at a Sun-beam.

The Light of Reason Is
a Diminutive Light

[104] This Candle of the Lord, 'tis *Lumen tenue & diminutum* [a feeble and diminished light]. A Lamp is no such dazling object. A Candle has no such goodly light, as that it should pride and glory in it. 'Tis but a brief and compendious flame, shut up, and imprison'd in a narrow compasse. How farre distant is it from the beauty of a Starre? How farre from the bright-nesse of a Sun? This Candle of the Lord when it was first lighted up, before there was any thief in it, even then it had but a limited and restrained light. God said unto it, Thus farre shall thy Light go. Hither shalt thou shine, and no farther.[1] *Adam* in innocency was not to crown himself with his own sparks. God never intended that a creature should rest satisfied with its own candle-light, but that it should run to the fountain of light, and sunne it self in the presence of its God. What a poor happinesse had it been for a man, only to have enjoyed his own Lamp? Could this ever have been a beatifical vision? Could this light ever have made a heaven fit for a soul to dwell in? The sparkling Seraphims and glittering Cherubims (if it were possible that the face of God should be eclipsed from them, that they should have no light, but that which shines from their own essences) Blacknesse, and darknesse, and gloominesse, a totall and fatal Eclipse, a present and perpetual night would rush in upon them, if the heaven were fuller of Stars then it is, and if this lower part of the world were adorned and illuminated with as many Lamps as 'tis capable of, yet would they never be able to supply the absence of one Sun. Their united light would not amount to so much as to make up one day, or one moment of a day. Let Angels and men contribute as much light as they can, let them knit

and concentricate their beams; yet neither Angelical Star-light, nor the sons of men with their Lamps and Torches could ever make up the least shadow of glory, the least appearance of heaven: the least fringe of happinesse. Lucifer that needs would be an Independent light that would shine with his own beams, you know that he presently sunk and fell into perpetual darknesse.[2] And *Adams* Candle aspiring to be a Sun, has burnt the dimmer ever since. God taking notice of it, and spying him in the dust; Lo (saies he) here lies the spark, that would needs become a God. There lies the glow-worm that would needs become a Sun. *Man is become like one of us,*[3] yet notwithstanding *Adams* light at first was a pure light, till he had soil'd it, 'twas a Virgin-light till he had deflower'd it. The breath [105] that God breath'd into him was very precious and fragrant, till he had corrupted it. אדם נשמח [the understanding of a man] the spirit of *Adam* (if we should render the words so) 'twas in a special manner נר יחוח *Lucerna Domini*[4] [the candle of the Lord], when God raised this goodly structure of man out of nothing, he built it most compleatly and proportionably; he left it *in statu integro & perfecto*[5] [in an integral and perfect state], for you cannot imagine that any obliquity, or irregularity should come from so accurate an hand as his was; when God printed the whole creation, there were no *errata* to be found, no blots at all. Every letter was faire and lovely, though some first and capital letters were flourisht more artificially then others; Other inferiour creatures would serve like so many consonants, but men were the vowels, or rather the diphthongs to praise him both in soul and body. When God first tun'd the whole creation, every string, every creature praised him; but man was the sweetest and loudest of the rest, so that when that string apostatized, and fell from its first tuning, it set the whole creation a jarring. When God first planted the soul of man, it was the garden of God himself, his spiritual *Eden,* he lov'd to walk in it; 'twas full of the fairest and choicest flowers, of the most precious and delicious fruits; 'twas water'd with all the fresh springs of heavenly influence: No weeds, nor briers, nor thornes to be found there. The understanding, that tree of knowledge, was very tall and stately, and reaching up to heaven. There was in man a *cognitio plena & lucida* [a complete and lucid knowledge], as the Schoolmen speak; *clara & fixa contemplatio intelligibilium*[6] [clear and steady contemplation of the intelligible]. The eye of the soul 'twas quick and clear, 'twas strong and fixt, God tried it by himself, by a Sun-beam, and found it genuine. How presently did *Adam* by this spy out the stamps and signatures that were upon the several creatures? when by an extemporary facility, he gave them such names as should interpret and comment upon their essences (nay according to the Schoolmens determinations) man in this his primitive condition, *habuit scientiam omnium naturaliter scibilium*[7] [knew all by nature]. As God framed him an elegant body, at its full height and stature, (though not with his head reaching up to heaven, as some did ridiculously phancy) so he gave him also a comely and amiable soul at its just ἀκμή [acme] endowed with all natural accomplishments and perfections; his Dove-like spirit dwelt in a spotlesse and beautiful temple. This makes the Protestant Divines very well determine, that *pronitas ad malum non fluit ex principiis naturae integrae*[8] [an inclination to evil does not originate in principles of unfallen nature]; for it would be a thought too injurious to the God of Nature, to imagine he should frame evill. Yet some of the Papists and some others do constantly affirm, that such a rational being as man is, considered *in puris naturalibus* [solely in his natural state], will have an unavoydable propensity unto evil, *ex necessaria materiae conditione* [by the necessary condition of matter], [106] and they bring forth such bold words as these. *Deum non posse creare hominem ex anima rationali, & materiali sensibili compositum, quin praeter divinam intentionem, homo ita constitutus habeat praecipitem inclinationem ad sensibilia,*[9] their meaning is this, by reason of that intimate and essential conjunction of the sensitive powers with the intellectual, there must needs arise some ataxy and confusion in the being of man, and too great a favouring of sensitive objects, unless that inferiour part of the soul be restrained *supernaturali quodam fraeno* [by a sort of supernatural rein] (as they speak;) and say they, it was thus chain'd up in a state of innocency, but now being let loose, 'tis extreamly wilde and unruly. How derogatory is this from the goodnesse and power of Gods creation, and from that accurate harmony and immaculate beauty that were to be found in such a noble being as man was in his native and original condition? *nec fraenum nec calcar desiderabatur*[10] [neither rein nor spur was required], for there was a just and regular tendency without the least swerving or deviation. There was no such tardity in the sensitive part as should need a spurre; nor yet any such impetuousnesse and violence as should require a bridle. This indeed must be granted, that upon the knitting and uniting of such a soul to such a body, of sensitives to intellectuals, there will naturally follow, *respectus & inclinatio ad sensibilia* [a consideration of, and tendency towards, sensible things]; and this is not *praeter, sed secundum intentionem divinam* [contrary, but according to, the intention of God]; but that this should be *praeceps, rebellis, & inordinata inclinatio*[11] [a violent, rebellious and disordered inclination], is so farre from being necessary, as that 'tis plainly contra-natural. For this sensitive appetite of man, is born *sub regno rationis* [under the rule of reason], and so is to be govern'd *sceptro rationis* [by the sceptre of reason]. By this golden Scepter, it was peaceably rul'd in a state of innocency. *Anima non aggravata erat a corpore*[12] [the soul was not oppressed by the body], (as the Schoolmen say) the body though it was not beautified and clarified in the same measure that a glorified body is; yet it was dutiful and obedient, and every way serviceable to the soul. The sensitive powers were not factious, but were willingly subject to the higher powers, to the intellectuals. The first bublings of the soul were pure and crystaline, and streamed out very freely and fluently without any murmuring, without any wavering, without any foaming. There were no violent motions, no violent perturbations which since have made such insurrections in the soul, and with their importunate breath endeavour as much as they can, to blow out this intellectual Lamp, this light of reason. There were *nullae passiones, quae respiciunt malum* [no passions which had evil as their object], (as the School tells us.) There was no slavish fear to bespeak and antedate grief. There was no palenesse to be seen, no tremblings nor shiverings, no tears nor sighs, no blushes nor the least tincture of shame. Paradise it had so much of the Lily, as't [107] had nothing of the Rose, yet there were *istiusmodi passiones quae ordinantur ad bonum*[13] [passions which were regulated towards the good]. Joy would dance and leap sometimes, love would embrace and twine about its dearest good; such pure and noble affections as live and dwell in the breasts of glorified beings were not banisht and excluded from this state of integrity. The Poets shadowed out this happy time in their golden age, though they mix some drosse in the description of it. Now man being constituted in this state of natural rectitude, his Candle shining clearly, his will following cheerfully, his affections complying most suitably, a sudden cloud presently rusht upon him, and blotted all his glory. And as the Orator stiled that Roman Magistrate, that was suddenly turned out of his place, *Consul vigilantissimus* [a most vigilant consul], because he did not sleep all the time of his Consulship (for he continued but a day in it)[14] in the very same sense, and only in this sense, man also was *vigilantissimus in honore* [most vigilant in honour], in the Psalmists language בל ילין[15] *non per noctabit,* he would not abide in honour, he did not lodge one night in honour. Though I am farre from laying such stresse upon those words, as they do, that will needs from thence measure the time so exactly, as that they'll tell you to a minute how long *Adam* enjoyed his first glory: This only we are sure of, it was a very brief and transient happinesse, a fading and withering glory; he had wasted his Oile presently, and the Lamp was going out, but that God dropt fresh oile into it, by the promise of a Messiah. The Schoolmen are very solicitous & desirous to know how *Adams* understanding being *in vigore viridi* [in its fresh vigour] could be entangled in such a snare, and deluded with such a miserable fallacy. *Aquinas* for his part determines *hominem in primo statu decipi non potuisse*[16] [man in his original innocence was not able to be deceived], which yet is altogether unconceivable, for how could he fall unlesse his head declin'd? 'Tis not very easily perceptible at any time, how there can be *defectus in voluntate* [a failure in the will], and yet not *Error in Intellectu* [an error in the intellect], much lesse can we tell how this should come to passe, when the will was so obediently disposed *ad nutum intellectus* [to the command of the intellect], when it gave such observance to all the commands and dictates of the understanding, as that did in a state of innocency. And to resolve the whole anomaly and irregularity of that first prevarication, only into the wills untowardnesse; what is it else then to say that *Adam* sinned *ex mera malitia, contra claritatem judicii*[17] [out of pure malice, against the clarity of his judgment]; which is to entertain a thought very groundlesse, uncharitable, and dishonourable to the first root of mankinde, and to make his transgression of the same dye with those damned Angelical spirits that were thrown into irrecoverable misery. Therefore *Zanchy,* that was one of the most scholastical amongst the Protestants, doth most judiciously conclude, that the understanding of *Adam* was defective in its office, by a negligent non-attend[108]ency.[18]

The eye was clear enough, the bowe was strong enough, but it was not vigilant enough, it was not bent enough; the balance was not deceitful, but he forgot to weigh things in it. Now man by this fall of his was not only *spoliatus supranaturalibus* [deprived of his supernatural gifts], but also *vulneratus in ipsis naturalibus*[19] [wounded in his very nature]. How soon is this beautiful creature withered! his spring is gone, his *May* is gone, his glosse and greennesse gone; the flower droops, the tree is neither so flourishing nor so fruitful, an untimely and disconsolate Autumne comes upon him. Thus the purest complexions are alwayes most fraile and brittle. Thus the highest conditions are most tottering and precipitious, and the noblest perfections, if built only upon natures bottome, are but voluble and uncertaine. There arises a sudden δυσκρασία [instability], a present ἀσυμμετρία[20] [lack of harmony], in the being of man. The Philosophers were very sensible of it, and groaned under it. You may hear them complaining of the τὰ νοσήματα περὶ τὴν ψυχὴν, of the languishings and faintings of the soul, of a νόθος λογισμὸς,[21] a spurious and adulterate kinde of reason. You may hear them complaining of an ἀπτηρία & πτερορρύησις,[22] a *defluvium pennarum.* The wings of the soul flag, many of the feathers are sick and drop away. And that soul which was wont to build its nest in the Starres, is now faine to build it in the dust. You may hear one Philosopher complaining of the κεφαλαλγία, his head, his understanding akes; another of the Ὀφθαλμία, his eye, his reason is dimm'd; a third of the καρδιαλγία, the *palpitatio cordis,* his soul trembles with doubts and uncertainties. You may see one grasping a cloud of Errors, another spending much of his time in untying some one knot, in solving some one difficulty; you may see some one pleasing himself, and sitting down in the shadow of his own opinion, another bending all his nerves and endeavours, and they presently snap asunder. You may see *Socrates* in the twilight, and lamenting his obscure and benighted condition, and telling you that his Lamp will shew him nothing but his own darknesse. You may see *Plato* sitting down by the waters of *Lethe,* and weeping because he could not remember his former notions. You may hear *Aristotle* bewailing himself thus, that his νοῦς ἐν δυνάμει[23] [potential reason] will so seldome come into act, that his *abrasa tabula*[24] has so few, and such imperfect impressions upon it, that his intellectuals are at so low an ebbe, as that the motions of *Euripus* will pose them.[25] You hear *Zeno* complaining that his στοά[26] [cloister] is dark, and *Epictetus* confessing that he had not the right *ansa*[27] [handle], the true apprehension of things; look upon the *Naturalists* head and you'll see it nonplust with an occult quality, feel the *Moralists* pulse, (his conscience I mean) and you'll finde it beating very slowly, very remissely; look upon the most speculative Eagles that stare the Sun in the face, that fly highest in contemplation, those that love to sport and play in the light; yet at length you may see the Sun striking them thorow with one of his [109] glorious darts, and chastizing their inquisitive eyes with one of his brightest beams. The Sun 'tis ready to put out this *Candle of the Lord*, if it make too neer approaches to it. Humane understandings are glad to wink at some dazling objects, as *vehemens sensibile* doth *destruere sensum* [an intense sense impression doth destroy the sense]: so *vehemens intelligibile* doth *perstringere intellectum* [an intense conceptual experience doth strain the intellect]. For in all knowledge there's required a due proportion between the *objectum cognoscibile* [knowable object], and the *virtus cognoscitiva* [knowing power], but when the several powers and faculties of the soul lost that comely proportion which they had amongst themselves, they lost also much of that correspondency and conformity which they had to their several objects. And the soul besides its own losse, had a share in the bodies losse also: for the body wanting much of that accurate and elegant composure which once it had, knowledge it self must needs be prejudic'd by it; that being amongst men founded in sense, and in some measure depending upon organical dispositions. So that the streitning and stopping of these windows, must needs prohibit light. Sin entered in first at a corporeal, then at an intellectual window, and stole away the heart; and the windows have been broken ever since. I know the generality of Philosophers do partly excuse the understanding, and do blame the objects for their exility and poverty, for their little diminutive Entity, for their want of intelligibility. But the subtil *Scotus* doth endeavour to invalidate that, by telling them, that *omnia eadem facilitate intelliguntur a Deo*[28] [all things are understood by God with equal facility]. Thus much is evident and undeniable, that the spying out of a little lurking object, doth argue the strength, and quicknesse, and clearnesse of the eye. The Sun discovers atomes, though they be invisible by candlelight, yet that makes them dance naked in his beams. Created understandings want spectacles to augment and majorate some objects. But the soul never meets with more difficulty then in the understanding of spiritual beings, although they have most of Entity, and so most of intelligibility. Yet the soul being imprison'd in a body not sufficiently clarified and refined, cannot so fully close and comply with incorporeal beings. This *Candle of the Lord* will discover more of spirituals when 'tis took out of the Lanthorne *in statu separato* [in a separate state], or when 'tis put into a clearer *in statu consummato* [in the perfected state]. But for the present how little doth it know of it self? How little of Angels? How little of God? And yet how much might be known of them? Look but a while, (if you can endure to look) upon so unlovely and unpleasant an object, I mean upon those black and prodigious Errors, that cover and bespot the face of these times. And they'll soon convince you of the weaknesse and dimnesse of this Lamp-light of the spirit of a man. *The Candle of the Lord,* though it be amongst them, yet 'tis not so powerful as to scatter and conquer their thick and palpable darkness. 'Tis not an easie, nor a sudden, nor a [110] delightful work to number so many errors, yet if I could reckon them up all, from the *blundering Antinomian,* to the *vagabond Seeker,* or the *wild Seraphick,*[29] set on fire of hell, they would all serve for so many fatal examples of the miserable weaknes of mens understanding. 'Tis true, they do not follow *the Candle of the Lord,* for then reason would have guided them better. But this very consideration shewes the weaknesse of their candle-light, for if it had been a brighter 'twould not have been so soon put out. 'Tis easie to blow out a candle, but who can put out a Starre? or who can extinguish the Sun? And men can shut up natural light, but who can imprison a Star? or who can shut up the Sun? This faint and languishing candle-light does not alwayes prevaile upon the will, it doth not sufficiently warme and inflame the affections. Men do not use to warme their hands at a candle, 'tis not so victorious and over-powering as to scatter all the works of darknesse. It will be night for all the candle; the Moralists were not only frigid in their devotions, but some of them were very dissolute in their practises. When you think upon these things, sure you'll willingly subscribe to the forementioned particular, which you may do very safely, that the spirit of a man 'tis but a Candle. *Lumen exile & diminutum* [a meagre and diminished light].

CHAPTER 13

The Light of Reason Discovers Present,
Not Future Things

[III] 'Tis *lumen explicans praesentia, non aperiens futura,* for did you ever hear of such a Lamp as would discover an object, not yet born nor yet in being? Would you not smile at him that should light up a Candle to search for a futurity? 'Tis the glorious prerogative of the Divine understanding, to have such a fair, and open, and unlimited prospect, as that in one glorious twinkling of an intellectual eye, he can see the whole compasse and extent, and latitude of being; and the whole duration of being: for Eternity at one draught doth swallow up the whole fluency of time, and is infinitely above those temporal conditions of past, present, and to come; *Nullum tempus occurrit Regi*[1] [royal prerogative is not subject to time], (say the Lawyers) *Nullum tempus occurrit Deo* [God is not subject to time], say the Philosophers. An intellectual Sun, doth not *occidere, & redire* [set and rise again], but makes one bright and perpetual day, and by its pure and un-interrupted irradiations, doth paraphrase, and comment upon all objects, so as to uncloud and reveale the most obscure contingency, and to make it present, and naked, and visible. For as the Schoolmen tell us, *Scientia Dei ad omnia praesentialiter se habet*[2] [the knowledge of God comprehends all things as present], His knowledge being all one with his essence, without the least shadow of change. Insomuch as that which with men is a fu-turity and contingency, with him is always present and extant; which speaks for the certainty and infallibility of his prescience, though it be con-versant about such things, as seeme to us most casual and fortuitous. For even we our selves know these things certainly, when they are in act, and in being, because that then they lose their volubility and contingency, and

126

put on reality and necessity: according to that unquestionable rule, *Omne quod est quando est necesse est esse*[3] [whatever is, necessarily is, when it is], a contingency when 'tis *extra suas causas* [beyond its causes], when 'tis actualy produc'd having a *determinatum esse* [determinate essence], it may then also have a determinate cognoscibility.[4] Now God always thus sees a contingency *in termino, in eventu, in periodo* [in its issue]; whereas created understandings look upon it, *in medio, in motu, in itinere*[5] [in its process]. Nay such is the poverty & imperfection of mans knowledge, that many things which are in their own nature necessary and demonstrable; yet perhaps they [112] know them, *per modum probabilitatis & non per modum necessitatis* [only as probable, and not as necessary]. But such is the height & transcendency of the Divine understanding, as that such things as are in their own natures most dubious and hovering between *esse* and *non esse* [being and non-being]; yet God knows even these *per modum infallibilem* [infallibly], and plainly perceives which way they will encline, when men see only an equipoise and neutrality. So that the whole rise of contingency flows from the wavering of second causes. And though *scientia Dei* be *causa rerum* [God's knowledge be the cause of things]; yet being but *causa remota* [a remote cause], it doth not take away contingency; But God himself sees that some things will *evenire contingenter* [occur contingently]: For he doth not only *cognoscere res* [know the thing itself], but *ordinem & modum rerum* [the order and measure of things]. And knows that there are some *causae intermediae* [intermediate causes], which are *impedibiles* and *defectibiles* [liable to weakness and defect] (as the Schoolmen speak somewhat rudely) and by vertue of these, there arises a contingency.[6] Thus in a Syllogisme, though the *major* be necessary, yet if the *minor* be contingent, the conclusion will be so also, and will *sequi deteriorem partem* [follow the weaker premise]; though the first cause be certain, yet if there be obstructions in the second, you cannot promise your self what the effect will be. Though the spring of motion cannot fail, yet if the wheels may possibly break, the progresse will be very uncertain to all but to God himself. For other understandings only know that the wheels may break, but God he sees whether they will break or no, so that which in respect of creatures is *periculosae plenum opus aleae*[7] [a work of hazardous risk], in respect of God is *fixum & τετράγωνον*, determined and immoveable in his everlasting thoughts. Angelical beings cannot reach to so high a perfection of knowledge as this is. For *futurum quatenus futurum,* is *objectum improportionatum intellectui Angelico* [the future as such is an object not fitted for the angelic intellect], as acute *Suarez* doth abundantly evince.[8] The Philosophers finde difficulty enough in explaining the manner how God hath a certain and infallible prescience of these future uncertainties. And they finde it a plain impossibility for the Angels to have any such knowledge, for they neither have *aeternitatem intuitus* [an eternal intuition], which should *ambire in objecto suo omnes differentias temporis,* which should remove all succession, all *prius & posterius* [before and after], and make a compleat simultaneity, nor yet have they *plenitudinem rationis representativae* [a fulness of representative reason], they have no such boundlesse and infinite *species* as the Divine essence is, by which God beholds all things.[9] Angels have neither light enough of their own to manifest a future object, nor an eye strong enough to pierce into it. They cannot infallibly foretel their own motions, because God can alter them and over-power them, much lesse can they know the determinations of God himself, or any operations that [113] depend upon a free agent, till they bud and blossome in some actual discoveries and appearances. Nor are they so well acquainted with the whole context and coherence of natural agents, with all those secret twinings and complications as to spy out beforehand those events which are brought forth in a casual and unusual and very unlikely manner. Whensoever then they have any prescience of future contingencies, 'tis only by revelation from God himself. They may see the face of a future object *in speculo divino* [in a divine mirror], but yet that's *speculum voluntarium* [a wilful mirror], and shews only what it pleaseth, and when, and to whom it pleaseth. The wicked Angels know this well enough, that they for their parts have no knowledge of future uncertainties, though they desire to have it as much as any, and they pretend to it as much as any; yet you know how cautelous they were in their Oracular responsals, as that elegant Moralist *Plutarch* doth most excellently shew in several places.[10] They always drew a curtain before their predictions, and wrapt them up in obscurity, which plainly argued a consciousnesse of their own ignorance in respect of future events. The good Angels are so fill'd with their present happinesse, they are so quieted with the enjoyment of God himself, as that they are not at all solicitous, or inquisitive about future events, but they cheerfully entertain and drink in all those beams that come flowing from the face of their God, and they desire no more then he is pleased to communicate to them, nay indeed they can desire no more, for he gives them as much as they are capable of. Now if Angelical understandings are not so wide and comprehensive as to graspe and take in such objects, what mean then the sons of men to aspire and reach after the knowledge of them? if those tall and eminent beings, standing upon the mount of God cannot see them, how shall the sons of men that are of a lower stature hid in a valley, how shall they behold them? Yet there was alwayes in the generality of mankinde, a prurient desire, and hankering after the knowledge of future events. Men still stretch out the hand to the forbidden tree, they long for the fruit of it, and would fain be plucking some apples from it. Nay, men long for the greenest apples, for the precocious knowledge of events before they come to their just ripenesse and maturity.[11] The desire of this sets the Astrologer a lighting his candle at the Stars. O how doth he flatter himself in his own imaginary twincklings, and how doth he perswade the more simple & credulous part of the world that he can discover every future atome, that he can put those capital Stars, those golden letters together, and spell out all the fates of Kingdomes and persons? It makes the *Augur* (the κορακομάντις as the Greeks call him) chatter with the birds in their own dialect, and as if he were their Scholiast, he writes Comments and Expositions upon their language; O how devoutly will he listen to a prophetical Crow? how will he criticize upon the harsh accents of the screech-Owle? upon the dismal and melancholy notes of the night-Raven? [114] It makes the *Auspex* watch the birds in their several postures, and to be as diligent and judicious a spectator of them, as the other was an Auditor. He can interpret every fluttering, he can tell you all their journeys, where they lodg'd, where they baited last, what tree they visited, what bough they staied longest upon; and at length he will pluck some pens out of their sacred wings, for the writing of all his learned predictions. It moved the *Exspex* to consult with the inwards, to search into the bowels of things; he'll but look upon a Liver, and will presently tell you the colour and complexion of all affairs. It caus'd the *Aruspex* to behold the behaviour of the dying sacrifice, and from the quietnesse or strugling of those sensitive creatures, to foretel the reluctancies or facilities in higher matters. It set the *Chiromancer* a studying to read those lines that seem to be scribled upon his hand, and to explain them with his own interlineary glosses; and to look upon them as natures M S S. as an Enchiridion of natures penning, in which she gave him a brief Synopsis of all such passages of his life, as should come into being afterward. It moved the *Interpreter of dreams* to set up his seat of Judicature in those gates of fancy, the *Porta Cornea* [gate of horn] I mean, and the *Porta Eburnea*[12] [gate of ivory], and as if the night were to enlighten the day, he will regulate all his waking motions by those slumbring intimations, yet usually the interpretation of the dream is the more non-sensical dream of the two. Some others will needs cast lots for their fortunes, and think that the judgement of a Dye is infallible, will undertake no matters of moment til they be predetermined by it; *Jacta est alea,*[13] *& per praesentem sortem judicant de futura* [the die is cast, and they judge the future by the present lot]. A rare device to finde out one contingency by another, to lose one arrow, and to shoot another after it. These are some of those many methods and contrivances, which the sons of men have contriv'd to themselves, for the finding out of future events. What should I tell you of the rest of the γεωμαντία [earth prophecy], and the πυρομαντία [fire prophecy], of the ὑδρομαντία [water prophecy], and the νεκρομαντία [necromancy], and βελομαντία [javelin prophecy], of the λιβανομαντία [incense prophecy], of the κοσκινομαντία [sieve prophecy], which are all but the various expressions of the same madnesse? What should I tell you of those several Nations that have been enamor'd with these follies? the Assyrians, the Caldeans, the Persians, the Grecians, the Romans, have had always amongst them several professors of these vanities. You see how fain the sons of men would have some key or other to unlock and open these secret and reserved passages, which Providence hath wisely shut up, and hid from the eyes of men. But *Aquinas* passes this censure upon them all, *Hujusmodi artes non utuntur patrocinio intellectus bene dispositi secundum virtutem*[14] [arts of this kind do not enjoy the patronage of a virtuous intellect]. And that sacred Author is much of the same minde; *Frustra illud quaeris in terris quod solus Deus novit in* [115] *Coelis* [you seek vainly on earth for that which God alone knows in heaven]. Yet this tree of knowledge is fair to the eye, and pleasant to the taste, the soul doth relish all notional dainties with delight, and these prenotions and anticipations of things are the more sweet and delicious to the palates and tastes of men, because most of their being is treasur'd up in their future condition. They have no satisfaction, no Sabbath, nor quiet in their present state, and therefore they would fain know what the next day, and what the next yeer, and what the next age will bring forth. The desires, the prayers, the hopes, the endeavours, the councels of men, they all look towards the future. For (as *Mirandula* the younger doth well observe) the soul of man, 'tis *trium temporum particeps. Tempus praeteritum memoriae, praesens intellectui, futurum voluntati congruit & respondit*[15] [participant in three times. Past time corresponds to memory, present time to understanding, and future time to will]. God therefore that he may keep such a creature as man is in a waiting and obedient posture, in a posture of dependance and expectation, he doth chuse gradually and leisurely to discover to him, πολυμερῶς καὶ πολυτρόπως[16] [at sundry times and in divers manners] those thoughts which he hath concerning him. God will have man in this sense *in Diem vivere* [to live for the day], to entertain fortune by the day, (as the noble *Verulam* saith that Prince did whose life he writes and commemorates)[17] τὸ σήμερον μέλει μοὶ, τὸ δ᾽ αὔριον τίς οἶδε[18] [I care for today; who can know tomorrow]? 'tis a speech that may be took in a better sence, then *Anacreon* e're meant it. And so may that of the Latin Lyrick, *Quid sit futurum cras fuge quaerere*[19] [do not ask what may come tomorrow]. And the Heroical Poet shews them the necessity of this sobriety and temperance in knowledge; for saith he, *Nescia mens hominum fati sortisque futurae*[20] [the mind of man is ignorant of fate and future fortune]; for mens knowledge naturally enters in at the gate of sense, but a future object can have no admission there. And as the minde cannot recal *objectum totaliter praeteritum* [an object totally obliterated], when there is no remaining *Species,* neither the least print or *vestigium* [trace] of it; so neither can it present an object that's altogether future, and hath no such colour as can move and strike the intellectual eye; such effects indeed as are stored up in pregnant and eminent and necessary causes, may be easily and certainly foreknown by visible and unquestionable demonstrations. The foretelling of an Eclipse may be done without an Oracle, and may be believed though there be no miracle to seal and confirm it. Such effects as lurk in probable causes, that seem to promise very fairly, may be known also in an answerable, and proportionable manner, by strong and shrewd conjectures; hence spring all the *praenotiones Medicorum, Nautarum, Pastorum* [predictions of doctors, sailors, and shepherds], as the fore-mentioned *Mirandula* tells us.[21] Yet the great pretenders of the Antedating knowledge, do very frequently *& pro more* [customarily], deceive both them[116]selves and others in these more ordinary & easy scrutinies. This might cloath your Almanacks in more red, and put them to the blush for guessing at the weather no better, you may write upon them *nulla dies sine errato* [no day without its error]. Did they ne're threaten you with thunder and lightning enough to make a *Caligula* prepare new Laurels;[22] when yet the heavens prov'd very pacate and propitious? Did they ne're tell you of a sad discontented day which would weep its eyes out? which yet when 'twas born prov'd a *Democritus,* and did nothing but laugh at their ignorance and folly.[23] Did they ne're flatter you with fine pleasant temperate weather, καὶ κατέβη ἡ βροχὴ, καὶ ἔπνευσαν οἱ ἄνεμοι,[24] the rain descended, the windes arose, the hail beat, the Prediction fell, because 'twas built upon so weak a foundation. So that *Aquinas* for his part thinks, that the sensitive creatures, the Crows, and the Craines, and the Swallows, those flying Almanacks, that know their appointed times, are more happy and successeful in their predictions, & are better directed by their feeling the impression of some heavenly bodies then men are by their seeing of them.[25] Now if these *Anni specula* [mirrors of the year] be crackt and broken, and give such unequal representations of things most obvious, how then will they be ever able to shew you objects farre more imperceptible and immaterial, that depend upon the will and decrees of God himself? and upon the motions of most free and indifferent agents? This makes the great *Astrologo-mastix* [Scourge of astrologers], I mean the most noble and eminent *Mirandula* with indignation to conclude, that this blasing Art of theirs (that is Astrology abus'd, for so either he means, or ought to mean) 'tis at the best but *Domina & Regina Superstitionum* [the mistress and queen of superstitions], and he breaks out into such words as these, *Vanitas vanitatum Astrologia, & omnis superstitio vanitas*[26] [astrology is the vanity of vanities, and all superstition is vanity]; yet notwithstanding God hath provided some that shall give some faint resemblances of himself, in the knowledge of future things, by a participation of light from him. Ἔχομεν βεβαιότερον τὸν προφητικὸν λόγον ᾧ καλῶς ποιεῖτε προσέχοντες, ὡς λύχνῳ φαίνοντι ἐν αὐχμηρῷ τόπῳ²⁷ [we have also a more sure word of prophecy; whereunto ye do well that ye take heed, as unto a light that shineth in a dark place]. That I may borrow these words of the Apostle, This *Lumen propheticum* [prophetic light], 'tis *Lumen super naturale* [a supernatural light], Prophetical springings come not from the will of man, but from the breathings of the holy Ghost, they are *impressiones & signaturae divinae scientiae* [the impressions and signatures of the divine wisdom]. As God himself is ὁ ὤν, καὶ ὁ ἦν, καὶ ὁ ἐρχόμενος²⁸ [he which is, and which was, and which is to come], so he will have a Prophet to be a shadow of himself, Ὅς τ᾽ ἤδη τά τ᾽ ἐόντα τὰ τ᾽ ἐσσόμενα πρὸ τ᾽ ἐόντα,²⁹ which *Virgil* well translates, *Novit namque omnia vates, Quae sint, quae fuerant, quae mox ventura trahantur*³⁰ [for the prophet knows all things [117] that are, that have been, and that approach their time]. God thus revealing and communicating his minde to his Prophets doth clearly manifest, that he himself hath an exact knowledge of future events, he doth expressely shew that he doth *curare res humanas* [care for human affairs], that he is *actor & ordinator futurorum* [the agent and ordainer of the future]; That his providence doth over-rule the greatest contingencies. He doth therefore upbraid the Idols of the Heathens with their ignorance of these things אם אלהים נ ונרעה לאחור האחיות הנידו Ἀναγγείλατε ἡμῖν τὰ ἐπερχόμενα ἐπ᾽ ἐσχάτου, καὶ γνωσόμεθα ὅτι θεοί ἐστε [show the things that are to come hereafter, that we may know that ye are gods] *Isaiah* 41.23. Prophetical language is *divini sermonis character* [a mark of divine utterance], and doth necessarily require, *super humanam cognitionem*³¹ [superhuman knowledge], which makes me wonder at the great Doctor *Maimon,* that resolves the power of prophesying into nothing else then a healthful temper, a lively complexion of body, and a vigorous minde advanced with study and industry. An opinion which smells too strongly of the Garlick and Onions of that Countrey, the Egyptian superstition I mean, with which he was sufficiently acquainted; yet he tells us that it's the publick tenent of the Jewes, *sententia legis nostrae*³² [the judgment of our law], for so he entitles it, and withall adds that the Art of prophesying (for though he does not stile it so, yet he makes it so) 'tis *supremus gradus hominis, & summa per-*

fectio speciei[33] [the highest distinction of man, and the greatest perfection of the race]; the qualifications which he requires are these, men must be *idonei ad prophetiam ab ipsa conceptione & nativitate* [fit for prophecy from their conception and birth], there must be *dispositio & dexteritas naturalis* [a natural disposition and skill], there must be *optimus humor cerebri* [an excellent intellect], he must be *optimus vir in intellectualibus, & moribus suis perfectus* [superior in intellect and perfect in morality]. But his principal condition is, that there must be *summa facultatis imaginatricis perfectio* [the highest perfection of the imaginative faculty]; for saith he, if the influence of an *intellectus agens* [active intellect], (such a one as he falsely and vainly supposes) be pour'd out only upon the rational part of the soul, and doth not drop upon the fancy, either by reason of the scarcity of oile, or the incapacity of the fancy, there will be onely *secta sapientum speculatorum* [a sect of wise speculators]. Such men may be eminent for deep Contemplation, but they will ne're be famous for prophesying. If the fancy be onely quickned or heightned, then there will be *secta Politicorum, Jurisperitorum, Praestigiatorum, Incantatorum* [a sect of politicians, lawyers, mountebanks, magicians], But if the understanding, and fancy be both heightened to their due *apex, repente fiunt prophetae* [suddenly prophets appear]: onely this I had almost forgot which yet he thinks very convenient, that they should have good dyet for the time of their prophesying; for, as he tells you, according to the minde of the Jews, *Prophetia neque habitat inter* [118] *tristitiam neque pigritiam* [prophecy lives neither in sorrow nor indolence]; So that the *terrae filii*[34] the עַם אָרֶץ, the vulgar sort of people are no more fit to prophesy, *quam vel Asinus vel Rana* [than is an ass or a frog]. They are his own words turn'd into Latine. But surely this Doctor himself did not prophesy but dream all this while; How else did he think that such a noble and spiritual imployment, such a rare and glorious priviledge as this is, could be raised by the power of man out of the strength of nature, that nature that's so fallen and degenerated? And what means he *to limit the Holy one of Israel,*[35] *and to restraine the Spirit of the Almighty?* Grant that *Esay* was a Courtier, yet was not *Amos* an herdsman? and was not he also among the Prophets? Did he ne're hear of the weaker sex sometimes prophesying? which yet was neer famous for intellectuals. Does not this prophetical spirit breath when it pleaseth, and where it pleaseth, & how it pleaseth? Me thinks this second *Moses* should not be offended, though some of the ordinary people be Prophets. Or if natural endowments, or artificial preparations must be had, and if they of themselves be so potent, and energetical, how then comes Vision to fail, and how does Prophecy cease? Are there none that have their imagination strong enough, that have their understandings rais'd enough? that are of unquestionable integrity, and are not wanting in study and industry, and yet are no Prophets nor Prophets sons? Let then this *Candle of the Lord* content it self with its proper object. It findes work enough and difficulty enough in the discovery of present things, and has not such a copious light as can search out future events.

The Light of Reason Is a Certain Light

[119] 'Tis *Lumen certum.* Lamp-light as 'tis not glorious, so 'tis not deceitful, though it be but a faint and languishing light. Though it be but a limited and restrained light, yet it will discover such objects as are within its own sphere with a sufficient certainty. The letters of Natures law, are so fairly printed, they are so visible and capital, as that you may read them by this Candle-light; yet some weak and perverse beings not fit to be honoured with the name of men, slight all the workings and motions of Reason, upon this account, that they are Rolling and fluctuating, that they are treacherous and unconstant. And they look upon Logick which is nothing else but the just advancement of reason, an Art of Ripening and mellowing reason, an art of Clarifying and refining of the minde, yet they look upon it as an intelectual kinde of jugling, an artificial kinde of cheating and cozening their understanding: Nor were it a wonder if onely the dregs of people, the rude lump of the multitude, if they onely were sunk and degenerated into this folly, But I meet with a famous and ancient sect of Philosophers that delight in the name of *Scepticks,* who by a strange kinde of Hypocrisy, and in an unusual way of affectation pretend to more ignorance then they have, nay then they are capable of. They quarrel with all Arts and Sciences, and do as much as they can to annihilate all knowledge and certeinty; and professe nothing but a Philosophical kinde of neutrality, and Lukewarmnesse. *Socrates* did not please them; for he shewed himself but a Semisceptick, one that was too confident in saying that he did *hoc tantum scire, se nihil scire* [know this much, that he knew nothing]; for they will not allow so much knowledge as that comes to, this they tell you, that they don't know this, whether they know any thing or no. There was

one sort of Academicks, that came very neer them, their motto was, οὐ καταλαμβάνω,[1] their meaning was that they could not graspe or comprehend any object. *Lucian* (that unhappy wit) makes himself very merry with them, and laughs at one of them, that had a servant that prov'd a fugitive and ran away from him, his Master (sayes he) is very unfit to runne after him δραπέτην μεταδιώκειν; for he will alwayes cry, οὐ καταλαμβάνω, οὐ καταλαμβάνω,[2] I cannot reach him, I cannot come neer him; yet if these Academicks by their ἀκαταληψία[3] [want of apprehension] meant no more then this, that the whole Intelligibility of any entity, could not be exhausted by them, [120] that they could not perfectly and powerfully pierce into any object as to discover all that was knowable in it, their opinion then was not onely tolerable, but very commendable, and undeniable; for only God himself, doth thus καταλαμβάνειν[4] [comprehend]. There is not enough in any created lamp to give such a bright displaying of an object. Nor is there vigour enough in any created eye, so to pierce into the pith and marrow of being, into the depth and secrecy of being. But if their minde was this (as 'tis generally thought to be) that there was nothing in being so visible as that their understanding could pierce it with certainty and satisfaction, such an Error as this was very derogatory to the plenitude and exuberancy of beings that streams out in a cleer cognoscibility, and 'twas very injurious to their own rational capacities, which were not made so strait and narrow-mouth'd as not to receive those notions that continually drop from being: But they were contriv'd and proportion'd for the well-coming and entertaining of truths, that love to spin and thred themselves into a fine continuity, as if they meant to pour themselves into the soul without spilling. But the Scepticks will bid you ἐπέχειν[5] [suspend judgment], and will desire you not to believe one word of this. They have no lesse then ten several bridles, *ad compescendum & cohibendum assensum*[6] [for checking and repressing assent]; *Sextus Empiricus,* that grand Sceptick will give you a sight of them all, from whence they were stil'd οἱ ἐφετικοὶ[7] men that did check and constrain knowledge, that whereas the οἱ Δογματικοὶ [Dogmatists] their adversaries *ex Diametro* [diametrical], did lay down their determinations in a more positive & decretorious manner, these οἱ σκεπτικοὶ [Sceptics] would take time to consider, and no lesse then all their life-time. They chose to be so many perpetual Questionists that would pose themselvs, & rub themselves, and stay themselves finally, and would by no means be perswaded to commence or take any degree in knowledge. Πάντα ἐστὶν ἀόριστα⁸ [all things are undetermined], that was the summe of all their Philosophy. Their most radical and fundamental principle, if they may be said to have any such, was this, τῷ παντὶ λόγῳ τὸν λόγον ἴσον ἀντικεῖσθαι,⁹ that all propositions were in *aequilibrio* [equilibrium], that there was nothing could encline the Balance this way or that, that there was an ἰσοσθένεια μαχομένη πρὸς πίστιν καὶ ἀπιστίαν,¹⁰ there was an exact equality of reason, for the affirmation or negation of any Proposition. *Lucian* brings in one of them with a paire of Balances in his hand, crowding three or four Arguments for the affirmative into one scale, and just as many for the negative into the other, and then telling them his meaning in these words, ζυγοστατῶ ἐν αὐτοῖς τοὺς λόγους καὶ πρὸς τὸ ἴσον ἀπευθύνω, καὶ ἐπειδὰν ἀκριβῶς ὁμοίους τε καὶ ἰσοβαρεῖς ἴδω, τότε δὲ ἀγνοῶ τὸν ἀληθέστερον.¹¹ I have took (saith he) a great deal of pains in weighing of controversies, and yet finde in them such an undistinguishable equipoise as that there is not in me the least inclination to one side more [121] then the other. This they tearm an Ἀδιαφορία [an indifference], an ἀρρεψία¹² [equipoise], a speculative kind of ἀπροσωποληψία,¹³ an impartiality in respect of al things. In morals they call it Ἀπραγμοσύνη [freedom from practical judgments]; for as they would not acknowledg any *verum* or *falsum* [truth or falsity], so neither would they trouble themselves about any *turpe* or *honestum* [shame or honour], οὐ μᾶλλον οὕτως ἢ ἐκείνως, ἢ οὐδετέρως [never preferring this to that, nor any third thing to either]. They had no better Ethicks then that speech would amount to; yet they had some lawes amongst them, some customes and rules of life, but they did not observe them as τὰ βεβαίως γνωστά, things that were fixt and fit to be establisht, they were farre from being irreversible, like those of the Medes and Persians, but they put them under the head of τὰ φαινόμενα [appearances], lawes *pro tempore,* such shadowes and appearances as they would for the present please themselves in.¹⁴ And after all debates, after all their siftings and discussing of affaires, they would conclude no otherwise then this. Ταχὰ δὲ ἐστὶ, ταχὰ δὲ οὐκ ἐστιν, ἐνδέχεται καὶ οὐκ ἐνδέχεται, ἔξεστι μὲν εἶναι ἔξεστι δὲ μὴ εἶναι¹⁵ [perhaps it is, perhaps it is not; possibly it is, possibly it is not; maybe it is, maybe it is not], which were all but so many frigid expressions of their hesitancy and stammering opinion. Yet this they call'd στάσις διανοίας[16] [mental balance], a judicious pawsing and deliberation which they did farre preferre, or rather seeme to preferre, before the daring rashnesse of others, that were more dogmatical and magisterial, κενεῆς οἰήσιος ἔμπλεοι ἀσκοί[17] (as they call'd them) swelling bladders, empty bottles, that were stopt, and seal'd up as if they had some precious liquor in them, when as they were fill'd with nothing but aire and winde. There was more modesty and lesse ostentation, as they thought, in their ἀπορία [doubt], which they esteem no small temperance and sobriety in knowledge. An intellectual kinde of continence and virginity to keep their minde pure and untoucht, when as other understandings were ravisht & deflower'd with the violence of every wanton opinion. Whereas demonstrations did not move these men at all, for as they tell you, they alwayes run, either εἰς τὸν διάλληλον or εἰς τόν ἄπειρον τρόπον[18] [into circular reasoning or endlessly to infinity], they either rest in a *medium* equally obscure, which must needs be invalid and inefficacious, or else there will be no period at all, but a *processus in infinitum;* if you expect that they should acquiesce and rest contented with first principles, they know no such things, they tell you they are only some artificial pillars, which some faint and tired understandings have set up for themselves to lean upon, they won't be fetter'd with an Axiome, nor chained to a first principle, nor captivated by a common notion. As they break the most binding cords of demonstrations asunder, so they threaten to make these pillars of truth to tremble; to prove by a first principle (say they) 'tis but *petitio principii,* 'tis τὸ ζητούμενον συναρπάζειν, 'tis to beg a truth, not to [122] evince it. If you tell them that these common notions shine with their native light, with their own proper beams; all that they return will be this, that perhaps you think so, but they do not. Yet that they might the better communicate their mindes, they allow'd their schollers to take some things for granted, for a while upon this condition, that they would distrust them afterwards. But these doubters, these Scepticks were never so much convinc'd, as when they were quickened and awaked by sensitive impressions. This made some laugh at *Pyrrhon,* though not the Author, (as is falsely supposed by some) yet a principal amplifier and maintainer of this Sect, (whence they had their name of οἱ

Πυῤῥώνειοι [Pyrrhonists],) who when a dog was ready to bite him, he beat him away, and ran as fast as he could from him; Some that took notice of it, gave him a smiling reproof, for his apostatizing from Scepticisme, but he returns him this grave answer, *ὥς χαλεπὸν εἴη ὁλοσχερῶς ἐκδῦναι ἄνθρωπον*[19] [that it was difficult to strip oneself entirely of human nature]; Where he spoke truth before he was aware, for his words are *Πυῤῥωνείας ὑποτύπωσις*, (as I may so phrase them) a brief description of the whole drift and intention of that Sect, which was *ἐκδῦναι ἄνθρωπον* [to strip off human nature], for they had sufficiently put off Reason, and they did endeavour indeed to put off Sense as much as they could: Yet the Sceptical writer *Sextus Empiricus* confesses, that the *ἀνάγκη τῶν παθῶν*, the vehemency & importunity of sensitives, *ἀβουλήτους ἡμᾶς ἄγουσιν εἰς συγκατάθεσιν*,[20] they are (saith he) so urgent and cogent, as that they do extort some kinde of assent from us, *λιμὸς μὲν ἐπὶ τροφὴν ἡμᾶς ὁδηγεῖ, δίψος δὲ ἐπὶ πόμα*,[21] when we seem to be hungry (saith he) perhaps we go to our meat, and when we have made a shew of eating, at length we seem to be satisfied, all such matters of sense they resolve into their *τὰ φαινόμενα*, into some kinde of appearances that do for the present affect them.[22] *Φαίνεται ἡμῖν γλυκάζειν τὸ μέλι*,[23] honey seems to be pretty sweet and pleasant to them, but whether it do not dissemble, whether it be as it seems to be, that they question. I finde that *Pyrrhon* the great promoter and propagator of this Sect was at first a Painter by his trade, and it seems he was very loath *ab arte sua recedere*[24] [to abandon his art], for he looks upon every being as a picture and colour, a shadow, a rude draught and portraicture, a meere representation, that hath nothing of solidity or reality. These pictures of his drawing enamor'd many others, for this Sect was patroniz'd by men of acutenesse and subtilty, the wits of the age, *magna ingenia, sed non sine mixtura dementiae*,[25] *mala punica, sed non sine grano putrido* [great geniuses, but not without a touch of madness; pomegranates, but with rotten seed], I could name you Authors of good worth and credit, who tell you that *Homer* and *Archilochus* and *Euripides,* and the Wise men of *Greece* were all Scepticks, yet those proofs which they bring to evidence and evince it, are not so pregnant and satisfying, but that you may very lawfully doubt of it, and yet be [123] no Scepticks neither. But *Francis Mirandula* reckons many very learned men that were deeply engaged in this Sect,

and some others that did very neere border upon it.[26] *Protagoras* among
the rest, whom *Plato* frequently mentions, and whom *Aristotle* confutes,
who was of this minde that all opinions were true, *Sextus Empericus* passes
this censure upon him, that he was too positive and dogmatical in assert-
ing this;[27] but if he had only question'd and deliberated upon it, whether
all opinions were not true, he had then been a rare and compleat Sceptick.
The ground that *Protagoras* went upon, was this, Πάντων πραγμάτων μέτρον εἶναι τὸν ἄνθρωπον[28] [man is the measure of all things]. By μέτρον
[measure] he meant nothing else but κριτήριον [criterion], and *Aristotle*
thus explains the words, ὁποῖα γὰρ ἑκάστῳ φαίνεται πράγματα τοιαῦτα
καὶ εἶναι,[29] for he made appearance of the whole essence & formality of
truth. So that according to him severall opinions were but the various discoveries and manifestations of truth. There was one *verum quod ad te pertinet* [truth relative to you], and another *verum quod ad illum pertinet*
[truth relative to him]. Honey was as truly bitter to a feaverish palate, as it
was sweet and delicious to an ordinary taste. Snow was as truly black, in
respect of *Anaxagoras,* as it was white in the eye and esteem of another.[30]
Thus saith he,[31] mad men, wise men, children, old men, men in a dream,
and men awake, they are all competent Judges of these things that belong
to their several conditions; for (as he tells us) truth varies according to several circumstances, that's true to day, which is not true to morrow, and
that's true at *Rome,* that's not true at *Athens;* that's true in this age, that's
not true in the next: That's true to one man, that's not true to another.
There's none of you but can spie out such a weak fallacy as this is; and if
he meant to have spoken truth, he would have said no more then this, that
every man thinks his own opinion true. For as the will cannot embrace an
object unlesse it be presented *sub umbra boni* [as a good], so neither can
the understanding close and comply with any opinion, unlesse it be disguised, *sub apparentia veri* [under the appearance of truth]; But to make
appearance the very essence of truth, is to make a shadow the essence of
the Sun, 'tis to make a picture the essence of a man. I shall say no more to
Protagoras then this, that if any opinion be false, his cannot be true, but
must needs be the falsest of all the rest. Yet the end that these Scepticks
propound to themselves, was (if you will believe him,) ἀταραξία καὶ με-
τριοπάθεια,[32] a freedom from jarres and discords, from Heresie and Ob-

stinacy, to have a minde unprejudic'd, unprepossest, the avoiding of perturbations, a milky whitenesse and serenity of soul; a fair marke indeed,
but how a roving Sceptick should ever hit it, is not easily imaginable, for
what Philosophy more wavering and voluble? was there ever a more reeling
and staggering company? was there ever a more tumbling and tossing generation? What shall I say to these old Seekers,[33] to this wanton [124] and
lascivious Sect, that will espouse themselves to no one opinion, that they
may the more securely go a whoring after all? If they be resolv'd to deny
all things (as they can do it very easily, and have seem'd to do it very compendiously) truly then they have took a very sure way to prevent all such
arguments as can be brought against them; yet because they seem to grant
appearances, we will at least present them with a few φαινόμενα [appear-
ances], and we will see how they will move them and affect them. 'Twere
well then if *Pyrrhon*, the fore-mentioned Painter, would but tell us,
whether a picture would be all one with a face, whether an appearance be
all one with a reality, whether he can paint a non-entity or no, whether
there can be an appearance where there is no foundation for it, whether all
pictures do equally represent the face, whether none can paint a little better then he used to do, whether all appearances do equally represent being?
whether there are not some false and counterfeit appearances of things? If
so, then his ἀδιαφορία[34] [indifference], must needs be took away, or if
there be alwayes true and certain appearances of things, then his doubting
and ἀπορία[35] [uncertainty] must needs vanish. When he is thirsty, and
chooses rather to drink then abstaine, what then becomes of his ἀδιαφορία
[indifference]? if he be sure that he is athirst, and if he be sure that he
seems to be athirst, what then becomes of his ἀπορία [uncertainty]? When
the dog was ready to bite him, if he was indifferent, why did he run away?
if it were an appearance, why did he flee from a shadow? why was the
Painter afraid of colours? If his sense was only affected, not his understanding, how then did he differ from the sensitive creature? from the creature that was ready to bite him? if he tels us that he was the hansomer
picture of the two who was it then that drew him so fairly, was it an appearance also? Doth one picture use to draw another? when he perswades
men to encline to his Scepticisme, what then becomes of his ἀδιαφορία
[indifference]? when he makes no doubt nor scruple of denying certainty,

what then becomes of his ἀπορία [uncertainty]? but not to disquiet this same *Pyrrhon* any longer, I shall choose more really to scatter those empty fancies by discovering the true original and foundation, the right progresse and method of all certainty.

Now God himself, that eternal and immutable being, that fixt, and unshaken Entity, that τὸ ὄντως ὂν καὶ τὸ βεβαίως ὄν,[36] must needs be the fountaine of certainty, as of all other perfections; and if other things be compared to him, they may in this sense, without any injury to them, be stiled τὰ φαινόμενα [appearances], in respect of the infinite reality and weighty and massy solidity, that is in his most glorious being, by vertue of which, as himself hath everlastingly the same invariable knowledge of all things, so he is also the most knowable and intelligible object, a sunne that sees all things, and is in it selfe most visible. An Atheist must needs be a Sceptick; for God himself is the onely [125] immoveable verity upon which the soul must fix and anchor. Created beings, shew their face a while, then hide it again, their colour goes and comes, they are *in motu & fluxu* [in motion and flux], God is the onely durable object of the soul. Now that the soul may have a satisfactory enjoyment of its God, and that it may be accurately made according to his image, God stamps and prints as resemblances of his other perfections, so this also of certainty upon it; How else should it know the minde of its God? how should it know to please him, to believe him, to obey him? with what confidence could it approach unto him, if it had onely weak & wavering conjectures? Nay God lets the soul have some certaine acquaintance with other beings for his own sake, and in order to his own glory. Nor is it a small expression of his wisdome and power, to lay the beginnings of mans certainty so low, even as low as sense; for by means of such an humble foundation the structure proves the surer and the taller. 'Tis true there is a purer and nobler Certainty in such beings as are above sense, as appeares by the Certainty of Angelical knowledge, and the knowledge of God himself; yet so much certainty as is requisite for such a rational nature as man is, may well have its rising and springings out of sense, though it have more refinings and purifyings from the understanding. This is the right proportioning of his certainty to his being; for as his being results out of the mysterious union of matter, to immateriality: so likewise his knowledge and the certainty of his knowledge (I

speake of naturall knowledge) first peeps out in sense, and shines more
brightly in the understanding. The first dawnings of certainty are in the
sense, the noon-day-glory of it is in the Intellectuals. There are indeed frequent errours in this first Edition of knowledge set out by sense; but 'tis
then onely when the due conditions are wanting, and the understanding
(as some printers use to do) Corrects the old *Errata* of the first Edition,
and makes some new Errours in its owne. And I need not tell you, that 'tis
the same soul that moves both in the sense and in the understanding, for
νοῦς ὁρᾷ & νοῦς ἀκούει[37] [it is the mind that sees, the mind that hears],
and as it is not priviledged from failings in the motions of the sense, so
neither is it in all its intellectual operations, though it have an unquestionable certainty of some, in both. The certainty of sense is so great as that an
Oath, that high expression of certainty, is usually and may very safely be
built upon it. Mathematical demonstrations chuse to present themselves
to the sense, and thus become Ocular and visible. The Scepticks that were
the known enemies of certainty, yet would grant more shadow and appearance of it in sense, then any where else, though erroneously. But sense,
that rackt them sometimes, and extorted some confessions from them,
which speculative principles could never do. Away then with that humour
of *Heraclitus* that tells us κακοὶ μάρτυρες ἀνθρώποισιν ὀφθαλμοί,[38] mens
eyes (sayes he) are but weak and deceitful witnesses. Surely he speaks onely
of his owne watery and [126] weeping eyes, that were so dull'd and blur'd,
as that they could not clearly discerne an object. But he might have given
others leave to have seen more then he did. Nor can I tell how to excuse
Plato for too much scorning and sleighting these outward senses, when
that he trusted too much inwardly to his owne fancy. *Sextus Empiricus* pro-
pounds the question, whether he were not a Sceptick,[39] but he onely
shew'd himself a Sceptick by this, for which he mov'd such a question. 'Tis
sure that *Plato* was sufficiently dogmatical in all his assertions, though this
indeed must be granted, that some of his principles strike at certainty, and
much indanger it; for being too fantastical and Poetical in his Philosophy,
he plac't all his security in some uncertaine airy and imaginary Castles of
his own contriving and building and fortifyng. His connate Ideas (I mean)
which *Aristotle* could not at all confide in, but blowed them away presently; and perceiving the proud emptinesse, the swelling frothinesse of

such Platonical bubles, he was faine to search for certainty somewhere else, and casting his eye upon the ground he spyed the bottome of it, lying in sense, and laid there by the wise dispensation of God himself, from thence he lookt up to the highest top and *Apex,* to the πτερύγιον and pinacle of certainty plac't in the understanding. The first rudiments of certainty were drawn by sense, the compleating and consummating of it was in the understanding. The certainty of sense is more grosse and palpable, the certainty of intellectuals, 'tis more cleere and Crystalline, more pure and spiritual. To put all certainty or the chiefest certainty in sense, would be excessively injurious to reason, and would advance some sensitive creatures above men, for they have some quicker senses then men have; sense 'tis but the gate of certainty, (I speak all this while but of humane certainty) the understanding 'tis the throne of it. *Des-Cartes* the French Philosopher resolves all his assurance, into thinking that he thinks,[40] why not into thinking that he sees? and why may he not be deceived in that as in any other operations? And if there be such a virtue in reflecting and reduplicating of it, then there will be more certainty in a super-reflection, in thinking that he thinks that he thinks, and so if he run *in infinitum,* according to his conceit he will still have more certainty, though in reality he will have none at all, but will be fain to stop and stay in Sceptisme, so that these refuges of lyes being scatter'd, first principles and common notions with those demonstrations that stream from them, they onely remaine, as the nerves of this assurance, as the souls of natural Plerophory;[41] and he that will not cast Anchor upon these, condemnes himself to perpetual Sceptisme; which makes me wonder at a passage of a Right honourable of our own;[42] Though whether he be the Authour of the passage, you may take time to consider it: But this it is, (the sense of it I mean) That absolute contradictions may meet together, in the same respect *Esse & non esse* [being and non-being] it seemes are espoused in a most neer and conjugal union, and live together very [127] affectionately and imbracingly; O rare and compendious Synopsis of all Sceptism! O the quintessence of *Sextus Empiricus* and the Pyrrhonian ὑποτύπωσις [*Outlines*] of all their ἐποχὴ [suspension of judgment] and ἀπορία [uncertainty] of their ἀφασία [non-assertion] and ἀοριστία[43] [indefiniteness], that which is the most paradoxical of all; you have all this in a book that calls it self by the name of truth: yet let none be so vaine as to imagine that this is in the least measure spoken to the disesteem of that noble Lord, who was well known to be of bright and sparkling intellectuals, and of such singular and incomparable ingenuity, as that if he had liv'd till this time, we cannot doubt but he would have retracted it, or at least better explain'd it before this time. However I could not but take notice of so black an Error that did crush and break all these first principles, and had an irreconcileable Antipathy against reason and certainty, though it hid it self under the protection of so good and so great a name. Certainty 'tis so precious and desirable, as where God hath given it, 'tis to be kept sacred and untoucht; and men are to be thankful for these Candles of the Lord, for this *Lumen certum,* set up, not to mock and delude them, but to deal truly and faithfully with them.

☙ CHAPTER 15 ☙

The Light of Reason Is Directive

[128] 'Tis *Lumen dirigens,* this νόμος γραπτὸς¹ [written law], 'tis a light for the feet, and a Lanthorn for the paths. For the understanding, 'tis the τὸ ἡγεμονικὸν,² the leading and guiding power of the soul. The will looks upon that as *Laeander* in *Musaeus* lookt up to the Tower for *Hero's* Candle, and calls it as he doth there λήχνον ἐμοῦ βιότοιο φαεσφόρον ἡγεμονῆα³ [a lamp which, while I live, is my illumination and guide]. Reason doth *facem praeferre,* it carries a Torch before the will, nay more then so, 'tis an eye to the blinde; for otherwise 'twere in vain to light up a Candle for a *Caeca potentia* [blind power], to see withal. Intellectuals are first in motion αἱ πύλαι φωτὸς, these gates of light must first be set open before any glorious and beautiful object can enter in for the will to court and embrace. The will doth but echo to the understanding, and doth practically repeat the last syllable of the *ultimum dictamen* [final decision], which makes the Moralist well determine *virtutes morales non possunt esse sine intellectualibus* [moral virtues cannot exist without intellectual powers]; for to the presence of moral vertues there are necessarily pre-required *Intelligentia & prudentia* [intelligence and prudence], the one being the knowledge of *principia speculativa* [theoretical principles], as the other of *principia operativa* [practical principles]. That action must needs be hopeful and promising when the understanding aimes before the will shoots; but he that in an implicit way rushes upon any performance, though the action it self should prove materially good, yet such a one deserves no more commendation for it, then he would do that first put out his eyes, and then contingently hit the mark. Other creatures indeed are shot more violently into their ends, but man hath the skill and faculty of directing himself, and is

147

(as you may so imagine) a rational kinde of arrow, that moves knowingly and voluntarily to the mark of its own accord. For this very end God hath set up a distinct lamp in every soul, that men might make use of their own light: all the works of men they should *olere lucernam*,[4] smell of this Lamp of the Lord, that is to illuminate them all. Men are not to depend wholly upon the courtesie of any fellow-creature; not upon the dictates of men; nay not upon the votes and determinations of Angels; for if an Angel from heaven should contradict first principles, though I will not say in the language of the Apostle, *let him be accursed*,[5] yet this we may safely say, that all the sons of men are bound to [129] dis-believe him. All arguments drawn from testimony and authority, (created authority I mean) were alwayes lookt upon as more faint and languishing, then those that were fetcht from reason. Matters of fact indeed do necessarily depend upon testimony, but in speculations and opinions none is bound so farre to adore the lamp of another, as to put out his own for it. For when any such controversie is mov'd, when any Author is quoted and commended, all the credit and esteem that is to be given him, is founded either in the Reason, which he doth annex to his assertion, or else in this more remote and general reason, that such a one had a very clear and bright lamp, that *the Candle of the Lord* did shine very eminently in him; therefore what he saies is much to be attended to, for in his words, though there should not be *ratio explicata* [an explicit reason], yet it is to be supposed that there's *ratio subintellecta* [an implicit reason]. So that the assent here is ultimately resolv'd into the reason of him that speaks, and the other that receives it; for he that complies with a naked testimony, makes a tacit acknowledgement of thus much, that he is willing to resigne up himself to anothers reason, as being surer and fuller then his own; which temper and frame of spirit is very commendable in a state of inchoation: for χρὴ τὸν μανθάνοντα πιστεύειν [a learner must have trust], knowledge in the cradle cannot feed it self; knowledge in its infancy must suck at the breasts of another: And babes in intellectuals must take in the ἄδολον γάλα[6] [sincere milk], those spoonfuls of knowledge that are put in their mouths, by such as are to nurse and to educate them. *Paul* when he sits at the feet of *Gamaliel* must observe the prints and footsteps of the Hebrew Doctor, and must roll himself *in pulvere sapientum*[7] [in the dust of the wise]. Knowledge in its non-age, in its pupil-age and minority must hide it self under the wing and protection of a guardian. Men use at first to borrow light, and to light their candle at the light of anothers; yet here I finde some licence and encouragement given to these first beginners, to these setters up in learning to be ξητητι-κοὶ,[8] modestly inquisitive into the grounds and reasons of that which is delivered to them.

Thus that sacred writer *Hierom* commends *Marcella* though one of the weaker sex, upon this account, that she was wont to search and examine his doctrine, *ita ut me sentirem* (says he) *non tam discipulum habere quam judicem*[9] [so that I felt I did not have a pupil so much as a critic]. Nay, a farre greater then *Hierome* honours the Bereans, with the title of οἱ εὐγε-νέστεροι,[10] a more noble and generous sort of Christians that would bring even Apostolical words to the touch-stone. Why is it not then lawful for them that are *in statu adulto,* that are come to some pregnancy and maturity in knowledge, to look upon the stamp and superscription of any opinion, to look any opinion in the face? The great and noble *Verulam* much complains (and not without too much cause) of those sad obstructions in learning, which arose upon the extreme doting upon some [130] Authors, which were indeed men of rare accomplishments, of singular worth and excellency, and yet but men, though by a strange kinde of Ἀπο-θέωσις [apotheosis], a great part of the world would have worshipt them as gods.[11] The Canonizing of some profane Authors, and esteeming all other as Apocryphal, hath blasted many buds of knowledge, it has quencht many sparks and beams of light, which otherwise would have guilded the world, with an Orient and unspotted lustre. Farre be it from me to drop one word that should tend to the staining and eclipsing of that just glory that is due to the immortal name of *Aristotle.* There are those that are envious and ungrateful enough, let them do it if they please; yet this I shall say, and it shall be without any injury to him, that to set him up as a Pope in Philosophy, as a visible head of the truth militant, to give him a negative voice, to give him an arbitrary power, to quote his texts as Scripture, to look upon his works as the irreversible decrees of Learning, as if he had seal'd up the Canon, so that whoe're addes to him, or takes one word from him, must be struck with a present *Anathema;* to condemn all for Hereticks that oppose him, for Schismaticks that depart from him, for Apostates that deny him; what's all this but to forget that he was but *the Candle of the Lord,* and to adore him as a Sun in the firmament that was set to rule the day of knowledge? 'tis to make him an ὄν ὄντων[12] [the Being of beings] the *causa prima,* the first mover of Learning, or at least 'twas to make him such an *Intellectus agens*[13] [active intellect], as *Averroes* would have, that must enforme and quicken all that come after him. Could that modest Philosopher have foreseen and prophesied, that the world would thus flatter him, tis to be fear'd, that he would have thrown his works also, his legible self into *Euripus*[14] rather then they should have occasioned such excessive Idolatry and partiality; yet 'tis no fault of his, if the world would over-admire him; for that which first inhanc't the price and esteem of *Aristotle,* was that rich veine of reason that ran along and interlin'd most of his works. Let this therefore, and this only commend him still; for this is of indelible and perpetual duration; yet if these blinde admirers of him, could have followed him fully and entirely, they might have learnt of him a braver liberty and independency of spirit; for he scorned to enslave and captivate his thoughts to the judgement of any whatsoever; for though he did not deal violently and disingenuously with the works of his predecessors, (as some affirme) yet he dealt freely with them, and was not over-indulgent to them. He came like a Refiner amongst them, he purged away their drosse, he boyl'd away their froth and scum, he gathered a quintessence out of their rude and elementary principles. How impartially did he deal with his Master *Plato?* and not favour him in any of his Errors, and his words are answerable to his practises, you may hear him what he saith, and professes, τοὺς παλαιοὺς αἰδεῖσθαι μὲν δίκαιον, φρίττειν δὲ οὐκ ἄξιον,[15] to have a reverent esteeme of Antiquity is but fitting and equal, [131] but to stand in awe of it, is base and unworthy. *Potestas senatoria* [senatorial power] is very honourable and beneficial, but *dictatoria potestas* [dictatorial power], is not to be allowed in the Common-wealth of Learning;[16] yet such hath been the intolerable tyranny and oppression of the Roman faction, as that they have enjoyn'd and engaged as many as they could to serve and torture their wits, for the maintaining of whatever such a one as pleaseth them, shall please to say: for they care not how prejudicial or detrimental they prove to Learning, so that they may but train up their schollars in an implicit faith, in a blinde obedience, in a slavish acknowledgement of some infallible judge of controversies, and may shut up and imprison the generality of people in a dark and benighted condition, not so much as allowing them the light of their own Candle, this Lamp of the Lord that ought to shine in them. That great advancer of Learning whom I commended before, takes notice, that by such unhappy means as these, the more noble and liberal sciences, have made no progresse proportionable to that which more inferiour and mechanical Arts have done; for in these latter *ingenia multorum in unum coeunt* [the talents of many combine to one end], whereas in the former, *ingenia multorum sub uno succubuerunt*[17] [the talents of many are over-come by one]. What brave improvements have been made in architecture, in manufactures, in printing, in the *Pyxis nautica* [sailor's compass]? For here's no limiting and restraining men to Antiquity, no chaining them to old Authors, no regulating them to I know not what prescribed formes and Canons, no such strange voices as these. You must not build better then your predecessors have done, you must not print fairer then the first *Tullies* Offices, that ere was printed; 'Tis not lookt upon as a transgression and a *piaculum* [crime], if they should chance to be a little more accurate then they were that went before them. But in speculatives, in meere Mathematicks (which one would think were farre enough from any breach of faith or manners) yet here if a *Galilaeus* should but present the world with a handful of new demonstrations, though never so warily and submissively, if he shall but frame and contrive a glasse for the discovery of some more lights; all the reward he must expect from *Rome,* is, to rot in an Inquisition, for such unlicenced inventions, for such venturous undertakings. The same strain of cruelty hath marcht more vehemently and impetuously in sacred and religious matters, for here *Babylon* hath heated her furnace seven times hotter, whilest under the pompous name of a Catholique Church, under the glittering pretences of Antiquity and Authority, they have as much as they could put out all the Lamps of the Lord. And that Bestian Empire hath transform'd all its Subjects into sensitive and irrational creatures. A noble Author of our own tells us in his book *De Veritate,* that he for his part takes them for the Catholique Church, that are constant and faithful to first principles; that common notions are the bottome and foundation upon which the Church is built.[18] [132] Excuse our diffidence here great Sir, the Church 'tis built upon

a surer and higher Rock, upon a more Adamantine and precious foundation; yet thus much is acceptable and undeniable, that whoe're they are
that by any practices or customes, or traditions, or tenents, shall stop the
passage of first principles, and the sound reason that flowes from them,
they are in this farther from a Church then the Indians or the Americans,
whilst they are not only Antichristian, but unnatural. And of the two the
Church hath more security in resting upon genuine Reason, then in rely-
ing upon some spurious traditions; for think but a while upon those infinite deceits and uncertainties that such Historical conveyances are liable
and exposed to, I always except those sacred and heavenly volumes of
Scripture, that are strung together as so many pearls, and make a bracelet
for the Spouse to wear upon her hands continually: These writings the
providence of God hath deeply engaged it self to keep as the apples of his
own eye. And they do not borrow their certainty or validity from any Ecclesiastical or universal Tradition (which is at the most but previous and
preparatory) but from those prints of Divinity in them, and specially from
the seal of the same Spirit that endited them, and now assures the soul,
that they were Oracles breathed from God himself. As for all other sacred
Antiquity, though I shall ever honour it as much as any either did or can
do justly, and with sobriety; and shall always reverence a gray-headed
truth; yet if Antiquity shall stand in competition with this Lamp of the
Lord (though genuine Antiquity would never offer to do it) yet if it
should, it must not think much if we prefer Reason, a daughter of Eternity, before Antiquity, which is the off-spring of time.[19] But had not the
spirit of Antichristianisme by its early twinings and insinuations wound
and wrought it self into most flourishing and primitive times, into the bosome of a Virgin-Church, and had it not offered violence to the works of
some sacred writers, by detracting and augmenting according to its several
exigencies, by feigning and adulterating, by hiding and annihilating some
of them, as much as they could, (the ordinary tricks of Antichrist, which
he used always more subtilly, though of late more palpably) had it not
been for such devices as these, Antiquity had come flowing to us, in purer
and fuller streams, in more fair and kindly derivations, and so might have
run down more powerfully and victoriously then now it will. But Antichrist hath endeavoured to be the *Abaddon* and the *Apollyon*[20] of all sacred

antiquities, though the very reliques of those shining and burning lights that adorn'd the Church of God, have splendor enough to scatter the darknesse of Popery, that empty shadow of Religion, that arises *ob defectum Luminis* [from the absence of light]; yet Antiquity (setting aside those that were peculiarly θεόπνευστοι[21] [inspired]) was but the first dawning of light which was to shine out brighter and brighter, till perfect day. Let none therefore so superstitiously look back to former ages, as to [133] be angry with new opinions and displayings of light, either in Reason or Religion. Who dares oppose the goodnesse and wisdome of God? if he shall enamour the world with the beauty of some pearls and jewels, which in former times have been hid, or trampled upon? if he shall discover some more light upon earth, as he hath let some new Stars be found in the heavens; This you may be sure and confident of, that 'tis against the minde and meaning of Antiquity to stop the progresse of Religion and Reason. But I know there are some will tell us of a visible tribunal, of an infallible head of the Church borne to determine all controversies, to regulate all men, 'tis a wonder they do not say Angels too. Others more prudently and equally resolve the final judgement of Controversies into a general and oecumenical Councel, but I shall speak to them all, in the language of the Philosopher, Δεῖ τὸν νόμον ἄρχειν πάντων[22] [the law ought to rule all], and I shall explain it according to the minde of the learned *Davenant* in his discourse *de judice ac norma fidei & Cultus Christiani*[23] [On the Judge and Rule of Christian Faith and Conduct]: God only is to rule his own Church αὐτοκρατορικῶς καὶ νομοθετικῶς, *judicio autoritativo,* by a determining and Legislative power. Men that are fitted by God himself, are to guide and direct it ὑπηρετικῶς καὶ ἑρμηνευτικῶς, *judicio ministeriali,* in way of subserviency to him, by an explication of his minde, yet so as that every one may judge of this ἰδιωτικῶς καὶ ἀκροατικῶς, *judicio privato & practicae discretionis,*[24] by acts of their own understanding illuminated by the Spirit of God; for there are no representatives in intellectuals and spirituals. Men may represent the bodies of others, in Civil and Temporal affairs in the acts of a Kingdome, and thus a bodily obedience is alwayes due to just authority; but there is none can alwayes represent the minde and judgement of another in the vitals and inwards of Religion; for I speak not of representations in outward order and discipline. A general council does

and may produce *judicium forense* [a public judgment], but still there is reserved, to every single *individuum, judicium rationale*[25] [individual, rational judgment]; for can you think that God will excuse any one from Error upon such an account as this, such a Doctor told me thus; such a piece
of Antiquity enform'd me so, such a general Councel determin'd me to
this; where was thine own Lamp all this while? where was thy *ratio illuminata & gubernata, secundum normas bonae & necessariae consequentiae rationali creaturae impressas* [reason illuminated and directed by the logic
natural to rational creatures]? Yet this must be gratefully acknowledged
that these general Councels have been of publick influence, of most admirable use and advantage to the Church of God; though they are not of the
very Essence of it; for 'tis well known that there were none of them till the
dayes of *Constantine:* But herein is the benefit of Councels, that they are
(or ought to be) a comparing and collecting of many Lights, an uniting
and concentricating of the judgements of many holy, learned, wise [134]
Christians with the Holy Ghost breathing amongst them, though not alwayes so fully and powerfully as that they shall be sure to be priviledg'd
from every Error, but being all of them subject to frailty and fallibility, and
sometime the major part of them proving the pejor part, there is none
bound to give an extemporary assent to their votes and suffrages, unlesse
his minde also concurre with theirs. That worthy Divine of our own,
whom I mentioned before, speaks very fully and clearly to this, *Ad nudam
praescriptionem, aut determinationem alterius sine lumine privati judicii
nemo est qui credere potest etiamsi cupiat maxime*[26] [not even the most willing is able to believe on the mere dictate or determination of another,
without the light of private judgment]. The most eminent *Mirandula* will
give you the reason of it; for (saies he) *Nemo credit aliquid verum praecise
quia vult credere illud esse verum, non est enim in potentia hominis facere aliquid apparere intellectui suo verum, quando ipse voluerit*[27] [no one believes
precisely because he desires to believe, for it is not in the power of man to
make a thing appear true to his intellect whenever he pleases]. But before
there can be faith in any soul, there must be *cognitio propositionis credendae*
[a knowledge of the proposition to be believed], and there must be *inclinatio intellectus ad assentiendum huic propositioni revelatae, & cognitae*[28] [an
inclination   of   the   intellect   to   assent   to   this   proposition   when

revealed and ascertained]; Before you understand the termes of any proposition, you can no more believe it, then if it came to you in an unknown tongue. A Parrat may repeat the Creed thus, *Corvos poetas poetridasque picas cantare credas Pegaseium melos*[29] [one might think that ravens and magpies were poets and poetesses and sang an inspired song]. Though such at length may very safely conclude, as that talkative bird is reported to have done by a happy and extemporary contingency, *Operam & oleum perdidi*[30] [I have lost my labour and my oil]. This is the misery of those implicit believers amongst the Papists (and 'tis well if not among some Protestants too) that do *in aliorum sententias pedibus potius quam cordibus ire* [accept the opinions of others in a pedestrian fashion, rather than with their hearts], dancing in a circular kinde of faith, they believing as the Church believes, and the Church believing as they believe, &c. and this is with them, נל הארם[31] [the whole duty] the whole perfection of a Roman Catholique. Yet let none be so foolish or wicked as to think that this strikes at any thing, that is truly or really a matter of faith, when as it doth only detect the wretched vanity and deceit of a Popish and implicit credulity, which commands men to put out their Lamps, to pluck out their eyes, and yet to follow their leaders, though they rush upon the mouth of hell and destruction, whereas 'tis better to be an *Argus* in obedience, then a *Cyclops* a *monstrum horrendum, &c.*[32] [horrible monster]. An eye open is more acceptable to God then an eye shut. Why do they not as well command men to renounce their sense, as to disclaim their understandings? Were it not as easie a tyranny to [135] make you to believe that to be white which you see to be black, as to command you to believe that to be true, which you know to be false? Neither are they at all wanting in experiments of both; for Transubstantiation, that heap and croud of contradictions, doth very compendiously put out the eyes of sense and reason both at once: yet that prodigious Error was established in the Lateran Councel[33] under *Innocent* the third, which (as some contend) was a general and Oecumenical Councel. And if the Pope whom they make equivalent to all Councels, nay transcendent, if he in *Cathedra* shall think fit to determine, that the right hand is the left, they must all immediately believe him, under pain of damnation. So that first principles, common notions with the products and improvement of them, must needs be lookt upon as of bad consequence, of pernicious influence at *Rome;* what, to say that two and two makes four, that *totum's majus parte* [the whole is greater than the part] (especially if the Church shall determine against it) O dangerous point of Socinianisme! O unpardonable Heresie of the first magnitude! Rebellion against the Catholique Church! a proud justling against the Chair of infallibility! Away with them to the Inquisition presently, deliver them up to the Secular powers, bring fire and fagot immediately; *Bonners* learned demonstrations,[34] and the bloody discipline of the scarlet and purple Whore. No wonder that she puts out the Candle, *and loves darknesse rather then light, seeing her deeds are evil.*[35] She holds a Cup in her hand,[36] and won't let the world sip and taste, and see how they like it, but they must swallow down the whole *Philtrum* and potion without any delay at all. Thus you may see the weak reeds that *Babylon* leans upon, which now are breaking and piercing her thorow. But Religion fram'd according to the Gospel, did alwayes scorn and refuse such carnal supports as these are. That truth that must look the Sun in the face for ever, can you think that it will fear a Candle? must it stand in the presence of God, and will it not endure the tryal of men? Or can you imagine that the Spouse of Christ can be so unmerciful as to pull out her childrens eyes? though she may very well restrain their tongues sometimes, and their pens if they be too immodest and unruly; I shall need to say no more then this, that true Religion never was, nor will be, nor need be shy of sound Reason which is thus farre *Lumen dirigens* [a directive light], as that 'tis oblig'd by the will and command of God himself, not to entertain any false religion, nor any thing under pretence of Religion that is formally and irreconciliably against Reason. Reason being above humane testimony and tradition, and being only subordinate to God himself, and those Revelations that come from God; now 'tis expresse blasphemy to say that either God, or the Word of God did ever, or ever will oppose Right Reason.

CHAPTER 16

The Light of Reason Is
Calme and Peaceable

[136] 'Tis *Lumen tranquillum & amicum,* 'tis a Candle, not a Comet, it is a quiet and peaceable light. And though this Candle of the Lord may be too hot for some, yet the Lamp 'tis only maintain'd with soft and peaceable Oile. There is no jarring in pure intellectuals; if men were tun'd and regulated by Reason more, there would be more Concord and Harmony in the world. As man himself is a sociable creature, so his Reason also is a sociable Light. This Candle would shine more clearly and equally if the windes of passions were not injurious to it. 'Twere a commendable piece of Stoicisme, if men could alwayes hush and still those waves that dash and beat against Reason, if they could scatter all those clouds that soil and discolour the face and brightnesse of it, would there be such fractions and commotions in the State, such Schismes and Ruptures in the Church, such hot and fiery prosecutions of some trifling opinions? If the soft and sober voice of Reason were more attended to, Reason would make some differencies kisse and be friends, 'twould sheath up many a sword, 'twould quench many a flame, 'twould binde up many a wound. This Candle of the Lord 'twould scatter many a dark suspition, many a sullen jealousie. Men may fall out in the dark sometimes, they cannot tell for what, if the Candle of the Lord were but amongst them, they would chide one another for nothing then but their former breaches, ἡ ἐπιστήμη ἵστησι τὴν ψυχὴν [knowledge calms the soul] it calmes and composes a soul, whereas passion, as the grand Stoick *Zeno* paints it, is ὁρμὴ πλεονάζουσα καὶ παρὰ φύσιν τῆς ψυχῆς κίνησις.[1] An abounding and over-boyling *impetus,* a preternatural agitation of soul, *animi commotio aversa a recta ratione, & contra*

157

*naturam*² [a disturbance of the soul opposed to right reason and contrary to nature], as the Orator stiles it. The soul 'tis tost with passion, but it anchors upon Reason. This gentlenesse and quietnesse of Reason doth never commend it self more then in its agreeing and complying with faith, in not opposing those high and transcendent mysteries that are above its own reach and capacity; nay it had alwayes so much humility and modesty, waiting and attending upon it, that it would alwayes submit and subordinate it self to all such divine revelations as were above its own sphere. Though it could not grasp them, though it could not pierce into them; yet it ever resolv'd with all gratitude to admire them, to bow its head, and [137] to adore them. One light does not oppose another; *Lumen fidei & Lumen rationis,* may shine both together though with farre different brightnesse; *the Candle of the Lord,* 'tis not impatient of a superiour light, 'twould both *ferre parem & priorem* [endure an equal and a superior]. The light of the Sun that indeed is *Lumen Monarchicum,* a supreme and sovereign light, that with its golden Scepter rules all created sparkles, and makes them subject and obedient to the Lord and rule of light. Created intellectuals depend upon the brightnesse of Gods beams, and are subordinate to them, Angelical Star-light is but *Lumen Aristocraticum,* it borrows and derives its glory from a more vast and majestical light. As they differ from one another in glory, so al of them infinitly differ from the Sun in glory. Yet 'tis far above the *Lumen Democraticum,* that light which appears unto the sons of men, 'tis above their lamps & Torches, poor and contemptible lights, if left to themselves; for do but imagine such a thing as this, that this external and corporeal world should be adjudg'd never to see the Sun more, never to see one Star more. If God should shut all the windows of heaven, and spread out nothing but clouds and curtains, and allow it nothing but the light of a Candle, how would the world look like a *Cyclops* with its eye put out? 'Tis now but an obscure prison with a few grates to look out at; but what would it be then, but a capacious grave, but a nethermost dungeon? yet this were a more grateful shade, a pleasanter and more comely darknesse, then for a soul to be condemned to the solitary light of its own Lamp, so as not to have any supernatural irradiations from its God. Reason does not refuse any auxiliary beams, it joyes in the company of its fellow-Lamp, it delights in the presence of an intellectual Sun, which will so far favour it, as that 'twill advance it, and nourish it, and educate it; 'twill encrease it, and inflame it, and will by no means put it out. A Candle neither can nor will put out the Sun, & an intellectual Sun, can, but will not put out the Lamp. The light of Reason doth no more prejudice the light of faith, then the light of a Candle doth extinguish the light of a Star. The same eye of a soul may look sometimes upon a Lamp, and sometimes upon a Star; one while upon a first principle, another while upon a revealed truth, as hereafter it shall always look upon the Sun and see God face to face; Grace doth not come to pluck up nature as a weed, to root out the essences of men; but it comes to graft spirituals upon morals, that so by their mutual supplies and intercourse they may produce most noble and generous fruit. Can you tell me why the shell and the kernel may not dwell together? why the bodies of nature may not be quickened by the soul of grace? Did you never observe an eye using a prospective-glasse, for the discovering and amplifying and approximating of some remote and yet desirable object? and did you perceive any opposition between the eye and the glasse? was there not rather a loving correspondency and communion between them? why should there be any greater strife between Faith and Reason, seeing they [138] are brethren? do they not both spring from the same Father of Lights,³ and can the Fountain of love and unity, send forth any irreconcileable streams? do you think that God did ever intend to divide a rational being, to tear and rend a soul in pieces, to scatter principles of discord and confusion in it? If God be pleased to open some other passage in the soul, and to give it another eye, does that prejudice the former? Man you know is ordained to a choicer end, to a nobler happinesse, then for the present he can attain unto, and therefore he cannot expect that God should now communicate himself in such bright and open discoveries, in such glorious manifestations of himself, as he meanes to give hereafter. But he must be content for the present, to behold those infinite treasures of reserved love, in a darker and more shadowy way of faith, and not of vision: Nature and Reason are not sufficiently proportion'd to such blessed objects, for there are such weights of glory in them, as do *opprimere ingenium humanum* [overwhelm the human mind], there are such depths, such pleonasmes, such oceans of all perfections in a Deity as do infinitely exceed all intellectual capacity but its own. The most that mans Reason can do, is to fill the understanding to the brim, but faith that throws the soul into the Ocean, and lets it roll and bathe it self in the vastnesse and fulnesse of a Deity. Could the sons of men have extracted all the spirits of Reason, and made them meet and jump in one head; nay, could Angels and men have united and concentricated all their Reason, yet they would never have been able to spy out such profound and mysterious excellencies, as faith beholds in one twinckling of her eye. Evangelical beauties shine through a veile that's upon their face; you may see the precious objects of faith like so many pearls and diamonds sparkling and glittering in the dark. Reveal'd truths shine with their own beams, they do not borrow their Primitive and original lustre from this *Candle of the Lord,* but from the purer light, wherewith God hath cloathed and attir'd them as with a garment; God crowns his own Revelations with his own beams. *The Candle of the Lord* it doth not discover, it doth not oppose them, it cannot eclipse them. They are no sparks of Reasons striking, but they are flaming darts of heavens shooting, that both open and enamour the soul. They are Stars of Heavens lighting, men behold them at a great distance twinckling in the dark. Whatsoever comes in Gods name does *aut invenire viam, aut facere* [either discover or make a way]. Whatever God reveals in his Word, 'tis *supra providentiam rerum communem constitutum*[4] [above the ordinary providence of things]. 'Tis not in the road of nature, and therefore for the welcoming and entertaining of it (as a noble Author of our own doth very well observe,) *explicatur sensus quidam super-naturalis, & θαυμάσιος*[5] [a certain supernatural and wonderful sense is brought into play], there's an opening of a new window in the soul, an intellectual eye looks out at the window, and is much pleased and affected with the oriency of [139] that light that comes springing and rushing in upon it; as there's a *νόμος γραπτὸς* [written law], so there's an *εὐαγγέλιον γραπτὸν* [written gospel] too; the one 'tis written by the pen of nature; the other by the finger of the Spirit, for *ubi desinit natura, ibi incipit gratia* [grace begins where nature ends]; and this second Edition set out by Grace, 'tis *auctior & emendatior* [expanded and corrected], yet so as it doth not at all contradict the first Edition, that was set out by Nature; for this is the voice of Nature it self, that whatsoever God reveals must needs be true; and this common Principle is the bottome and foundation of all Faith to build upon. The soul desires no greater satisfaction then an αὐτὸς ἔφη [*ipse dixit*], for if God himself say it, who can question it? who dare contradict it? Reason will not, Reason cannot; for it does most immovably acknowledge a Deity, and the unquestionable truth of a Deity: in all believing there is an assent, a yielding to him that speaks by vertue of his own Authority; though he don't prove it, though he don't evince it. Now men themselves look upon't as a contempt and injury not to have their words taken, and Reason it self dictates thus much, that we are to believe such a one whom we have no reason to distrust; for without some Faith there would be no commerce nor traffiking in the world, there's no trading without some trusting. A general and total incredulity would threaten a present and fatal dissolution to humane society. Matters of fact are as certain in being and reality, as demonstrations; yet in appearance most of them can never be prov'd or evinc'd any other way then by meer testimony; much historical knowledge, many a truth has been lost and buried in unbelief, when as many a falsity in the mean time has prov'd more fortunate and triumphant, & has past currantly through the world under the specious disguise of probability; yet because no created being is infallible or authentical, because the sons of men are so easily deceived themselves, and are so apt and propense to deceive and impose upon others, 'twill be very lawful to move slowly and timerously, warily and vigilantly in our assents to them; for a sudden and precocious faith here, is neither commendable nor durable: But God being truth it self, an Eternal, Immutable truth, his word being *vehiculum veritatis* [the vehicle of truth]; and all Revelations flowing from him, shining with the prints and signatures of certainty, hence it is that his naked word is a demonstration; and he that won't believe a God, is worse then a Devil, he is the blackest Infidel that was e're yet extant. This sin is so unnatural, as that none but an Atheist can be guilty of it; for he that acknowledges a Deity, and knows what he acknowledges, sure he won't offer to make his God a liar. That which might otherwise seem to some to be against Reason, yet if it bring the seal of God in its forehead, by this you may know that 'tis not against Reason. *Abrahams* slaying of his son may seem a most horrid and unnatural act, against the νόμος γραπτὸς[6] [written law], against the *Candle of the Lord,* yet being commanded [140] and authorized by God himself, the Candle durst not oppose the Sun. That pat-

tern of faith the father of the faithful does not dispute and make Syllogismes against it; he does not plead that 'tis against common Notions, that
'tis against Demonstrations (for he had said false if he had said so,) but he
doth dutifully obey the God of Nature, that high and supreme Law-giver,
who by this call and voice of his did plainly and audibly proclaime, that
for *Abraham* to kill his son in these circumstances, was not against the Law
of Nature. So that all the stresse and difficulty will be to know whether
God reveals such a thing or no; for here Reason (corrupt reason I mean,)
is wont to slip and evade, and when it cannot frame a conceit adequate &
commensurate to some transcendent and superlative mysteries, it would
then fain cloud them and eclipse them, that it may quench and avoid the
dazling brightnesse of them. It would faine make them stoop and conde-
scend to its own capacity, and therefore it puts some inferiour notion upon
them. When it cannot grasp what God saith, it then presently questions
whether God say so or no, whether that be the minde of his Word. Hence
many may erre very deeply and dangerously, yet will acknowledge the
Scriptures, they will own and honour them as the Word of God; for they
are not yet arriv'd to that full perfection of Errour, as those lumps and
dunghills of all Sects, I mean that young and upstart generation of gross
Anti-Scripturists,[7] that have a Powder-plot against the Gospel, that would
very compendiously behead all Christian Religion at one blow, a device
which old and ordinary Hereticks were never acquainted withall. Though
they be not come to such an height as this, yet either by their flat and frigid
explicating, they do endeavour to dispirit and enervate the Word of God;
or else in a more violent and injurious manner, they do even ravish it, and
deflower the virginity of it; or else in a more subtle and serpentine manner,
they seek to bend the rule, and expound it to their purposes and advantages. The letter of the word, the *vagina verbi* [the sheath of the word] that
does not wound them, that does not strike them, and as for the edge they
think they can draw that as they please, they can blunt it as they list, they
can order it as they will. But the Law of sound Reason and Nature does
oppose such unworthy dealings as these are; for men look upon't very hei-
nously to have their words misinterpreted, to have their meaning wrested
and violenc'd. Can you think that the majesty of Heaven will allow or endure that a creature should study or busie it self in perverting his words,

in corrupting his meaning, in blending it and mixing it with the crude imaginations of their own braine? That Spirit which breath'd out the word at first, and which convinces and satisfies the soul, that 'tis the word of God; the very same Spirit is the Interpreter of it, he is the Commentator upon it. The text is his, and the glosse is his, and whosoever shall call this a private spirit, must needs be a bold blasphemer, a Jesuit, an Atheist. But they that know what the Spirit of God is, will easily grant that the [141] Spirit of God unsheaths his own sword, that he polishes Evangelical Pearls, that he anoints and consecrates the eye of the soul, for the welcoming and entertaining of such precious objects. 'Tis true indeed, that some explications are so impertinent and distorted, as that a prophane and carnal eye may presently discerne that there was either some violence or deceit used in them, as who cannot tell when any Author is extremely vext and wrong'd? but if there be any such obscurity as may give just occasion of doubting and diffidence, who then can be fitter to clear and unfold it, then the Author himself? nay, who can explaine his minde certainly but he himself? is it not thus in spirituals much rather? When God scatters any twilight, any darknesse there, is it not by a more plentiful shedding abroad of his own beams? such a knot as created understanding cannot unty, the edge of the Spirit presently cuts asunder; Nor yet is providence wanting in external means, which by the goodnesse and power of God, were annexed as *sigilla verbi* [seals of the word], miracles I mean, which are upon this account very suitably and proportionably subservient to Faith, they being above natural power, as revealed truths are above natural understanding. The one's above the hand of nature, as the other's above the head of nature; But Miracles, though they be very potent, yet they are not always prevalent, for there were many spectators of Christs Miracles, which yet like so many *Pharoahs* were hardened by them, and some of them that beheld them were no more moved by them, then some of them who only hear of them [and] will not at all attend to them. So that only the seal of the Spirit can make a firme impression upon the soul, who writes his own word upon the soul with a conquering and triumphant Sun-beam, that is impatient either of cloud or shadow. Be open therefore ye everlasting doors, and stand wide open ye intellectual gates, that the spirit of grace and glory, with the goodly train of his revealed truths may enter in.[8]

There's foundation for all this in a principle of nature; for we must still put you in minde of the concord that is betwixt Faith and Reason. Now this is the voice of Reason, that God can, and that none but God can assure you of his own mind; for if he should reveal his minde by a creature, there will still be some tremblings and waverings in the soul, unlesse he does withal satisfie a soul, that such a creature does communicate his minde truly and really as it is; so that ultimately the certainty is resolv'd into the voice of God, and not into the courtesie of a creature. This holy Spirit of God creates in the soul a grace answerable to these transcendent objects, you cannot but know the name of it, 'tis called Faith, *Super-naturalis forma fidei* [a super-natural form of faith], as *Mirandula* the younger stiles it, which closes and complies with every word that drops from the voice or pen of a Deity, and which facilitates the soul to assent to revealed truths; So as that with a heavenly inclination, with a delightful propension it moves to them as to a centre.[9] [142] Reason cannot more delight in a common notion or a demonstration, then Faith does in revealed truth. As the Unity of a Godhead is demonstrable and clear to the eye of Reason, so the Trinity of persons, that is, three glorious relations in one God is as certain to an eye of Faith. 'Tis as certain to this eye of Faith that Christ is truly God, as it was visible to an eye both of Sense and Reason that he is truly man. Faith spies out the resurrection of the body; as Reason sees the immortality of the soul. I know there are some Authors of great worth and learning, that endeavour to maintain this Opinion, that revealed truths, though they could not be found by reason, yet when they are once revealed, that Reason can then evince them and demonstrate them: But I much rather encline to the determinations of *Aquinas,* and multitudes of others that are of the same judgement, that humane Reason when it has strecht it self to the uttermost, is not at all proportion'd to them, but at the best can give only some faint illustrations, some weak adumbrations of them.[10] They were never against Reason, they were always above Reason. 'Twill be employment enough, and 'twill be a noble employment too, for Reason to redeeme and vindicate them from those thornes and difficulties, with which some subtle ones have vext them and encompast them. 'Twill be honour enough for Reason to shew that Faith does not oppose Reason; and this it may shew, it must shew this; for else οἱ ἔσω [those within], those that are within the inclosure of the Church will never rest satisfied, nor οἱ ἔξω [those without], Pagans, Mahumetans, Jewes, will ever be convinc'd.[11] God indeed may work upon them by immediate revelation; but man can only prevaile upon them by Reason; yet 'tis not to be expected, nor is it required, that every weak and new-born Christian, that gives reall assent, and cordial entertainment to these mysterial truths, should be able to deliver them from those seeming contradictions which some cunning adversaries may cast upon them. There are some things demonstrable, which to many seeme impossible, how much more easily may there be some matters of faith which every one cannot free from all difficulties. 'Tis sufficient therefore for such, that they so farre forth understand them as to be sure that they are not against Reason, and that principally upon this account, because they are sure God has revealed them. And others that are of more advanced and elevated intellectuals, may give such explications of them, as may disentangle them from all repugnancy, though they cannot display them in their full glory. Nor must the multitude or strength and wit of opposers fright men out of their Faith and Religion. Though the major part of the world do disesteeme and look upon them as meer contradictions; yet this being the censure of most unequal and incompetent judges, is not at all prejudicial to their worth and excellency; for to most of the world they were never revealed so much as in an external manner, and to all others that refuse and reject them, they were never powerfully revealed by the [143] irradiations of the Holy Ghost. So that one affirmative here is to be preferred before a whole heap of negatives; the judgement of one wise, enlighten'd, experienc'd, spiritualiz'd Christian is more to be attended to, then the votes and suffrages of a thousand gainsayers; because this is undeniable, that God may give to one that Eye, that Light, that discerning power, which he does deny to many others. 'Tis therefore a piece of excessive vanity and arrogancy in *Socinus,* to limit and measure all Reason by his own. Nor does this put any uncertainty in Reason, but only a diversity in the improvings of it, one Lamp differs from another in glory; and withal it laies down an higher and nobler principle then Reason is: for in things meerly natural, every rational being is there a competent Judge in those things that are within the Sphere & compasse of Reason, the Reason of all men does agree and conspire, so as that which implies an expresse and palpable contradiction, cannot be own'd by any; but in things above Nature and Reason, a paucity here is a better argument then a plurality; because Providence uses to open his Cabinets only for his Jewels. God manifests these mysterious secrets only to a few friends, his Spirit whispers to a few, shines upon a few, so that if any tell us that Evangelical mysteries imply a contradiction, because they cannot apprehend them, it is no more then for a blinde man confidently to determine, that it involves a contradiction to say there is a Sun, because he cannot see it. Why should you not as well think that a greater part of the world lies in Error, as that it lies in wickednesse? is it not defective in the choisest intellectuals, as well as in the noblest practicals? Or can any perswade himself, that a most eminent and refined part of mankinde, and (that which is very considerable) a Virgin-company which kept it self untoucht from the pollutions of Antichrist, upon mature deliberation, for long continuance upon many debatings, examinings, discussings, constant prayers unto God for the discovery of his minde, should all this while embrace meere contradictions, for the highest points of their Religion? or can any conceive that these Evangelical Mysteries were invented, and contriv'd, and maintain'd by men? Could the Head of a creature invent them? could the arme of a creature uphold them? have they not a Divine super-scription upon them? have they not an heavenly original? or can you imagine that Providence would have so blest and prosper'd a contradiction? as alwayes to pluck it out of the pawes of devouring adversaries? when the whole Christian world was ready to be swallowed up with Arrianisme, dare any to say that God then prepar'd an Arke only for the preserving of a contradiction? Providence does not use to countenance contradictions, so as to let them ride in triumph over Truth. The most that any opposer can say, if he will speak truth, is no more then this, that they seeme to him to imply a contradiction; which may very easily be so, if he want an higher principle of faith, suitable and answerable to these matters of faith, both of them (the principle and object I mean) being [144] supernatural, neither of them contranatural; for there is a double modesty in Reason very remarkable: As it does not *multa asserere* [assert much], so it does not *multa negare* [deny much]; as it takes very few things for certain, so it concludes very few for impossible; Nay, Reason though she will not put out her eye, for that's unnatural, yet she will close her eye sometimes, that faith may aime the better, and that's commendable: And Faith makes Reason abundant compensation for this; for as a learned Author of our own, and a great Patron both of Faith and Reason, does notably expresse it, Faith is a supply of Reason in things intelligible, as the imagination is of sight in things visible.[12] The imagination with her witty and laborious pensil drawes and represents the shapes, proportions and distances of persons and places, taking them only by the help of some imperfect description, and 'tis faine to stay here, till it be better satisfied with the very sight of the things themselves. Thus Faith takes things upon an heavenly representation and description, upon a word, upon a promise, it sees a heavenly *Canaan* in the Map before an intellectual eye can behold it in a way of cleere and open vision; for men are not here capable of a present Heaven, and happinesse of a compleat and beatifical vision; and therefore they are not capable of such mysteries in their full splendor and brightnesse; for they would make it, if they were thus unfolded, but they now flourish only in the latices,[13] as Christ himself the Head of these Mysteries; they do σκηνοῦν ἐν ἡμῖν[14] [dwell among us], they put a veile upon their face, out of pure favour and indulgence to an intellectual eye, lest it should be too much overcome with their glory; the veiles of the Law were veiles of obscurity, but the veiles of the Gospel are only to allay the brightnesse of it. 'Tis honour enough for a Christian, if he can but touch the hem of Evangelical Mysteries, for he will never see a full Commentary upon the Gospel, till he can behold the naked face of his God. Yet the knowledge which he hath of him here, *imperfecta cognitio rerum nobilissimarum* [an imperfect knowledge of the most splendid things], 'tis most pleasant and delicious. 'Tis better to know a little of God and Christ, then to see all the creatures in their full beauty and perfection. The gleanings of spirituals is better then the vintage of naturals and morals. The least spangle of happinesse is better then a globe of temporals. This sets a glosse and lustre upon Christian Religion, and highly commends the purity and perfection of it, above all other whatsoever, in that in hath τὰ βάθη τοῦ θεοῦ[15] [the deep things of God]. Christ tries all his followers by his own Sunbeams. Whereas the dull and creeping religion of *Mahomet* has nothing at all above Nature and Reason, though it may have many things against both; no need of Faith there, there are no Mysteries in his Alcoran, unlesse

of deceit and iniquity. Nothing at all *nisi quod de facili, a quolibet medi-
ocriter sapiente naturali ingenio cognosci potest* [except what may be known
to some extent by a moderately wise mind easily and naturally], as that [145]
solid Author[16] very well observes. And therefore that stupid imposter did
not seale his words with any miracles, for there was not one supernatural
truth to be sealed, nor could he have sealed it if it had been there, but only
he prosecutes it with a sword. *Mahomets* Loadstone[17] does not draw men,
but his sword that conquers them; he draws his sword, he bids them deliver up their souls, and tells them, that upon this condition he will spare
their lives. *Signa illa quae tyrannis & latronibus non desunt*[18] [those signs
which tyrants and thieves do not lack], as he speaks notably. But the very
principles of Christian Religion are attractive and magnetical, they enamour and command, they overpower the understanding, and make it glad
to look upon such mysterious truths as are reflected in a glasse, because it
is unable to behold them πρόσωπον πρὸς πρόσωπον[19] [face to face]. This
speaks the great pre-eminence of Mount *Sion* above Mount *Sina*.[20] In the
Law you have *the Candle of the Lord* shining; in the Gospel you have the
day-spring from on high,[21] the Sun arising. Nature and Reason triumph
in the Law, Grace and Faith flower out in the Gospel. By vertue of this
wise and free dispensation, weak ones chiefly receive the Gospel, for they
are as well able to believe as any other, nay they are apter to believe then
others. If it had gone only by the advancement of intellectuals, by the
heightenings and clarifyings of Reason, who then would have been saved
but the grandees of the world? the Scribes, the Pharisees, the Philosophers,
the Disputers? but God has fram'd a way that confounds those heads of
the world, and drops happinesse into the mouths of babes. There are some
understandings that neither spin nor toile, and yet *Solomon* in all his wisdome and glory was not clothed like one of these:[22] for this way of Faith
'tis a more brief & compendious way *Longum iter per Rationem, breve per
Fidem* [the road of reason is long, that of faith short]. Very few understandings much lesse all can demonstrate all that is demonstrable, but if
men have a power of believing, they may presently assent to all that's true
and certain. That which Reason would have been sweating for this many
a yeer, Faith sups up the quintessence of in a moment. All men in the
world have not equal abilities, opportunities, advantages of improving

their Reason, even in things natural and moral, so that Reason it self tels us, that these are in some measure necessitated to believ others. How many are there that can't measure the just magnitude of a Star, yet if they will believe an Astronomer, they may know it presently, and if they be sure that this Mathematician hath skill enough, and will speak nothing but truth, they cannot then have the least shadow of Reason to dis-believe him. 'Tis thus in spirituals, such is the weaknesse of humane understanding *pro hoc statu* [in its present state], as that they are necessitated to believing here; yet such is its happinesse, that it hath one to instruct it who can neither deceive nor be deceived. God hath chosen this way of Faith, that he may staine the pride and glory of man, that he may pose his [146] intellectuals, that God may maintaine in man great apprehensions of himself, of his own incomprehensiblenesse, of his own truth, of his own revelations, as that he may keep a creature in a posture of dependency, so as to give up his understanding, so as to be disposed and regulated by him. And if a Cherubim be ambitious of stooping, if Angelical understanding do so earnestly παρακύψαι[23] [stoop to look], me thinks then the sons of men might fall down at the beautiful feet of Evangelical mysteries, with that humble acknowledgment, *Non sum dignus solvere corrigiam hujus mysterii*[24] [I am not worthy to unloose the shoe latchet of this mystery]. Only let thy Faith triumph here, for it shall not triumph hereafter; let it shine in time, for it must vanish in eternity. You see then that Reason is no enemy to Faith, for all that has been said of Faith, it has been fetch out of Reason. You see there are mutual embraces twixt the Law and the Gospel, Nature and Grace may meet together, Reason and Faith have kissed each other.[25]

৩০৪ CHAPTER 17 ৩০৪

The Light of Reason Is a Pleasant Light

[147] 'Tis *Lumen jucundum;* All light is pleasant, 'tis the very smile of Nature, the glosse of the world, the varnish of the Creation, a bright paraphrase upon bodies. Whether it discover it self in the modesty of a morning blush, and open its fair and Virgin eye-lids in the dawning of the day, or whether it dart out more vigorous and sprightful beams, shining out in its noon-day glory; whether it sport and twinckle in a Star, or blaze and glore out in a Comet, or frisk and dance in a Jewel, or dissemble and play the Hypocrite in a gloworm, or Epitomize and abbreviate it self in a spark, or shew its zeale and the ruddinesse of its complexion, in the yolk of the fire, or grow more pale, pining and consuming away in a Candle; however 'tis pleas'd to manifest it self, it carries a commanding lustre in its face, though sometimes indeed it be veil'd and shadowed, sometimes 'tis clouded and imprison'd, sometimes 'tis soyl'd and discolour'd. Who will not salute so lovely a beauty with a χαῖρε φῶς [welcome light]; welcome thou first-borne of corporeal beings, thou Lady and Queen of Sensitive beauties, thou clarifier and refiner of the Chaos, thou unspotted beauty of the Universe. Let him be condemn'd to a perpetual night, to a fatal disconsolate grave, that is not enamour'd with thy brightnesse. Is it not a pleasant thing to behold a Sun?[1] nay, to behold but a Candle, a deputed light? a vicarious light? the ape of a Sun-beame? Yet there are some superstitious ones that are ready to adore it; how devoutly do they complement with a Candle, at the first approach? how do they put off the hat to it, as if with the Satyr they meant to kisse it. You see how pleasant the light is to them; Nay that learned Knight in his discourse of Bodies, tells us of one totally blinde, who yet knew when a candle came into the room, only by

170

the quickning & reviving of his Spirits.² Yet this Corporeal light, 'tis but a shadow, 'tis but a black spot to set off the fairnes of intellectual brightnes. How pleasant is it to behold an intellectual Sun? Nay, to behold but the Candle of the Lord? How pleasant is this Lamp of Reason, πᾶν φυσικὸν ἡδύ. All the Motions and Operations of Nature are mix'd and season'd with sweetnesse; Every Entity 'tis sugared with some delight; Every being 'tis roll'd up in some pleasure. How does the inanimate Being clasp and embrace its Centre, and rest there as in the bosome of delight? how flourishing is the pleasure of vegetatives? Look but upon the beauty and pleasure of a flower. Behold the Lilies of the [148] Valleyes, (and the Roses of *Sharon*,) *Solomon* in all his Pleasure was not cloathed like one of these.³ Go then to sensitive Creatures, and there you meet with pleasures in a greater height and exaltation. How are all the *Individua* amongst them maintained by acts of pleasure? How are they all propagated by acts of pleasure? Some of them are more merry and cheerful then the rest. How pleasant and jocund is the Bird? How musical is it? How does it sing for joy? did you never see the fish playing in its element? did you never see it caught with a bait of pleasure? does not *Leviathan* sport in the sea, and dally with the waves? If you look up higher to rational Beings, to the sonnes of men, you'l finde there a more singular and peculiar kinde of pleasure, whilest they have both a taste of sensitive delight, and a Participation of Intellectual. The soul and body enjoying a chaste and conjugal love, the pleasure of the soul is more vigorous and masculine, that of the body more soft and effeminate. The Nobler any Being is, the purer pleasure it hath proportion'd to it. Sensitive pleasure it hath more of dregs; Intellectual pleasure it hath more of Quintessence. If pleasure were to be measured by Corporeal senses, the Brutes that are more exquisite in sense then men are, would by vertue of that, have a choicer portion of happinesse then men can arrive to, and would make a better sect of Epicureans then men are ever like to do. But therefore Nature hath very wisely provided, that the pleasure of Reason should be above any pleasure of Sense; as much, and far more then the pleasure of a Bee is above the pleasure of the Swine. Have you not seen a Bee make a trade of pleasure, and like a little Epicure faring deliciously every day,⁴ whilest it lies at the breast of a flower, drawing and sucking out the purest sweetnesse? and because 'twill have variety of dishes and dainties, it goes from flower to flower, and feasts upon them all with a pure and spotlesse pleasure, when as the Swine in the mean time tumbles and wallowes in the mire, rolling it self in dirt and filthinesse. An Intellectual Bee that deflowers most elegant Authors, a learned Epicure that sups up more Orient pearles then ever *Cleopatra* did, one that delights in the embraces of truth & goodnes, hath he not a more refin'd and clarified pleasure, then a wanton Corinthian that courts *Lais,* then a soft *Sardanapalus* spinning amongst his Courtizans, then a plump *Anacreon,* in singing & dancing and quaffing & lascivious playing? τῶν ἡδονῶν τὰς σωματικὰς, αἱ πρακτικαὶ καὶ φιλότιμοι τῷ χαίροντι τῆς ψυχῆς δι᾽ ὑπερβολὴν καὶ μέγεθος ἐναφανίζουσι, καὶ κατασβεννοῦσι⁵ [in one who rejoices in the grandeur and superiority of the soul, the active and emulative pleasures of the body are obliterated and extinguished], as the elegant Moralist hath it: and 'tis as if he had said, the delights of a studious and contemplative Athenian, or of a courageous and active Lacedemonian, is infinitely to be preferr'd before the pleasure of a delicate Sybarite, or a dissolved Persian. The delight of a Philosopher does infinitely surpasse the pleasure of a Courtier. The choicest pleasure [149] is nothing but the *Efflorescentia veri & boni* [flowering of the true and the good], there can be no greater pleasure, then of an understanding embracing a most clear truth, and of a will complying with its fairest good, this is ἐν θυμῷ χαίρειν [to rejoice in spirit], as the Greeks call it; or as the Latines *in sinu gaudere;*⁶ all pleasure consisting in that Harmonious Conformity and Correspondency, that a faculty hath with its object, 'twill necessarily flow from this, that the better and nobler any object is, the purer and stronger any faculty is, the neerer and sweeter the union is between them; the choicer must be the pleasure that ariseth from thence. Now Intellectual Beings have the bravest object, the highest and most generous faculties, the strictest Love-knot and Union, and so can't want a pleasure answerable to all this. *Epicurus* himself (as that known writer of the Philosophers lives, who himself also was a favourer and follower of the Epicurean Sect, does represent him)⁷ that grand master of pleasure, though sometimes he seeme to steep all pleasure in sense, yet upon more digested thoughts he is pleased to tell us, that the supreme delight is stor'd and treasur'd up in intellectuals. Sometimes indeed he breaks out into such dissolute words as these, οὐ γὰρ ἐγώγε ἔχω τί νοήσω, ἀγαθὸν ἀφαιρῶν μὲν τὰς διὰ χυλῶν ἡδονὰς τὰς δι᾽ ἀφροδισίων, καὶ τὰς διὰ μορφῶν.[8] I know no pleasure, saith he, if you take away the bribes and flatteries of lust, the enticings & blandishments of sense, the graces and elegancies of Musick, the kisses and embraces of *Venus*. But afterwards he is in a farre different and more sober strain, and seems to drop a pearl, though his auditors prov'd swine, his words were these, οὐ τὰς τῶν ἀσώτων ἡδονὰς, καὶ τὰς ἐν ἀπολαύσει κειμένας. I meane not (saies he) the pleasures of a Prodigal, or those that are situated in a carnal fruition, ἀλλὰ νήφων λογισμοὺς, καὶ τὸ μέγιστον ἀγαθὸν φρόνησις. I intend a rational pleasure, a prudential kinde of pleasure, which makes him lay down this for an axiome, οὐκ ἔστιν ἡδέως ζῆν ἄνευ τοῦ φρονίμως καὶ καλῶς,[9] that is, there can be no pleasure unlesse it be dipt in goodnesse, it must come bubbling from a fountain of Reason, & must stream out vertuous expressions & manifestations, and whereas others in their salutations were wont to write χαίρειν [rejoice], he alwayes writ εὐπράττειν[10] [do good]. But that ingenuous Moralist[11] whom I mentioned before, who could easily spy out the minde of *Epicurus,* and who was of greater candor and fairnesse then to wrong his opinion, doth yet so farre lay it open and naked to the world, as that he notably detects the follies and vanities of that voluptuous Philosopher in that golden tractate of his, which he entitles οὐκ ἔστιν ἡδέως ζῆν κατ᾽ Ἐπίκουρον. *Non potest suaviter vivere secundum Epicuri decreta* [*One Cannot Live Pleasurably in Accordance with the Doctrine of Epicurus*], where he shews that this jolly Philosopher makes the body onely the proper centre of pleasure, and when he tells you that the minde hath a more rarified delight, he means no more then this, that the minde perceives the [150] pleasure of sense better then the sense does,[12] which makes the forementioned Author passe this witty censure upon them, τὴν ἡδονὴν καθάπερ οἶνον ἐκ τοῦ πονηροῦ ἀγγείου διαχέοντες,[13] they pour no pleasure upon the soul, but that which comes out of the impure and musty vessel of the body. The whole summe of *Epicurus* his Ethicks, which he stiles his Canonical Philosophy, is this, τὴν ἡδονὴν ἀρχὴν καὶ τέλος λέγομεν τοῦ μακαρίως ζῆν,[14] that pleasure was the (α) [alpha] and (ω) [omega] of all happinesse. To this purpose he wrote a multitude of books, and scattered them like so many of his Atomes, and the greedy appetite of his licencious followers was easily caught with these baits of pleasure, which made his opinions to be stiled *meretricia dogmata* [meretricious doctrines] that curl'd their locks, that painted their faces, that open'd their naked breasts, that cloath'd themselves in soft and silken apparel, to see if they could thus entice the world; they were δογματικαὶ σειρῆνες [doctrinal sirens] that with a melting and delicate voice, did endeavour to soften and win upon the hearts of men as much as they could; the quintessence of all his doctrine was this, *Dux vitae dia voluptas*[15] [divine pleasure is the guide of life], as *Lucretius* the Epicurean Poet sings. The practice of that frolick professour of pleasure, did sufficiently explain and comment upon his minde. His dwelling was in a garden, a fit place to crown with Rosebuds, δρέπειν κορυφὰς[16] to crop the tops of pleasure, to let no flower of the spring passe untoucht of him; here he was furnisht with all his voluptuous accommodations, and he might spread like a green and flourishing Bay-tree;[17] But amongst all his pleasure me thinks none should envie that (which yet the writer of his life is pleased to observe) that he was wont δὶς τῆς ἡμέρας ἐμεῖν ἀπὸ τροφῆς,[18] to vomit twice a day constantly after meales, by vertue of his excessive luxury. O rare Philosopher! that Head of a vomiting Sect, that lickt up his and their own filthinesse. Is this the work of an Athenian? is this his mixing of vertue with pleasure? will he call this ζῆν ἡδέως [living happily]; sure he will not call this ζῆν φρονίμως [living rationally]; yet his death was very conformable to his life, for he expir'd with a cup of wine at his mouth,[19] which puts me in minde of the end of the other carousing Epicure, that merry Greek *Anacreon;* who by a most emphatical *Tautopathy*[20] was chok'd with the husk and kernel of a Grape. So soone does the pleasure of an Epicure wither, so soone are his resolves blasted, he eats, and drinks, and dies before to morrow, αἱ ἡδοναὶ καθάπερ αὖραι, &c.[21] [pleasures are like breezes, etc.] they seeme to refresh and fan the soul with a gentle breath, but they are not certain, nor durable. Those corporeal delights (as that florid Moralist *Plutarch* tells us) ἔξαψιν ἅμα καὶ σβέσιν ἐν σαρκὶ λαμβάνουσιν,[22] like so many sparks, they make a crack and vanish; like some extemporary meteors, they give a bright and sudden coruscation, and disappear immediately. The pleasures of taste are but *in fine palati* [in the mouth], as that famous [151] Epicure *Lucretius* tells us.[23] Whereas intellectual joy shines with a fixt and undecaying brightnesse, and though these ἡδοναὶ ἔξω γραφόμεναι (as *Plato* calls them elegantly)[24]

these outward pictures of pleasure, though they lose their glosse and colour, yet the inward face of delight maintains its original and primitive
beauty. Sensitive pleasure is limited and contracted to the narrow point of
a τὸ νῦν [present experience], for sense hath no delight but by the enjoyment of a present object, when as intellectual pleasure is not at all restrained by any temporal conditions, but can suck sweetnesse out of time
past, present, and to come; the minde does not only drink pleasure out of
present fountains; but it can taste those streams of delight that are run
away long ago, and can quench its thirst with those streams, which as yet
run under ground. For does not memory (which therefore *Plato* calls
αἰσθήσεων σωτηρία[25] [preservation of perception]) does it not reprint and
repeat former pleasure? and what's hope but pleasure in the bud? does it
not antedate and prepossesse future delight? Nay, by vertue of an intellectual percolation, the waters of *Marah* and *Meribah* will become sweet and
delicious.[26] The minde can extract honey out of the bitterest object when
'tis past, how else can you construe it, *haec olim meminisse juvabit*[27] [some-
day we will rejoice to recall these trials]? Corporeal pleasure 'tis but drossie
and impure, the wine 'tis dasht with water, there is a γλυκυπικρότης [bit-
tersweet taste] (as *Plato* in his *Philebus* that book of pleasure doth very
plainly and fully explain it,) and the instance that there *Socrates* gives, is a
quenching of thirst, where there's a very intimate connexion betwixt vexation and satisfaction.[28] Tell me, you that crown your selves with Rose-
buds, do you not at the same time crown your selves with thornes? for they
are the companions of Rose-buds. But intellectual pleasure 'tis ἄλυπος,
ἀπαθής, εἰλικρινής[29] [without grief, or suffering, or impurity], clear and
crystaline joy, there's no mud in it, no feculency at all. Men are asham'd
of some corporeal pleasures, the crown of Roses 'tis but a blushing crown,
but who are blusht at intellectual delights? *Epicurus* his Philosophy was
very well term'd νυκτερινὴ φιλοσοφία [a philosophy of night], 'twas afraid
to come to the light, whereas intellectual pleasure need not fear the light,
or the Sun-shine. Men faint and languish with sensitive pleasures, *Membra
voluptatis dum vi labefacta liquescunt* [while their limbs relax and melt in
the embrace of pleasure] (as *Lucretius* himself upon much experience acknowledges.)[30] *Lassata viris nondum satiata*[31] [exhausted by men, yet not
satisfied], as the Satyrist speaks of the eminent wanton. Nay, such is the

state and temper of the body σώματος φαυλότης καὶ ἀφνία,[32] as that it will better endure extreme grief, then excessive pleasure. Did you ne're hear of the soft Sybariste, who complain'd in the morning of his wearinesse, and of his pimples, when he had lien all night only upon a bed of Roses; but who ever was tir'd with intellectual pleasure? who ever was weary of an inward complacency? or who er'e surfetted [152] of rational joy? Other pleasures ingratiate themselves by intermission, *Voluptates commendat rarior usus*,[33] whereas all intellectuals heighten and advance themselves by frequent and constant operations. Other pleasures do but emasculate and dispirit the soul, they do not at all fill it and satisfie it. *Epicurus* may fill his with one of his atomes, as well as with one of his pleasures. Whereas rational pleasure fills the soul to the brim; it oiles the very members of the body, making them more free and cheerful; Nay, speculative delight will make abundant compensation for the want of sensitive; 'twill turne a wildernesse into a Paradise. 'Tis like you have read of the Philosopher that put out his eyes, that he might be the more intent upon his study;[34] he shuts his windows that the candle might shine more clearly within; and though he be rather to be wondered at, then to be followed or commended, yet he did proclaim thus much by this act of his, that he preferred one beame of intellectual light before the whole glory of this corporeal world; How have some been enamoured with the pleasure of Mathematicks? when, saies *Plutarch,* did any Epicure cry out βέβρωκα [I have eaten] with so much joy as *Archimedes* did εὕρηκα[35] [I have found it]? How have some Astronomers built their nests in the Stars? and have scorn'd to let any sublunary pleasures rend their thoughts from such goodly speculations? the worst of men in the meane time glut themselves with sensitive pleasure, χαίρουσιν οἱ ἄφρονες καὶ οἱ δειλοὶ καὶ οἱ κακοὶ[36] [fools and wretches and the wicked are merry] (as he in *Plato* speaks.) *Apollo* laughs but once in a yeere, when as a fool laughs all the yeer long. And 'tis a great deal more consonant to sound Philosophy that rationality should be the spring of inward pleasure, then of outward risibility. Amongst all mental operations reflex acts taste pleasure best, for without some self-reflexion men cannot tell whether they rejoyce or no; now these acts are the most distant and remote from sense, and are the highest advancements of Reason: true pleasure, 'tis *res severa* [a serious matter] (as the grave Moralist *Seneca* speaks)[37] and 'tis *in profundo* [in the depth], where truth and goodnesse those twin-fountains of pleasure are. Sensitive pleasure makes more noyse and crackling, when as mental and noetical delight, like the touches of the Lute, make the sweetest and yet the stillest and softest musick of all. Intellectual vexations have most sting in them, why then should not intellectual delights have most honey in them? Sensitive pleasure 'tis very costly, there must be χορηγία πολυτελής,³⁸ much preparation and attendance, much plenty and variety, *Parcentes ego dexteras odi, sparge Rosas*³⁹ [I hate sparing hands; scatter the roses], 'tis too dear for every one to be an Epicure, 'tis a very chargeable Philosophy to put in practice, whereas rational delight freely and equally diffuses it self, you need not pay any thing for fountain-pleasure, the minde it self proves a *Canaan* that flows with milk and honey, other pleasure a sick man cannot relish, an old man cannot embrace it. *Barsillai* saies he's too old [153] to taste the pleasures of the Court.⁴⁰ A Crown of Rose-buds does not at all become the gray head. But this noetical pleasure 'tis a delight fit for a Senator, for a *Cato*, 'tis an undecaying, a growing pleasure, 'tis the only pleasure upon the bed of sicknesse; the minde of him that has the gowt may dance, 'tis the staffe for old age to leane upon; these are the *rosae in hyeme* [roses of winter], the delights of old age, how much is the pleasure of a wise *Nestor* above the pleasure of a wanton *Menelaus?* The more rational & spiritual any being is, the larger capacity it has of pleasure. Νοῦς ἐστι βασιλεὺς οὐρανοῦ καὶ γῆς⁴¹ [mind is king of heaven and earth] (saith *Plato*) and in a commendable sense it does *Terram coelo miscere* [mix earth and heaven], and extract what sweetnesse it can out of both. The purer Arts, the nobler Sciences have most pleasure annext to them, when as Mechanical Arts are more sordid and contemptible, being conversant about sensitive and corporeal objects. Seeing and hearing are the most pleasurable senses, because they receive their objects in a more spiritual and intentional manner, and are deservedly stil'd by the Naturalist *sensus jucunditatis*⁴² [the senses of pleasure]. Other senses are more practical, but these are more contemplative. Φάμεν γὰρ ὁράματα καὶ ἀκούσματα εἶναι ἡδέα [we affirm that the perceptions of eye and ear are sweet], as *Aristotle* tells us,⁴³ for these are the *sensus disciplinae* [senses of instruction], they are the αὐτάγγελοι *mentis* [direct instructors of the mind], they contribute most to Reason. The more any object is spiritual-

ized, the more delightful it is, there's much delight in the tragical representation of those things which in reality would be sights full of amazement
and horror. The ticklings of fancy are more delightful then the touches of
sense. How does Poetry insinuate and turne about the mindes of men?
Anacreon might take more delight in one of his Odes, then in one of his
Cups; *Catullus* might easily finde more sweetnesse in one of his Epigrams,
then in the lips of a *Lesbia*. *Sappho* might take more complacency in one
of her Verses, then in her practices. The neerer any thing comes to mental
joy, the purer and choycer it is. 'Tis the observation not only of *Aristotle,*
but of every one almost, "Ἔνια δὲ τέρπει καινὰ ὄντα.⁴⁴ Some things delight
meerly because of their novelty, and that surely upon this account, because
the minde which is the spring of joy, is more fixt and intense upon such
things. The Rose-bud thus pleases more then the blown Rose. This noetical pleasure doth quietly possesse and satiate the soul, and gives a com-
pos'd and Sabbatical rest. So that as the forementioned Philosopher has it,
χαίροντες σφόδρα οὐ πάνυ δρῶμεν ἕτερον.⁴⁵ Men that are took up with
intellectual joy, trample upon all other inferiour objects. See this in Angelical pleasure; those Courtiers of heaven much different from those on
earth, neither eat nor drink, nor come neere, nor desire to come neere any
carnal pleasures. The painted and feigned heaven of a *Mahomet,* would
prove a real hell to an Angel or glorified Saint. He plants a [154] fooles paradise of his own, there are trees of his own setting and watering, the fat
and juicey Olive, the wanton and sequacious Ivy, and though he would
not allow them Vines on earth (such was his great love of sobriety) yet he
reserves them for heaven;⁴⁶ what meanes that sensual and sottish imposter,
to give notice of heaven by an Ivy-bush? Does he think that Goats and
Swine, that *Mahomets* must enter into the new Jerusalem? This is just such
a pleasure and happinesse as the Poets, that loose and licentious generation
fancied and carved out as most agreeable to their Deities. They poure
them out *Nectar,* they spread them a table, they dish out *Ambrosia* for
them, they allow them an *Hebe,* or a *Ganymede* to wait upon them, and
do plainly transforme them to worse then sensitive beings, such is the froth
of some vain imaginations; such is the scum of some obscene fancies, that
dare go about to create an Epicurean Deity, conformable to their own lust
and vile affections. Judge in your selves, are these pleasures fit for a su-

preme being? is there not a softer joy, is there not a more downy happinesse for a spiritual being to lay its head upon? That conqueror of the
world had far wiser and more sober thoughts, when he distinguisht himself from a Deity by his sleep and lust.[47] And I begin to admire the just
indignation of *Plato,* who though neither he himself, (unlesse he be mis-
reported) could content himself with intellectual pleasure, no nor yet with
natural, yet he would banish from the *Idea* of his Common-wealth all such
scandalous and abominable Poetry, as durst cast such unworthy and dishonourable aspersions upon a Deity, and make their god as bad as themselves, as if they were to draw a picture of him by their own faces and complexions.[48] Yet as all other perfections, so the perfection of all true and real
pleasure, is enjoyed by God himself in a most spiritual and transcendent
manner. That which is honour with men, is glory with him; that which
we call riches, is in him his own excellency. His creatures which are very
properly (as the Philosopher stiled riches) $\pi\lambda\hat{\eta}\theta os$ $\dot{o}\rho\gamma\acute{a}\nu\omega\nu$[49] [a multitude
of instruments], all serviceable and instrumental to him, and so that which
amongst men is accounted pleasure, is with him that infinite satisfaction,
which he takes in his own Essence, and in his own operations. His glorious
decrees and contrivances, they are all richly pregnant with joy and sweetnesse. Every providential dispensation is an act of choicest pleasure; the
making of all beings, nay of all irregularities contribute to his own glory,
must needs be an act of supreme and sovereigne delight. The laughing his
enemies to scorne,[50] 'tis a pleasure fit for infinite justice, the smiling upon
his Church, the favouring and countenancing of his people,[51] 'tis a pleasure fit for mercy and goodnesse; Miracles are the pleasure of his omnipotency, varieties are the delight of his wisdome; Creation was an act of
pleasure, and it must needs delight him to behold so much of his own
workmanship, so many pictures of his own drawing; Redemption was an
expression of that singular delight and pleasure which he took in the sons
of men.[52] Such [155] heaps of pleasures as these are never enter'd into the
minde of an *Epicurus,* nor any of his grunting Sect, who very neer border
upon Atheisme, and will upon no other termes and condition grant a Deity, unlesse they may have one of their own modelling and contriving, that
is, such a being as is wholly immerst in pleasure, and that such a pleasure
as they must be judges of; a being that did neither make the world, nor

takes any care of it, for that they think would be too much trouble to him, too great a burden for a Deity, 'twould hinder his pleasure too much. May they not a great deale better tell the Sun, that it's too much trouble for it to enlighten the world; may they not better tell a Fountaine that it's too much pains for it to spend it self in such liberal eruptions, in such fluent communications? Or shall naturall agents act with delight *ad extremum virium* [to their highest capacity], and shall not an infinite, and a free, and a rational agent choose such operations as are most delightful to him? would not *Epicurus* himself choose his own pleasure? and will he not allow a Deity the same priviledge? will he offer to set limits to a being which he himself acknowledges to be above him? must he stint and prescribe the pleasures of a God? and measure out the delights of the first being? who should think that an Athenian, that a Philosopher could thus farre dimme *the Candle of the Lord?* and could entertain such a prodigious thought as this, that the Sun it self is maintain'd with the same Oile, as his decayed and corrupted Lamp is? That gallant Moralist *Plutarch* does most notably lay the axe to the root of this abominable Error, for, saith he, If *Epicurus* should grant a God in his full perfections, he must change his life presently, he must be a swine no longer, he must uncrown his rosy head, and must give that practical obedience to the dictates of a God which other Philosophers are wont to do; whereas he looks upon this as his fairest Rose-bud, as the most beautiful flower in his garden of pleasure, that there's no providence to check him, or bridle him; that he is not so subject or subordinate as to stand in awe of a Deity.[53] But that brave Author (whom I commended before) shews the inconsistency of this tenent with true and solid pleasure;[54] For grant, O Epicure, that thou dost not care for a Deity in a calme, yet what wilt thou do in a storme? when the North-winde blows upon thy garden, and when the frost nips thy tender Grapes. Thou dost not care for him in the spring, but wouldst thou not be glad of him in the winter? will it be a pleasure then that thou hast none to help thee? none to guide thee, none to protect thee? Suppose a Ship ready to be split upon a rock, or to be soop't[55] up of a wave, would this then be a comfort and encouragement to it, or would it take pleasure in this, μήτε τινὰ κυβερνήτην ἔχειν μήτε τοὺς διοσκούρους, that it has no Pilot to direct it, it has no tutelar Deities to minde the welfare of it? but it must rush on as

well as it can; thou blinde and fond Epicure, thou knowest not the sweetnesse of pleasure, that might be extracted out of providence, which is not
φοβερόν τι σκυθρωπὸν, 'tis not a [156] supercilious and frowning authority,
but 'tis the indulgent and vigilant eye of a father, 'tis the tender and affectionate care of a Creator. One blossome of Providence hath more joy and
pleasure in it, then all thy Rose-buds. Where is there more delight then in
the serving of a God? Look upon the Sacrifices, what mirth and feastings
are there? ἀλλ᾽ οὐκ οἴνου πλῆθος οὐδὲ ὄπτησις τῶν κρεῶν τὸ εὐφραῖνον ἐν
ταῖς ἑορταῖς, 'Tis not the abundance of wine, nor the abundance of provision that makes the joy and pleasure there, ἀλλὰ καὶ ἐλπὶς ἀγαθὴ καὶ
δόξα τοῦ παρεῖναι τὸν θεὸν, εὐμενῆ καὶ δέχεσθαι τὰ γινόμενα κεχαρι-
σμένως, it's the presence of a propitious Deity, accepting and blessing his
worshippers, that fills the heart with greater joy then an Epicure is capable
of. Never was there a Sect found out that did more oppose true pleasure,
then the Epicureans did; they tell us that they take pleasure in honour, τὴν
εὐδοξίαν ἡδὺ ἡγοῦνται, they look upon it as a lovely and delightful thing;
yet by these tenents and practices of theirs, they quite staine and blot their
honour, & so lose that piece of their pleasure which they pretend to. They
say (if you'l believe them) that they take pleasure in friends, when as yet
they constitute friendship, only κατὰ τὴν κοινωνίαν ἐν ταῖς ἡδοναῖς[56] [as
a partnership in pleasure], they must be boon companions, that must
drink and be merry together, and run into the same excesse of riot. Have
not sensitive creatures as much friendship as this amounts to? They tell us
they love the continuation of pleasure, why then do they deny the immortality of the soul? Δεῖ τὸν αἰῶνα μὴ εἶναι,[57] 'tis the voice of Epicurus
and his swinish Sect, There must be no eternity. What, are they afraid their
pleasure should last too long? or are they conscious (as they may very well
be) that such impure pleasure is not at all durable? δὶς γὰρ οὐκ ἔστι γίνε-
σθαι, 'tis the voice of the same impure mouth, There is no repetition of life:
what's he afraid of having his pleasures reiterated? does he not expect a
crown of Rose-buds the next spring? or is he so weary (as well he may be)
of his pleasure, as that he will preferre a non-entity before it? This sure was
the minde and desire of that Epicurean Poet *Lucretius,* though a Roman
of very eminent parts, which yet were much abated by a *Philtrum* that was
given him; a just punishment for him, who put so much of his pleasure in

a cup; and this desperate slighter of Providence, at length laid violent hands upon himself.[58] Are any of you enamour'd with such pleasure as this? you see what's at the bottome of an Epicures cup: you see how impatient a rational being is of such unworthy delights, and how soon 'tis cloy'd with them. You see the misery of an Epicure, whose pleasure was only in this life, and yet would not last out this life neither. But all rational pleasure, tis not of a span long, but reaches to perpetuity. That Moralist whom I have so often mentioned, reckons up whole heaps of pleasure, which spring from the continuation of the soul. Ἀυτὰρ ἐγὼ καὶ 'κεῖθι φίλου μεμνήσομ' ἑταίρου.[59] There (saies he) shall I have the pleasure of seeing all my [157] friends again, there I shall have the pleasure of more ennobled acts of Reason; γλυκὺν γεύσας τὸν αἰῶνα,[60] there shal I taste the so much long'd for sweetnesse of another world. οὐδὲ ὁ Κέρβερος, οὐδὲ ὁ Κώκυτος, &c.[61] [neither Cerberus nor Cocytus, etc.]. The fear of future misery cannot more terrifie a guilty soul (the fear of which 'tis like made *Epicurus* put off all thoughts of another life as much as he could, for else the fear of that would have been a worm in his Rose-bud of pleasure); but the fear of that has not more horror and amazement in it, then the hope of future happinesse has joy and delight annext to it.

Hoc habet animus Argumentum divinitatis, quod cum divina delectant[62] [the soul has an argument for her divine nature in the fact that divine things delight her], as that serious Moralist *Seneca* speaks most excellently. The soul by the enjoyment of God comes neer the pleasure of God himself.

The Platonists tell us that *Voluptatis Generatio fit ex infiniti & finiti copulatione* [the generation of pleasure results from the union of the infinite and the finite], because the object of real pleasure must be αὐταρκὲς, τέλειον, ἱκανὸν, καθαρὸν, νοητὸν, μονειδὲς, ἀδιάλυτον, τὸ ὄντως ἀγαθόν[63] [sufficient in itself, perfect, fitting, pure, comprehensible, unmixed, indissoluble, essentially good]. An intellectual eye married to the Sun, a naked will swimming, and bathing it self in its fairest good, the noblest affections leaping and dancing in the purest light, this speaks the highest *apex* and eminency of noetical pleasure; yet this pleasure of heaven it self, though by a most sacred and intimate connexion it be unseparably conjoyn'd with happinesse, yet 'tis not the very essence and formality of it, but does rather flow from it by way of concomitancy and resultancy.

That which most opposes this pleasure, is that prodigious and anomalous delight (not worthy the name of delight or pleasure) which damn'd spirits and souls degenerate farre below the pleasure of *Epicurus,* that delight which these take in wickednesse, in malice, in pride, in lies, in hypocrisie; all which speaks them the very excrements of *Beelzebub,* the Prince of Devils. But you that are genuine Athenians, fill your selves with noetical delights, and envie not others their more vulgar Beotick pleasures; envie not the ranknesse of their Garlick and Onions, whilest you can feed and feast upon more Spiritual and Angelical dainties. Envy not the wanton Sparrows, nor the lascivious Goats, as long as you can meet with a purer and chaster delight in the virginity of intellectual embraces.

Do you devoure with a golden Epicurisme, the Arts and Sciences, the spirits and extractions of Authors; let not an Epicure take more pleasure in his garden then you can do in your studies; you may gather flowers there, you may gather fruit there. Convince the world that the very pith and marrow of pleasure does not dwell in the surface of the body, but in a deep and rational centre. Let your triumphant reason trample upon sense, and let no corporeal pleasures move you [158] or tempt you, but such as are justly and exactly subordinate to Reason; you come to *Athens* as to a fountain of learned pleasure; you come hither to snuff *the Candle of the Lord* that is within you, that it may burn the clearer and the brighter. You come to trim your Lamps, and to pour fresh Oile into them; your very work and employment is pleasure. Happy Athenians (if you knew your own happinesse). Let him be condemn'd to perpetual folly and ignorance, that does not prefer the pleasent light of *the Candle of the Lord* before all the Pageantry of sensitive objects, before all the flaunting and Comical joy of the world.

Yet could I shew you a more excellent way, for the pleasures of natural reason are but husks in comparisen of those Gospel-delights, those mysterious pleasures that lie hid in the bosome of a Christ; those Rose-buds that were dy'd in the bloud of a Saviour, who took himself the Thorns, & left you the roses. We have only lookt upon the pleasure of a candle, but there you have the Sun-shine of pleasure in its full glory.

The Light of Reason Is
an Ascendent Light

[159] 'Tis *Lumen ascendens*—ὃν ὤφελεν αἰθέριος Ζεὺς Ἐννύχιον μετ᾽ αἔθ-λον ἄγειν ἐς ὁμήγυριον ἄστρων¹ [it would have been fitting had heavenly Zeus, after the dark struggle, raised it into the assembly of the stars], as *Musaeus* sings in the praise of *Hero's* Candle. Yet I mean no more by this, then what that known saying of Saint *Austin* imports, *Fecisti nos (Domine) ad te, irrequietum erit cor nostrum donec redit ad te*² [you have made us, Lord, for yourself; our heart will be restless until it return to you]. The Candle of the Lord it came from him, and 'twould faine returne to him. For an intellectual lamp to aspire to be a Sun, 'tis a lofty straine of that intolerable pride which was in *Lucifer* and *Adam:* but for *the Candle of the Lord,* to desire the favour, and presence, and enjoyment of a beatifical Sun, this is but a just and noble desire of that end which God himself created it for. It must needs be a proud and swelling drop that desires to become an Ocean; but if it seeks only to be united to an Ocean, such a desire tends to its own safety and honour. The face of the soul naturally looks up to God, *coelumque tueri Jussit, & erectos ad sidera tollere vultus*³ [who ordained that man gaze at heaven, and raise his upturned face to the stars], tis as true of the soul as of the body. All light loves to dwell at home with the Father of lights.⁴ Heaven 'tis *Patria luminum* [the fatherland of lights], God has there fixt a tabernacle for the Sun,⁵ for 'tis good to be there, 'tis a condescension in a Sunne-beam that 'twill stoop so low as earth, and that 'twill gild this inferiour part of the world; 'tis the humility of light that 'twill incarnate and incorporate it self into sublunary bodies; yet even there 'tis not forgetful of its noble birth and original, but 'twill still look upwards to the Father of lights. Though the Sun cover the earth with its healing

and spreading wings, yet even those wings love to flie aloft, and not to rest upon the ground in a sluggish posture. Nay, light when it courteously salutes some earthy bodies, it usually meets with such churlish entertainment, as that by an angry reverberation, 'tis sent back again, yet in respect of it self 'tis many times an happy reflection and rebound, for 'tis thus necessitated to come neerer heaven. If you look but upon a Candle, what an aspiring and ambitious light is it? though the proper figure of flame be Globular and not Pyramidal, (as the noble *Verulam* tells us in his History of Nature)[6] which appears by those celestial bodies, those fine and rarified flames, (if we may so call them with the [160] Peripateticks leave) that roll and move themselves in a globular and determinate manner: yet that flame which we usually see puts on the form of a Pyramide, occasionally and accidentally, by reason that the aire is injurious to it, and by quenching the sides of the flame crushes it, and extenuates it into that form, for otherwise 'twould ascend upwards in one greatnesse, in a rounder and compleater manner. 'Tis just thus in *the Candle of the Lord;* Reason would move more fully according to the sphere of its activity, 'twould flame up towards heaven in a more vigorous and uniforme way, but that it is much quencht by that εὐτερίστατος ἁμαρτία[7] [sin which easily besets us], and the unrulinesse of the sensitive powers will not allow it its full scope and liberty, therefore 'tis fain to spire up, and climbe up as well as it can in a Pyramidal forme, the bottome and basis of it borders upon the body, and is therefore more impure and feculent; but the *apex* and *cuspis* of it catches at heaven, and longs to touch happinesse, thus to unite it self to the fountain of light and perfection. Every spark of Reason flies upwards, this divine flame fell down from heaven, and halted with its fall, (as the Poets in their Mythology tell us of the limping of *Vulcane*)[8] but it would faine ascend thither againe by some steps and gradations of its own framing.

Reason 'tis soon weary with its fluttering up and down among the creatures, *the Candle of the Lord* does but waste it self in vain in searching for happines here below. Some of the choicest Heathens did thus spend their Lamps, & exhaust their Oile, and then at length were faine to lie down in darknesse & sorrow; their Lamps did shew them some glimmering appearances of a *Summum bonum* at a great distance, but it did not sufficiently direct them in the way to it, no more then a Candle can guide a traveller that is ignorant of his way. You may see some of the more sordid Heathen toyling and searching with their Candle in the mines and treasuries of riches, to see if they could spy any veine of happinesse there, but the earth saith, 'Tis not in me. You may see others among them feeding and maintaining their Candle with the aire of popular applause, sucking in the breath and esteem of men, till at the length they perceived that it came with such uncertain blasts, as that they chose rather to cloyster themselves up in a Lanthorn, to put themselves into some more reserved and retired condition, rather then to be exposed to those transient and arbitrary blasts, which some are pleased to entitle and stile by the name of honours. You might see some of them pouring the Oile of gladnesse into their Lamps, till they soon perceived that voluptuous excesse did but melt and dissolve the Candle, and that pleasures like so many thieves, did set it a blazing, and did not keep it in an equal shining. You might behold others, and those the most eminent amongst them, snuffing their Candles very exactly and accurately, by improving their intellectuals and refining their morals, till they sadly perceived that when they were [161] at the brightest, their Candles burnt but dimly and blewly, and that for all their snuffing they would relapse into their former dulnesse. The snuffings of Nature and Reason will never make up a day, nor a Sun-shine of happinesse; all the light that did shine upon these Ethiopians did only discover their own blacknesse, yet they were so enamour'd with this natural complexion, as that they look't upon't as a piece of the purest beauty.

Nature *Narcissus*-like loves to look upon its own face, and is much taken with the reflexions of it self. What should I tell you of the excessive and hyperbolical vapourings of the Stoicks in their adoring and idolizing of Nature, whilest they fix their happinesse in the τὰ ἐφ' ἡμῖν,[9] in their own compasse and sphere; these were (as I may so terme them) a kinde of Pharisees among the Heathen, that scorn'd precarious happinesse, like so many arbitrary and independent beings; they resolv'd to be happy how they pleas'd, and when they list. Thus do fond creatures boast of their decayed Lamps, as if they were so many Sunnes, or at least Stars of the first magnitude. The Stoicks spoke this more loudly, yet the rest of the Heathen whispered out the same, for they were all of the Poets minde,— *Natura beatis Omnibus esse dedit, si quis cognoverit uti*[10] [nature grants to all the means to be happy, if only we knew how to use them]. And they would all willingly subscribe to those words of *Salust*. *Falso de natura queritur humanum genus*[11] [the human race complains of nature falsely], which indeed if understood of the God of Nature, they were words of truth and loyalty; but if they meant them (as certainly they did) of that strength which was for the present communicated to them, they were but the interpreters of their own weaknesse and vanity. Yet 'tis no wonder to hear any of the Heathen Rhetoricating in the praise of Nature; it may seem a more tolerable piece of gratitude in them to amplifie and extoll this gift of their Creatour; 'tis no wonder if such a one admire a Candle, that ne're saw a nobler light. But for such as are surrounded and crown'd with Evangelical beams, for men that live under Gospel-Sun-shine, for them to promise themselves and others that they may be saved by the light of a candle, a Stoick, an Academick, a Peripatetick shall enter into heaven before these. Yet I finde that in the very beginning of the fifth Century, *Pelagius* an high Traitor against the Majesty of Heaven, scattered this dangerous and venomous Error, endeavouring to set the Crown upon Natures head, and to place the creature in the throne of God and grace. The learned *Vossius*[12] in his *Historia Pelagiana* (a book full fraught with sacred Antiquity) gives us this brief representation of him, that he was, *humani arbitrii decomptor, & Divinae Gratiae contemptor*, a trimmer of Nature, and an affronter of grace. His body was the very type of his soul, for he wanted an eye, he was but μονόφθαλμος [one-eyed]: to be sure he wanted a spiritual eye to discern the things of God. He was a *Scot* by Nation, a Monk by profession, a man exemplary in Morals, and not contemptible [162] for learning, for though *Hierom* vilifie him in respect of both, yet *Chrysostom* gives him a sufficient *Commendamus*, and *Augustine* himself will set his hand to it, that learned adversary of his full of grace and truth, & the very hammer that broke his flinty and rebellious Errour in pieces. If you would see the rise, and progresse, and variations of this Errour, how it began to blush and put on more modesty in Semipelagianisme; how afterwards it cover'd its nakednesse with some Popish fig-leaves; how at length it refin'd it self and drest it self more handsomely in Arminianisme, you may consult with the forementioned Author, who kept a relique of his Pelagian History in his own breast, whilest it left upon him an Arminian tincture. This spreading

Errour leaven'd the great lump and generality of the world, as the profound *Bradwardin* sighs, and complains; *Totus pene mundus post* Pelagium
abiit in errorem[13] [almost the whole world followed Pelagius into error]:
for all men are born Pelagians; Nature is predominant in them: it has took
possession of them, and will not easily subordinate it self to a superior
principle. Yet Nature has not such a fountain of perfection in it self, but
that it may very well draw from another; this Heathenish principle after
all its advancements and improvements, after all its whitenings and purifyings, it must stand but afar off in *Atrio Gentium* [in the court of the Gen-
tiles], it cannot enter into the Temple of God, much lesse into the *Sanctum
Sanctorum,* it cannot pierce within the veile.

The ennoblement of intellectuals, the spotlesse integrity of Morals,
sweetnesse of dispositions, and the candor of Nature, they are all deservedly amiable in the eye of the world. The Candle of *Socrates,* and the candle of *Plato,* the Lamp of *Epictetus,* they did all shine before men, and
shine more then some that would fain be call'd Christians. Nature makes
a very fine show, and a goodly glittering in the eye of the world, but this
Candle cannot appear in the presence of a Sun; all the paintings and var-
nishings of Nature, they please and enamour the eyes of men, but they
melt away at the presence of God. The Lamp of a Moralist may waste it
self in doing good to others, and yet at length may go out in a snuffe, and
be cast into utter darknesse. The harmonious composing of natural faculties, the tuning of those spheres, will never make up an heaven fit for a
soul to dwell in. Yet notwithstanding whatsoever is lovely in nature is acceptable even to God himself, for 'tis a print of himself, and he does proportion some temporal rewards unto it; the justice of an *Aristides,* the good
laws of a *Solon* or a *Lycurgus,* the formal devotion of a *Numa Pompilius,*
the prudence of a *Cato,* the courage of a *Scipio,* the moderation of a *Fabius,*
the publick spirit of a *Cicero,* they had all some rewards scattered among
them. Nor is there any doubt but that some of the Heathen pleased God
better then others. Surely *Socrates* was more lovely in his eyes then *Aristophanes, Augustus* pleased him better then *Tiberius, Cicero* was more acceptable to him then *Catiline,* for there were more [163] remainders of his
image in the one then in the other, the one was of purer and nobler influence then the other. *Minus malus respectu pejoris est bonus* [the less wicked

is, compared with the more wicked, good], the one shall have more miti-gations of punishment then the other; *Socrates* shall taste a milder cup of wrath, when as *Aristophanes* shall drink up the dregs of fury; if divine jus-tice whip *Cicero* with rods, 'twill whip *Catiline* with Scorpions. An easier and more gentle worm shall feed upon *Augustus,* a more fierce and cruel one shall prey upon *Tiberius;* if justice put *Cato* into a prison, 'twill put *Cethegus* into a dungeon. Nor is this a small advantage that comes by the excellencies & improvements of Nature, that if God shall please to beau-tifie and adorne such an one with supernatural principles, and if he think good to drop grace into such a soul, 'twill be more serviceable and instru-mental to God then others. Religion cannot desire to shine with a greater glosse and lustre, it cannot desire to ride among men in greater pomp and solemnity, in a more triumphant Chariot, then in a soul of vast intellec-tuals, of Virgin and undeflowered morals, of calme and composed affec-tions, of pleasant and ingenuous dispositions. When the strength of Na-ture, and the power of godlinesse unite, and concentricate their forces, they make up the finest and purest complexion; the soundest and bravest constitution, like a sparkling and vigorous soul, quickening and informing a beautiful body. Yet this must be thought upon, that the different im-provement even of Naturals, springs only from grace. For Essentials and Specificals (which are meer Nature) they are equal in all, but whatsoever singular or additional perfection is annext to such a one, flows only from the distinguishing goodnesse of an higher cause; that *Socrates* was any bet-ter then *Aristophanes,* was not nature, but a kinde of common gift and grace of the Spirit of God, for there are the same seminal principles in all. *Augustus & Tiberius* were hew'n out of the same rock; there are in *Cicero* the seeds of a *Catiline:* and when the one brings forth more kindely and generous, the other more wilde and corrupted fruit, 'tis accordingly as the countenance and favourable aspect of heaven is pleased to give the in-crease; for as the Philosophers tell us, *Motio moventis praecedit motum mo-bilis* [the motion of the mover precedes the motion of the moved], was there any propension or inclination to goodness in the heart of a *Cicero* more then of a *Catiline?* 'twas only from the first mover, from the finger of God himself that tuned the one more harmoniously then the other. As take two several Lutes, let them be made both alike for essentials, for matter and

form; if now the one be strung better then the other, the thanks is not due
to the Lute, but to the arbitrary pleasure of him that strung it; let them be
both made alike and strung alike, yet if the one be quickened with a more
delicate and graceful touch, the prevailing excellency of the musick was
not to be ascribed to the nature of the Lute, but to the skill and dexterity
of him that did move it and prompted it into such elegant sounds. The
[164] several degrees of worth in men that are above radicals and fundamen-
tals of nature, they are all the skill and workmanship, the fruits and productions of common grace; For *Omnis actio particularis habet originem ab
agente universali*[14] [every particular action springs from a universal agent].
Now if the universal agent did only dispense an equal concourse in an
equal subject, all the operations and effects that flow from thence must
needs be equal also; if then there be any eminency in the workings of the
one more then of the other, it can have no other original then from that
noble influence, which a free and supreme agent is pleased to communicate in various measures; so that naked Nature of it self is a most invalid
and inefficacious principle, that does crumble away its own strength, and
does wear and waste by its motions, and for every act of improvement it
depends only upon the kindnesse of the first being. They that tell you Nature may merit Grace and Glory, may as well tell you (if they please) that
a Candle by its shining may merit to be a Star, to be a Sun. Nor yet is
Nature alwayes constant to its own light; it does not deal faithfully with
its intimate and essential principles. Some darlings of Nature have abundantly witnessed this, whilest they have run into some unnatural practices,
that were the very blushes of Nature; if then Nature cannot tell how to live
upon earth, will it ever be able to climbe up to heaven? *Si nesciat servire,
nescit imperare* [if it does not know how to serve, it will not know how to
rule], if it be not faithful in a little, do you think that it shall be made Ruler
over much? no certainly, moral endowments when they are at the proudest
top and *apex,* can do no more, then what that great Antipelagian *Prosper*
tells us, *Mortalem vitam honestare possunt, aeternam conferre non possunt*[15]
[they can make our mortal life honourable; they cannot confer immortal-
ity]. God has ordeined men to a choycer end, then these natural faculties
can either deserve, or obtaine, or enjoy. Natures hand cannot earn it; *Natures hand cannot reach it, Natures eye cannot see it.* That glorious and ul-

timate end, which must fill and satiate the being of man, is the beatifical vision of God himself. Now there is no natural power nor operation proportioned to such a transcendent object as the face of God, as the naked essence of a Deity. Inferior creatures may, & do move within the compasse of their natures, and yet they reach that end which was propounded and assigned to their being: but such was the special and peculiar love of God, which he manifested to a rational nature, as that it must be advanc't above it self by a *supernaturale auxilium* [supernatural aid], before it can be blest with so great a perfection, as to arrive to the full end of its being. Yet God has toucht nature with himself, and drawes it by the attractive and magnetical vertue of so commanding an object as his own essence is, which makes Nature affect and desire somewhat supernatural, that it may make neerer approaches unto happinesse; for this end God did assume humane nature to the divine, that he might make it more capable of this perfection, and [165] by a strict love-knot and union might make it partaker of the divine nature; not that 'tis changed into it, but that it has the very subsistence of its happinesse by it. Every being does naturally long for its own perfection, and therefore a rational nature must needs thus breath and pant after God, and the neerer it comes to him, the more intensely and vehemently it does desire him, for as they tell us, *Motus naturalis velocior est in fine,*[16] the neerer a body approaches to its centre, the more cheerful and vigorous is its motion. The Understanding that sees most of God, desires to see more of him; its eye will never leave rolling till it fix it self in the very centre of the Divine essence. Nature that has but some weake glimpses of him, and so it has but faint and languishing velleities after him. Ὁι μὲν ἐκ φύσεως νεύουσι πρὸς τὸ ἀγαθὸν[17] [those who naturally move towards the good], as he speaks of the Heathens, they seem to nod after a *summum bonum.* What the states and conditions of those Heathens was and is in order to eternal happinesse, we cannot easily nor certainly determine; yet thus much may be safely granted, though we say not with the Pelagians, that the emprovements of nature can make men happy; nor yet with the Semi-Pelagians that natural preparations and predispositions do bespeak & procure Grace; nor yet with the Papists and Arminians, that works flowing from Grace do contribute to more Grace & Glory, yet this we say, that upon the improvement of any present strength, God out of his free goodnesse, may if he please give more. As God freely gave them nature (which makes *Pelagius* sometimes call Nature Grace) and as he freely, and out of his Grace gave them some emprovement of Nature, so he might as freely give them supernatural strength if it so please him. Yet a creature cannot come to heaven by all those improvements which are built upon Natures foundation; for if it should accurately and punctually observe every jot and tittle of Natures Law, yet this natural obedience would not be at all correspondent or commensurate to a supernatural happinesse, which makes Saint *Augustine* break out into such an expression as this; *Qui dicit hominem servari posse sine Christo, dubito an ipse per Christum servari possit*[18] [I doubt whether he who says that man can be saved without Christ, can himself be saved by Christ]; for this is the only way, the new and living way, by which God will assume humane nature to himself, and make it happy. Yet notwithstanding their censure is too harsh and rigid, who as if they were Judges of eternal life and death, damne *Plato* and *Aristotle* without any question, without any delay at all; and do as confidently pronounce that they are in hell, as if they saw them flaming there. Whereas the infinite goodnesse and wisdome of God might for ought we know finde out several wayes of saving such by the Pleonasmes of his love in Jesus Christ; he *might* make a *Socrates* a branch of the true Vine, and *might* graffe *Plato* and *Aristotle* into the fruitful Olive; for it was in his power, if he pleased, to reveale Christ unto them, and to infuse faith into them after an extra[166]ordinary manner; Though indeed the Scripture does not afford our charity any sufficient ground to believe that he did; nor doth it warrant us peremtorily to conclude the contrary. *Secreta Deo,* it does not much concerne us to know what became of them; let us then forbear our censure, and leave them to their competent Judge. But when we mention *Socrates, Plato* and *Aristotle,* and the more eminent and refined ones among the Heathens, you must be sure not to entertain such a thought as this, that the excellency of their intellectuals and morals did move and prevail with the goodnesse of God to save them more then others of the Heathen, as if these were *dispositiones de congruo merentes salutem aeternam*[19] [dispositions meriting eternal salvation congruously], this indeed were nothing but Pelagianisme a little disguised; whereas you must resolve it only into the free grace of God, that did thus distinguish them here in time, and might more distinguish them eternally, if it pleased him to bestow a Saviour upon them. Which grace of God is so free, as that it might save the worst of the Heathens, and let go the rest; it might save an *Aristophanes* as well as a *Socrates,* nay before a *Socrates,* as well as a Publican before a Pharisee: not only all Heathen, but all men are of themselves in equal circumstances in order to eternal happinesse; 'tis God only that makes the difference, according to his own determinations, that were eternal and unconditional. Yet I am farre from the minde of those Patrons of Universal Grace, that make all men in an equal propinquity to salvation, whether Jewes, or Pagans, or Christians; which is nothing but dight and guilded Pelagianisme, whilest it makes grace as extensive and Catholick, a principle of as full latitude as nature is, and resolves all the difference into created powers and faculties. This makes the barren places of the world in as good a condition as the Garden of God, as the inclosure of the Church: It puts a Philosopher in as good an estate as an Apostle; For if the *remedium salutiferum* [healing remedy] be equally applied to all by God himself, and happinesse depends only upon mens regulating and composing of their faculties; how then comes a Christian to be neerer to the Kingdome of Heaven then an Indian? is there no advantage by the light of the Gospel shining among men with healing under its wings?[20] Surely, though the free grace of God may possibly pick and choose an Heathen sometimes, yet certainly he does there more frequently pour his goodnesse into the soul where he lets it streame out more clearly and conspicuously in external manifestations. 'Tis an evident signe that God intends more salvation there, where he affords more means of salvation; if then God do choose and call an Heathen, 'tis not by universal, but by distinguishing grace. They make Grace Nature, that make it as common as Nature. Whereas Nature when 'twas most triumphant, shining in its Primitive beauty and glory, yet even then it could not be happy without Grace. *Adam* himself besides his *integritas naturae* [integral nature], had also *adjutorium gratiae* [the help of grace], for as the Schoolmen [167] explain it, though he had *vires idoneas ad praestanda omnia naturalia; reipsa tamen nihil praestitit sine auxilio gratiae*[21] [powers capable of performing all natural acts, yet in fact he performed nothing without the help of grace]. As, if you expect any goodly and delicious clusters from a Vine, besides its own internal forme which we'll stile Nature, there must be also *auxilium gratiae* [the help of grace], the Sun must favour it and shine upon it, the raine must nourish it, and drop upon it, or else Nature will never be pregnant and fruitful. *Adams* Candle did not shine so clearly, but that Grace was fain to snuffe it. Nature, though 'twere compleate and entire, yet 'twas faine to strengthen and support it self by its twinings about Grace, and for want of the powerful support and manu-tenncy[22] of Grace, Nature fell down presently; it startled from it self, and apostatiz'd like a broken bowe. What meane the Pelagians to tell us of a *Naturalis Beatitudo* [natural beatitude], when as Nature now is surrounded with so many frailties and miseries, so many disorders and imperfections? Yet were it as green and flourishing as ever it was when 'twas first planted in Paradise, yet even then 'twould be too remote from happinesse, for perfect happinesse excludes and banishes all futurity and possibility of misery, which Nature never yet did, nor could do. And happinesse never flows out till the Sunne look upon it, till it see the face of God himself, whom Natures eye will ne're be able to behold. Yet Oh! how desirous is Nature of this? how inquisitive is humane Nature into the causes of things, and esteems it no smal piece of its beatitude if it can finde them out? *Foelix qui potuit rerum cognoscere causas*[23] [happy is he who is able to discover the causes of things]. What a goodly sight is it then to behold the first cause of all being, and its own being? how faine would an intellectual eye behold him that made it! Nature longs to see who 'twas that first contrived it, and fram'd it, and fashion'd it; the soul would fain see its Father of Spirits. The Candle would faine shine in the presence of him that lighted it up.

Yet Nature cannot see the face of God and live. *Ante obitum nemo supremaque funera foelix*[24] [before death and the final funeral no man is happy]. The Moralists happiness is dormant in the night-time, for there's no *operatio secundum virtutem* [virtuous action] then, nor can the soul while 'tis clogg'd with a fraile body, climbe to the ἀκρότης [pinnacle] of goodnesse or happiness; the soul here has not a perfect enjoyment of inferiour objects, much lesse of God himself; it has but a shadowy sight of Angels *propter connaturalitatem intellectus nostri ad phantasmata*[25] [because of the natural attraction of our intellect to phantasms]; and if natures eye cannot look upon the face of a twinkling Starre, how will it behold the brightnesse of a dazling Sunne? that general knowledge which it hath of God here is mixt with much error and deceit.

Nor can Faith look upon the divine essence; 'tis a lovely grace indeed, yet it must die in the Mount like *Moses;* it cannot enter into the Land of promise; 'tis [168] *auditui magis similis quam visioni*[26] [more like hearing than seeing], it hears the voice of its God, it does not see his face, it enflames the desire of the soul, it does not quench it, for men would faine see what they beleeve; the object of Faith is obscure and at a distance, but the face of God is all presence and brightnesse. Happinesse it consists in the noblest operation of an intellectual being, whereas in beleeving there is *imperfectissima operatio ex parte intellectus, licet sit perfectio ex parte objecti*[27] [a most imperfect operation on the part of the intellect, although there is perfection on the part of the object].

Nor yet is the divine essence seen in a way of demonstration, for then only a Philosopher should see his face, such only as had skil in Metaphysicks, who yet may be in misery for all that, for demonstrations are no beatifical visions. The damned spirits can demonstrate a Deity, and yet they are perpetually banisht from his face: there can be no demonstration of him *a priore,* for he is the first cause, and all demonstrations fetcht from such effects as flow from him, they do only shew you that he is, they do not open and display the divine essence, for they are not *effectus adaequantes virtutem causae*[28] [effects proportionate to the power of the cause]. To see God in the creatures, 'tis to see him veil'd, 'tis to see him clouded. The soul will not rest contented with such an imperfect knowledge of its God, it sees him thus here, and yet that does not hush and quiet rational desires, but does increase and inlarge them. Such things as last long, are perfected slowly, and such is happinesse; the knowledge of men here 'tis too green and crude, 'twon't ripen into happinesse, till the Sun shine upon it with its blessed and immediate beams. God therefore creates and prepares a *Lumen Gloriae*[29] [light of glory] for the soul, that is, such a supernatural disposition in an intellectual eye, by which 'tis clarified and fortified, and rightly prepared for the beholding the divine essence, which makes *Dionysius* the falsely supposed *Areopagite,* very fitly describe happinesse by this, 'tis στάσις ἐν θείῳ φωτὶ[30] [standing in the light of God], the souls sunning of it self in the *Lumen Gloriae*. Some will have that of the Psalmist to be sung in the praise of this light, *In lumine tuo videbimus lumen*[31] [in thy light shall we see light]. That Seraphical Prophet does thus most excellently represent it: *The Sunne shall be no more thy light by day, neither for brightnesse shall the Moone give light unto thee, but the Lord shall be unto thee an everlasting light, and thy God thy glory,* Isai. 60. v. 19.[32] You have it thus rendered in the Apocalypse: Καὶ ἡ πόλις οὐ χρείαν ἔχει τοῦ ἡλίου, οὐδὲ τῆς σελήνης ἵνα φαίνωσιν αὐτῇ. ἡ γὰρ δόξα τοῦ θεοῦ ἐφώτισεν αὐτήν[33] [And the city had no need of the sun, neither of the moon, to shine in it, for the glory of God did lighten it]. This *lumen gloriae,* which is *similitudo quaedam intellectus divini*[34] [a kind of reflection of the divine intellect] (as the Schoolmen speak,) this light 'tis not so much for the discovering of the object, (for that's an intellectual Sun cloathed with all perfection and brightnesse,) as [169] 'tis for the helping and advancing of a created understanding, which else would be too much opprest with the weight of glory; but yet this augmentation of the visive faculty of the soul, by the *Lumen Gloriae,* 'tis not *per intentionem virtutis naturalis,* but 'tis *per appositionem novae formae:* 'tis not the raising and screwing of nature higher, but 'tis the adding of a new supernatural disposition that may close with the divine essence; for as *Aquinas* has it, *Ipsa divina essentia copulatur intellectui, ut forma intelligibilis,*[35] humane understanding is as the matter accurately predisposed by the *Lumen Gloriae,* for the receiving of the divine essence, as an intelligible forme stamps an impression of it self upon it; it prints the soul with that *summum bonum* which it has so much long'd for.

So that though there be still an infinite disproportion between God and the creature *in esse naturali* [in nature], yet there is a fit and just proportion between them *in esse intelligibili* [in intellect]. Though an eye be enabled to behold the Sun, yet this does not make it all one with the Sun, but it keeps its own nature still as much as it did before.

Nor is this vision a comprehensive vision, for a finite being will never be able fully to graspe an infinite essence; 'tis true indeed, it sees the whole essence of God, not a piece of his face only, for all essence is indivisible, especially that most simple and pure essence of God himself, but the soul does not see it so clearly, and so strongly as God himself sees it; hence degrees of happinesse spring, for the *Lumen Gloriae* being variously shed amongst blessed souls, the larger measure they have of that, the brighter sight have they of the divine essence. Several men may look upon the same face, and yet some that have more sparkling eyes, or some that stand neerer may discerne it better; if a multitude of spectators were enabled to behold the Sunne, yet some of them that have a more strong and piercing eye might see it more cleerly then the rest. In this glasse of the divine essence glorified souls see all things else that conduce to their happinesse; as God by seeing himself the cause and fountain of beings, sees also all effects that come streaming from him; so these also looking upon the Sunne, must needs see his beams; they see the Sunne, and see other things by the Sun: they see there *omnium rerum genera & species* [the genera and species of all things], they there behold *virtutes, & ordinem universi*[36] [the powers and order of the universe]. Yet because they do not see the essence of God clearly and perfectly, (that is, comprehensively) so neither can they see all those treasures of mysterious wisdome, of unsearchable goodnesse, of un-limited power, that lie hid in the very depth of the divine essence. *Non vident possibilia, nec rationes rerum, nec ea quae dependent ex pura Dei vo-luntate*[37] [they do not see possible things, nor the reasons of things, nor those things which depend on the pure will of God], as the Schoolmen do well determine; yet all that a glorified understanding sees, it's in one twin-kling of its eye, for it sees all by one single *species,* by the divine [170] essence. It forgets its wrangling *Syllogismes,* it leaves its tardy *demonstrations* when it once comes to an intuitive knowledge. *Non movetur de uno intelligibili in aliud, sed quiescit in actu unico*[38] [it does not move from one intelligible to another, but rests in one act], for the state of happinesse is a Sabbatical state. The soul rests and fixes it self in one act of perpetual enjoyment, and by this participation of simultaneity it partakes of eternity, for that is *tota simul*[39] [all at once].

Whether this glorious happinesse be more principally situated in an act of the understanding, or of the will, I leave the *Thomists* and *Scotists* to discusse it; only this I will say in the behalfe of *Aquinas,* that the will can-not enjoy this happinesse any other wayes, then as 'tis a rational appetite.[40] For there is a blinde appetite of good in every being, which yet neither has nor can have such happinesse. As therefore the operations of the will, so the happinesse of the will also seemes to be subordinate to that of the un-derstanding. But it is enough for us that an intire soul, an whole rational being is united to its dearest, fairest, and supreme object in a way of pure intuitive speculation, in a way of sweetest love and fruition. Nor could nature of it self reach this, for an inferiour nature cannot thus unite it self to a superiour, but only by his indulgence raising it above it self.

This *Candle of the Lord* may shine here below, it may and doth aspire, and long for happinesse; but yet it will not come neere it, till he that lighted it up, be pleased to lift it up to himself, and there transforme it into a Starre, that may drink in everlasting light and influence from its original and fountain-light.

NOTES

In the following notes the expression "quoted in" indicates the editors' opinion that Culverwell drew the quotation from the secondary source named.

The Epistle Dedicatory

1. *Susceptours:* godfathers. OED discovers in Dillingham's use of the term the first example of the metaphoric meaning of supporter or maintainer.

To the Reader

1. Gen. 16:1–16.
2. See chap. 1, n. 19.
3. 1 Sam. 21:9.
4. 1 Tim. 6:16.

Courteous Reader

1. Nathaniel's younger brother, Richard, one of the first two Campden exhibitioners at St. Paul's School, followed him to Cambridge, receiving his B.A. in 1638 and his M.A. in 1642. He was ordained deacon in 1642, and priest in 1662. Richard was successively Fellow (1640), Tutor (1643–47), and Junior Dean (1645–46) of Trinity College. Although his medical history of hypochondria ("the ruines of a crazy body") was sufficiently complicated to be recorded by Dr. Pratt in 1645 (British Library: Sloane MS587, ff. 1–12), he subsequently became rector of Grundisburgh in Suffolk (1648) and survived until 1688.

2. Deut. 25:5–10.

3. See chap. 8, n. 16. Richard's letter continually echoes the text of the *Discourse;* only the more obvious instances have been noted.

4. An allusion to two passages in the New Testament which cite classical authors: Acts 17:28 (Aratus and Epimenides), and 1 Cor. 15:33 (Menander). Cf. chap. 11, n. 75.

5. Josh. 9:23.

6. Exod. 18:17–24.

7. After the capture of Jerusalem, Pompey is said to have entered the Temple and even the Holy of Holies. See Dion Cassius, *Roman History,* XXXVII, 15 and Josephus, *Jewish Wars,* XIV, 4.

8. The "court of the Gentiles" was the area of the temple at Jerusalem more frequently called "the outer court" (Ezek. 40:17). See Acts 17:28 and chap. 11, n. 75. Culverwell uses the expression on p. 188.

9. Rom. 1:19.

10. 1 Pet. 1:12.

11. Rom. 11:33.

12. See chap. 17, n. 34.

13. Phil. 3:14.

14. 1 Cor. 10:9.

15. Prov. 30:13.

16. *Compurgatours:* one who testifies to or vindicates another's innocence, veracity, or accuracy.

17. Rom. 11:33.

Chapter 1

1. The Vulgate reads "lucerna Domini spiraculum hominis," and the AV "the spirit of man is the candle of the Lord." Culverwell's use of the term "understanding" is apparently original, for it is not found in any of the chief English translations; however, his version receives support from the *Biblia Hebraica Eorundem Latina Interpretatio* brought out by Santes Pagninus in 1528: "Lucerna Domini mens hominis." (Pagninus' footnote advises that "mens" is "animus.") Culverwell quotes the Greek of the Septuagint correctly, and then provides the variant readings of subsequent translators of the second century. Aquila was a proselyte to Judaism who lived in the reign of Hadrian (117–38). His translation, which was extremely literal, appears to have been

designed to undermine the support which the Septuagint version gave to the views of the Christian church. Theodotion was also a Jewish proselyte, but he produced a free revision of the Septuagint rather than an independent translation. Symmachus reacted against the literalism of Aquila and attempted to express the sense of the Hebrew original rather than provide an exact verbal rendering. The researches of Origen in the following century brought to light three other anonymous translations, and these he added to his scholarly version of the Septuagint, *Hexaplorum Quae Supersunt.* In its six columns, the Hexapla contained (1) the Hebrew, (2) the Hebrew transliterated, (3) Aquila, (4) Symmachus, (5) the Septuagint and variants from the three minor translators, (6) Theodotion. See H. B. Swete, *An Introduction to the Old Testament in Greek,* rev. ed., 1914, 31–55, and 59–86. Much of this material was made available in Culverwell's period in the notes by Peter Morinus to the Roman edition of the Septuagint (Rome, 1587), and in J. Drusius, *Veterum Interpretum Graecorum in totum vetus Testamentum Fragmenta* (Arnheim, 1622). The relevant entry in Drusius' edition reads: "נר. A. Sym. Th. λύχνος: lucerna. caeteri. λαμπτήρ: fax sive lucerna."

2. Bacon, *The Advancement of Learning* (*Works,* III, 350): " . . . out of the contemplation of nature, or ground of human knowledges, to induce any verity or persuasion concerning the points of faith, is in my judgement not safe: *Da fidei quae fidei sunt* [give unto Faith that which is Faith's]: . . . we ought not to attempt to draw down or submit the mysteries of God to our reason; but contrariwise to raise and advance our reason to the divine truth." See also Bacon, *Works,* III, 218 and IV, 342.

3. Gen. 27. "If the understanding will not consent to a revelation, until it see a reason of the proposition, it does not obey at all, for it will not submit, till it cannot choose. In these cases Reason and Religion are like *Leah* and *Rachel:* Reason is fruitful indeed, and brings forth the first-born, but she is blear-ey'd, and oftentimes knows not the secrets of her Lord; but *Rachel* produces two children, *Faith* and *Piety,* and *Obedience* is *Midwife* to them both, and *Modesty* is the *Nurse.*" Jeremy Taylor, *Ductor Dubitantium* (London, 1660), 50. See note 11 below.

4. Luke 16:26.

5. Rom. 16:16; 1 Cor. 16:20; and elsewhere.

6. Cf. Ps. 85:10, and 169 below.

7. Gen. 1:16.

8. Faustus Socinus (1539–1604) was a Sienese nobleman who settled in Poland and became a spokesman for religious reform throughout Europe. The

faith which he and his friends evolved was marked by scripturalism and rationalism in about equal proportions. They held that the Bible was a complete and perfect revelation of the will of God, yet they also insisted that reason was necessary for the comprehension of this revelation. This emphasis on reason led them to deny two of the basic articles of traditional Christianity, the divinity and the atoning sacrifice of Christ. Apart from John Biddle and Paul Best, Socinianism found little militant support in England, but the Socinian literature which filtered into the country throughout the century had a pervasive effect. "Socinianism" became a term of reproach among orthodox divines—it was used against Chillingworth by Francis Cheynell and against Whichcote by Tuckney—and Culverwell wishes to dissociate his defense of reason from the more extreme rationalism of the continental writers. See H. J. McLachlan, *Socinianism in Seventeenth-Century England* (Oxford, 1951).

9. Dan. 4:33.

10. Rom. 8:22.

11. Gen. 29:17; AV has "tender eyed" but Douay "blear-eyed."

12. Deut. 24:1.

13. Acts 3:2; Ps. 84:10.

14. Ps. 55:14.

15. Rom. 1:20.

16. Pindar, *Olympian Odes*, VI, 4, 5.

17. A reference to Samuel Hoard, *Gods Love to Mankind* (London, 1633), which was answered by Bishop John Davenant, *Animadversions . . . upon a treatise intitled Gods Love to Mankind* (London, 1641). John Arrowsmith, Master of St. John's College and later of Trinity College, in a posthumous work edited by William Dillingham and Thomas Horton, *Armilla Catechetica* (Cambridge, 1659), 317, recommended Davenant's book in which "the reader will not onely meet with the doctrine of *Predestination* modestly handled, but also with ample satisfaction to most of those wicked cavils which flesh and bloud have been wont to suggest against it."

18. Culverwell is probably thinking of John Eaton's *Honey-comb of free Justification by Christ Alone* (London, 1642); Eaton, according to Ephraim Pagitt, *Heresiography* (London, 1645), 89, was "the first Antinomian among us." The remaining phrases appear to be merely characteristic slogans from the literature of left-wing Puritanism. Cf. William Prynne, *A Fresh Discovery of some Prodigious New Wandring-Blasing-Stars, & Firebrands, Stiling themselves New-Lights, Firing our Church and State into New Combustions* (London, 1645), 1: "those *New-Lights* and *Sectaries,* sprung up among us, who (being many of

them *Anabaptists*) have all new-christned themselves of late, by the common name of *Independents*," and the anonymous pamphlet, *A True and Perfect Picture . . . a Short View of the New-Lights that have Brake forth since Bishops Went Downe* (London, 1648).

19. 1 Sam. 17:26 and 51; Whichcote employs the story in a similar manner in his second letter to Tuckney: "I deserve as little to be called a Socinian, as David for extorting Goliath's sword out of his hand, and cutting the master's head off with it, did deserve to be esteemed a Philistine." Cf. Richard Hooker, *Of the Laws of Ecclesiastical Polity*, III, 8, x: "'The Word of God is a two-edged sword,' but in the hands of reasonable men; and Reason, as the weapon that slew Goliath, if they be as David was that use it."

20. Robert Francis Bellarmine (1542–1621) was a Jesuit theologian, writer, and cardinal. He held the chair of controversies at the Roman College, and his most influential work was *Disputationes de Controversiis Christianae Fidei*, 1586–93. A dispute with James I over the oath of allegiance made him well-known in England; his most serious English opponent in theological matters was William Whitaker.

21. Isa. 57:20.

22. Acts 19:28.

23. Acts 17:23; Charles Hotham in his *Ad Philosophiam Teutonicam Manuductio* (London, 1648, tr. 1650), an oration delivered at the commencement at Cambridge in 1647, addresses the members of the university and his fellow-students as "you noble Athenians."

24. As Dillingham observes in the preface "To the Reader," Culverwell did not live to complete this plan.

Chapter 2

1. 1 Sam. 10:23, Septuagint.

2. James 1:17.

3. Eccles. 1:14; AV translates "vexation of spirit" and the Vulgate "afflictio spiritus," but Culverwell's version (depastio spiritus) retains the literal sense of the Hebrew: "feeding on wind."

4. Compare Bacon's use of this story of Solomon and Prov. 20:27 in the first pages of *The Advancement of Learning* (*Works*, III, 265–66).

5. Prov. 3:17.

6. Eccles. 12:13.

7. Prov. 20:27: as the English and Latin translations suggest, Culverwell has reversed the order of the Hebrew words, although such a reversal would not give the meaning he indicates.

8. The linking of Prov. 20:27 with Gen. 2:7 is not unusual in Renaissance biblical commentaries; cf., e.g., Cornelius Jansen the Elder, *Commentaria in Proverbia Salomonis* (London, 1586), and Ralph Baynes, *In Proverbia Salomonis* (Paris, 1555), although it is rare in English commentaries of the early seventeenth century; but see Henry Ainsworth, *Annotations upon Genesis* (London, 1621).

9. This definition is quoted from Santes Pagninus, *Thesaurus Linguae Sanctae sive Lexicon Hebraicum* (Geneva, 1614), col. 1715. Culverwell relies mainly on this lexicon and its quotations from rabbinical sources in the following discussion of the various meanings of the three Hebrew words for soul: נשמה (neshamah), רוח (ruach), and נפש (nephesch).

10. Pagninus, *Thesaurus,* col. 1715: a popular false etymology repeated by Ainsworth, *Annotations,* sig. B4: "The *breath* here is in Hebrew Neshamah, which hath affinitie with *Shamajin heavens:* usually it signifieth eyther the breath of God or of men, not of other things: and so it is put for man's *minde,* or reasonable *soule* [Proverbs 20:27]. And this *Mind* is the *Lord's Candle, searching all the inward roomes of the belly.*" Cf. also Edward Leigh, *Critica Sacra* (London, 1642), s.v.

11. Pagninus, *Thesaurus,* cols. 1715 and 1658.

12. Acts 17:25, quoted in Pagninus, *Thesaurus,* col. 1715.

13. 1 Cor. 15:44, 45: "It is sown a natural body; it is raised a spiritual body. There is a natural body, and there is a spiritual body. And so it is written, The first man Adam was made a living soul, the last Adam was made a quickening spirit." Culverwell closely paraphrases Pagninus, *Thesaurus,* cols. 1659 and 1715; cf. Ainsworth, *Annotations,* sig. B4.

14. Culverwell may have discovered the names of the three souls in Valentine Schindler, *Lexicon Pentaglotton* (Frankfort, 1612), col. 1147.

15. Pagninus, *Thesaurus,* col. 2654.

16. See Pagninus, *Thesaurus,* col. 2654, and Schindler, *Lexicon,* cols. 1709–10: "Per metonymiam . . . *animae affectus,* seu *motus animi bonus* aut *malus.*" Cf. also Diogenes Laertius, *Lives,* VIII, 30: "The soul of man, he [Pythagoras] says, is divided into three parts, intelligence [νοῦς], reason [φρήν], and passion [θυμός]."

17. Pagninus, *Thesaurus,* col. 1715.

18. 2 Cor. 5:17.

19. In Prov. 20:27.

20. See Gen. 2:7 and Pagninus, *Thesaurus,* col. 1715; cf. n. 8 above.

21. Schindler, *Lexicon,* col. 1177; Culverwell repeats Schindler's use of Hebrew characters to express the Arabic phrase for "breath of life."

22. John Calvin, *Commentary on the First Book of Moses called Genesis,* tr. John King (Edinburgh, 1847), 112: "Whatever the greater part of the ancients might think, I do not hesitate to subscribe to the opinion of those who explain this passage of the animal life of man; and thus I expound what they call the vital spirit, by the word *breath* . . . here mention is made only of the lower faculty of the soul, which imparts breath to the body, and gives it vigour and motion. . . . Now we know that the powers of the human mind are many and various. Wherefore, there is nothing absurd in supposing that Moses here alludes only to one of them; but omits the intellectual part, of which mention has been made in the first chapter." Bacon comments on the same passage in *De Augmentis Scientiarum* (*Works,* IV, 396): "For touching the first generation of the rational soul, the Scripture says, 'He hath made man of the dust of the earth, and breathed into his nostrils the breath of life'; whereas the generation of the irrational soul, or that of the brutes, was effected by the words, 'Let the water bring forth, let the earth bring forth.' Now this soul (as it exists in man) is only the instrument of the rational soul, and has its origin like that of the brutes in the dust of the earth. For it is not said that 'He made the body of man of the dust of the earth,' but that 'He made man'; that is the entire man, excepting only the breath of life." See also Thomas Aquinas, *Summa Theologica,* I, qu. 75, art. 6.

Chapter 3

1. Thomas Bradwardine (ca. 1290–1359), Archbishop of Canterbury, author of *De Causa Dei contra Pelagium,* ed. H. Savile (London, 1618); he is appropriately linked here with Saint Augustine as a defender of the Christian doctrine of grace.

2. John Selden (1584–1654), *De Jure Naturali* (London, 1640); Hugo Grotius (1583–1645), *De Jure Belli ac Pacis* (Paris, 1625); Claudius Salmasius (1588–1653), *Epistola ad Andream Colvium, super Cap. xi primae ad Corinth. Epist. De Caesarie Virorum et Mulierum Coma* (Leiden, 1644). The dialogue *De Coma* was published at Leiden a year later and the two were sometimes bound together, as in the British Library copy.

3. Aristotle, *Physics,* II, i. Culverwell gives the Latin form of this definition just below: "*principium motus & quietis.*"

4. Thomas Aquinas, *Commentaria in Octo Physicorum Aristotelis Libros* (Venice, 1551), 16 (commentary on book II, chap. i).

5. Thomas Aquinas, *Summa Theologica,* I–II, qu. 91, art. 2: "Hence the Psalmist . . . in answer . . . says: *The light of thy countenance, O Lord, is signed upon us* thus implying that the light of natural reason, whereby we discern what is good and what is evil, which is the function of the natural law, is nothing else than an imprint on us of the Divine light."

6. Plutarch, *On the Pleasures of Philosophers,* 875B.

7. Plutarch, *Against Colotes,* 1111F.

8. Plato, *Laws,* X, 888E.

9. Plato, *The Sophist,* 265C.

10. Plato, *Laws,* X, 889A.

11. Ibid., 892B.

12. Ibid., 892D ff.

13. Ibid., 892B.

14. Ibid., 890D.

15. Plato, *The Sophist,* 265C.

16. Ps. 123:2.

17. 2 Peter 1:4.

18. Thomas Fowler's explanation of "natura naturans" in his edition of Bacon's *Novum Organum* (Oxford, 1889), 344, is worth repeating: "Natura Naturata is the actual condition of a given object or quality, or of the aggregate of all objects and qualities, the Universe, at any given time; Natura Naturans is the immanent cause of this condition, or aggregate of conditions, and is regarded as producing it by a continuous process. Hence, Natura Naturans is related to Natura Naturata as cause to effect." See also Thomas Aquinas, *Summa Theologica,* I–II, qu. 85, art. 6.

19. Plutarch, *On Affection for Offspring,* 495C.

20. A central principle of Aristotle's teleological philosophy; see, e.g., *On the Heavens,* II, xi.

21. Durandus of Saint-Pourcain (ca. 1270–1332), *In Petri Lombardi Sententias Theologicas Commentariorum,* II, dist. 1, qu. 5: "Utrum Deus agat immediate in omni actione creaturae." The metaphors of clock and organ are Culverwell's.

22. Cf. Sir Thomas Browne, *Religio Medici,* I, 16, 17; ed. L. C. Martin (Oxford, 1964), 15, 16: "Nor do I so forget God, as to adore the name of

Nature; which I define not with the Schooles, the principle of motion and rest, but, that streight and regular line, that setled and constant course the wisdome of God hath ordained the actions of his creatures, according to their severall kinds. . . . This is the ordinary and open way of his providence . . . there is another way full of Meanders and Labyrinths, . . . and that is a more particular and obscure method of his providence, directing the operations of individuals and single Essences; this we call Fortune, that serpentine and crooked line, whereby he drawes those actions his wisdome intends in a more unknowne and secret way."

23. Plutarch, *Symposiacs,* 732E.

24. Seneca, *De Beneficiis,* IV, 8.

25. See, e.g., Galen, *Of the Movement of Muscles* in *Medicorum Graecorum Opera,* ed. D. C. G. Kuhn (Leipzig, 1821–30), IV, 452, quoted in Grotius, *De Jure,* II, xii, 26 (2).

26. Aristotle, *Categories,* VIII, 9a.

27. Grotius comments on 1 Cor. 11:14 in *De Jure,* II, xii, 26 (2): "In this passage, and elsewhere at times, the law of nature has been used to designate that which is everywhere the accepted custom. So in the writings of the Apostle Paul nature herself is said to teach that it is disgraceful for a man to wear long hair, though nevertheless this is not repugnant to nature, and has been customary among many nations."

28. Salmasius, *Epistola ad Andream Colvium,* 718; 1 Cor. 11:14 is also discussed in *De Coma,* 51 ff.

Chapter 4

1. Thomas Aquinas, *Summa Theologica,* I–II, qu. 90, art. 1, quoted in Suárez, *De Legibus,* I, i, 1.

2. Rom. 8:2.

3. Rom. 7:23; the text is cited by Suárez, *De Legibus,* I, i, 3.

4. Suárez employs the phrase *lex fomitas* in *De Legibus,* I, i, 3, and refers the reader to Thomas Aquinas, *Summa Theologica,* I–II, qu. 90, art. 1, and qu. 90[91], art. 6.

5. This argument appears frequently in Suárez, *De Legibus;* see I, i, 5; II, xvii, 6; I, iii, 8: "'Law' is to be attributed to insensate things, not in its strict sense, but metaphorically. Not even brute animals are capable of law in a strict sense, since they have the use neither of reason nor of liberty; so that it is only

by a like metaphor that natural law may be ascribed to them." For the history of this idea, see E. Zilsel, "Genesis of the Concept of Physical Law," *Philosophical Review,* 51 (1942), 245–79.

6. Suárez, *De Legibus,* I, i, 5.

7. Plato, *Laws,* II; viewing music both literally and figuratively, Plato in the second book examines its role in education and maintains that "the criterion of music should be pleasure; not, however, the pleasure of any chance person; rather I should regard that music which pleases the best men and the highly educated as about the best, and as quite the best if it pleases the one man who excels all others in virtue and education."

8. Plato, *Minos* (also known as *De Legibus*), 318B.

9. Aristotle, *Problems,* XIX, 28.

10. Plato, *Minos,* 313B; the next three Greek quotations are from the following parts of the same source: 313C, 314E, 315A. Compare Cudworth's discussion of the same source in *A Treatise concerning Eternal and Immutable Morality* (London, 1731), 285.

11. ὂν ὄντων does not occur in Aristotle's works, nor is it likely to come from any other classical author. The Platonic ὂν ὄντως (true being), *Phaedrus* 247E and *The Sophist* 266E have probably combined with the biblical trope "king of kings" found in Deut. 10:17; Dan. 2:47; and 1 Tim. 6:15 to produce the idea and the phrase. Robert Burton attributes the Latin equivalent (ens entium) to Aristotle in *The Anatomy of Melancholy,* pt. III, sect. 4, memb. 1, subsect. 2.

12. Demosthenes, *Against Aristogeiton,* I, 16.

13. Plato, *Minos,* 317C.

14. James 2:8.

15. Plutarch, *To an Uneducated Ruler,* 780E.

16. Suárez, *De Legibus,* I, i, 6; Suárez provides a free paraphrase of Thomas Aquinas, *Summa Theologica,* I–II, qu. 96, art. 4.

17. See Suárez, *De Legibus,* II, iv, 4, and Thomas Aquinas, *Summa Theologica,* I–II, qu. 93, art. 3.

18. See the discussion in Plato, *Laws,* 662C–663B.

19. The image of the golden chain had its origin in Homer, *Iliad,* VIII, 18–27, and was given currency by Plato, *Theaetetus,* 153C. English writers could find it in Chaucer, *Knight's Tale* (I-A-2987–93). As a symbol of divine order the golden chain was popular in the seventeenth century, being used by Milton in *Prolusion* I, Sir Thomas Browne in *Religio Medici,* I, 18, Drummond of Hawthornden in *A Cypress Grove,* II, and twice by Bacon in *De Augmentis*

Scientiarum (*Works*, I, 525, 545, or IV, 322, 342). The first use of the image by Bacon may have been in Culverwell's mind: "Nor need we wonder if the horns of Pan reach even to the heaven, seeing that the transcendentals of nature, or universal ideas, do in a manner reach up to divinity. And hence the famous chain of Homer (that is, the chain of natural causes) was said to be fastened to the foot of Jupiter's throne."

20. This and the following Greek passage are from Plato, *Minos*, 317B and 316E, respectively.

21. See Plato, *Gorgias*, 488 ff.

22. Aristotle, *Rhetoric to Alexander*, I (1420a).

23. Thomas Aquinas, *Summa Theologica*, I–II, qu. 90, art. 4, quoted in Suárez, *De Legibus*, I, xii, 3.

24. Suárez, *De Legibus*, I, xii, 5.

25. Suárez provides a full discussion of this subject in *De Legibus*, I, iv, 5, and I, v, 22–25: "strictly speaking . . . the binding obligation imposed by law is derived from the will of the legislator."

26. Suárez, *De Legibus*, I, vii, 8.

27. The passage is from Horace, *Satires*, I, iii, 98, but Grotius in *De Jure*, Prolegomena, 16, claims that it expresses the view of Carneades. Culverwell, ignoring the note in which Grotius identifies the source of the words, attributes them to Carneades himself. Cf. Selden, *De Jure*, I, vi (81).

28. Judg. 9:14, 15.

29. Mal. 4:2.

30. Plutarch, *To an Uneducated Ruler*, 780F.

31. Ibid., 780F–781A.

32. Plato, *Minos*, 321C, which cites a phrase used by Homer, *Iliad*, II, 85, and elsewhere.

33. Amos 5:24.

34. Ahitophel spun a "web" of evil counsel in an attempt to catch David and Absalom (2 Sam. 16–17); Haman's "web" was a law for the persecution of the Jews which he persuaded King Ahasuerus to pass (Esther 3:8–15); Herod's "web" took the form of a plot to destroy the promised Messiah by slaughtering the children (Matt. 2:16).

35. Suetonius, *De Vita Caesarum*, V, *Flavius Domitianus*, 3: "In the beginning of his Empire his manner was, to retire himself daily into a secret place for one hour, and there to do nothing else but to catch flies and with the sharp point of a bodkin or writing steel prick them through." (Trans. Philemon Holland, 1606.)

36. Plato, *Laws*, I, 628C.

37. Aristotle, *Politics*, III, xi, 4–5.

38. Ibid., III, xi, 5–6.

39. A fragment by Epicharmus of Syracuse cited by Plutarch, *Moralia*, 98C, 336B, 961A. The phrase was popular with another Platonist of the period, Peter Sterry, who uses it in a manuscript now at Emmanuel College (MS 295, Pinto vii). The entire fragment reads, "The mind sees and the mind hears; everything else is deaf and blind."

40. Suárez, *De Legibus*, I, iv, 6.

41. The hieroglyphic is described by Plutarch, *Of Isis and Osiris*, 10, and discussed by Macrobius, *Saturnalia*, I, 12. Erasmus employs the figure in *Of the Education of a Christian Prince*, ed. L. K. Born (New York, 1965), 186.

42. Homer, *Iliad*, XVIII, 250: "Then among them wise Polydamus was first to speak, the son of Penthous, for he alone looked at once before and behind."

43. This and the two following Greek passages are from Plato, *Laws*, I, 645A.

44. See Suárez, *De Legibus*, I, vii–viii.

45. See ibid., I, xi, and I, iv, 12: "it is still needful to state that, with respect to the command of one person over another the only necessary requisite, following the act of will on the part of the lawmaker . . . is that the lawmaker should manifest, indicate or intimate this decree and judgment of his, to the subjects to whom the law itself relates."

Chapter 5

1. Thomas Aquinas, *Summa Theologica*, I–II, qu. 91, art. 2, quoted in Suárez, *De Legibus*, I, iii, 9.

2. Suárez, *De Legibus*, II, i, 1: "ab aeterno solum fuit Deus."

3. Job 38:11; quoted in Suárez, *De Legibus*, I, i, 2; II, ii, 10; and II, iii, 7.

4. Terms drawn from Plato and the neo-Platonists are joined here with newly coined words (Νομοειδεῖς) and echoes of the New Testament (James 2:8: Royal Law), to summarize an idealist view of law. See, e.g., Plato, *Cratylus*, 401D, *Laws*, 777D, and Plotinus, *Enneads*, III, i, 8, 8 and I, viii, 13, 11, and n. 63 in chap. 17.

5. Luke 11:27.

6. Gen. 49:3.

7. Rom. 1:20.

8. Suárez, *De Legibus,* II, i, 3.

9. Cicero, *De Legibus,* II, iv, 8, quoted in Suárez, *De Legibus,* II, i, 2, and Selden, *De Jure,* I, viii (95–96).

10. Plutarch, *To an Uneducated Ruler,* 781B.

11. Dan. 7:9, 13.

12. Plato, *Minos,* 319D and 320D; in the second passage the phrase is attributed to Hesiod, although it does not occur in our text of Hesiod and is not quoted by any other writer.

13. Ps. 45:7.

14. Exod. 34.

15. Thomas Aquinas, the "Angelic Doctor," and Bonaventure, the "Seraphic Doctor."

16. Suárez, *De Legibus,* II, i, 3.

17. Ibid., II, ii, 5, 9: "God is not subject to it; on the contrary, He remains always exempt from law, so that He is able to act as He wills. . . . "

18. The idea is found in Suárez, *De Legibus,* II, ii, 10–12, and II, iv, 1; see also Thomas Aquinas, *Summa Theologica,* I–II, qu. 93, art. 5, 6.

19. Augustine, *De Civitate Dei,* II, xix, quoted in Suárez, *De Legibus,* II, iii, 6.

20. See Suárez, *De Legibus,* II, ii, 9 and II, iii, 3, 10: "law consists in a decree of the [divine] will . . . an idea . . . resides in the intellect . . . an idea has only the character of an exemplar in relation to God himself, so that He works in accordance with it, while it serves (so to speak) merely as a concrete pattern for the works of God; whereas the divine law as law has rather a dynamic character, giving rise to an inclination or obligation to action."

21. Thomas Aquinas, *De Veritate,* qu. 5, art. 1, ad. 6, as quoted and paraphrased in Suárez, *De Legibus,* II, iii, 12.

22. Suárez, *De Legibus,* II, iii, 12.

23. See, e.g., ibid., II, i, 9, and II, iv, 10: "regarded strictly, as being eternal, it [the eternal law] cannot be said actually to bind; but it may be said to have a potentially binding character (if we explain the matter thus), or to suffice of itself for the imposition of a binding obligation. . . . Thus it also follows that the eternal law never binds through itself and apart from every other law, and that, on the contrary, it must necessarily be united with some other law in order actually to bind."

24. James 1:17.

25. Rom. 2:15.

Chapter 6

1. Culverwell quotes Suárez's paraphrase (*De Legibus*, II, xvii, 3) of the *Institutes* of Justinian, I, ii, and the *Digest* of Justinian, I, i, 3.

2. Culverwell quotes Selden's reference to Justinian's *Digest*, I, i, 3, 4 and paraphrases Selden's reflections upon it: Selden, *De Jure*, I, iv (43).

3. The lawyers' distinction between the law of nature and the law of nations is discussed in Suárez, *De Legibus*, II, xvii, 3, and in Selden, *De Jure*, I, v (60).

4. Rom. 2:15.

5. Rom. 1:20.

6. Aristotle, *On the History of Animals*, IX, vii.

7. Cicero, *De Finibus Bonorum et Malorum*, II, 110 (chap. 33).

8. Aristotle, *Nicomachean Ethics*, X, ii, 1.

9. Suárez, *De Legibus*, II, xvii, 6, 7.

10. Ps. 19:1.

11. Almost certainly a punning reference to Archbishop Laud, who had been executed January 10, 1645, the previous year.

12. Hesiod, *Works and Days*, 276–79, quoted in Grotius, *De Jure*, I, i, 11 (1).

13. Ovid, *Metamorphoses*, X, 324–28, quoted in Selden, *De Jure*, I, v (69).

14. Juvenal, *Satires*, XV, 146–49, quoted in Grotius, *De Jure*, I, i, 11 (1), note.

15. Cf. chap. 2, 20 above.

16. Cicero, *Pro Milone*, iv, 10.

17. Grotius, *De Jure*, II, xxi, 11 (3), quoted in Selden, *De Jure*, I, iv (59), where Culverwell found it.

18. *Ecloga Basilicorum*, II, 131 (126), quoted in Selden, *De Jure*, I, iv (57).

19. Grotius, *De Jure*, II, xx, 1 (1).

20. Eustathius, *On the Odyssey*, I, 318 and XII, 382, quoted in Selden, *De Jure*, I, iv (57).

21. See Selden, *De Jure*, I, iv (50–51).

22. Selden, *De Jure*, I, iv (53 ff.).

23. Selden, in *De Jure*, I, iv (56), quotes this passage from Maimonides, *Guide of the Perplexed*, III, xl, in which Exod. 21:28, 29 is cited and discussed.

24. Josephus, *Antiquities of the Jews*, IV, 281, paraphrased in Selden, *De Jure*, I, iv (56); Selden's interpretation is quoted next.

25. 1 Cor. 9:9.

26. Suárez, *De Legibus*, II, ii, 11.

27. Plato, *Gorgias*, 486A, and *Laws*, XI, 934A, quoted in Grotius, *De Jure*, II, xx, 4 (1) and (3).

28. Seneca, *De Ira,* I, xix, quoted in Grotius, *De Jure,* II, xx, 4 (1).

29. "in compensationem ... in emendationem ... in exemplum"; see Grotius, *De Jure,* II, xx, 6 (1), and Selden, *De Jure,* I, iv (57).

30. Clement of Alexandria, *Tutor,* I, viii, 70, quoted in Grotius, *De Jure,* II, xx, 6 (1).

31. Plutarch, *On the Delayed Vengeance of the Deity,* IV, xvi, 550A–559F, quoted in Grotius, *De Jure,* II, xx, 6 (2).

32. Hierocles, *On the Golden Verses of Pythagoras,* 27–29, quoted in Grotius, *De Jure,* II, xx, 1 (2).

33. Demosthenes, *Orations,* lix, 77, quoted in Grotius, *De Jure,* II, xx, 9 (1).

34. Deut. 31:12.

35. Grotius, *De Jure,* II, xx, 9 (1).

36. Seneca, *De Ira,* II, 26, quoted in Grotius, *De Jure,* II, xx, 5 (1).

37. Grotius, *De Jure,* I, i, 10 (1).

38. St. John Chrysostom, *On the Statues,* xiii (Migne, XLIX, col. 131). Selden's quotation of this homily in *De Jure,* I, viii (100), may well have sent Culverwell to the original text, from which he continues to draw.

39. Chrysostom, *On the Statues,* xiii (Migne, XLIX, col. 140).

40. Ibid., xii (Migne, XLIX, col. 132).

41. Ibid., xii (Migne, XLIX, col. 132).

42. Gen. 5:22.

43. 2 Pet. 2:5.

44. Exod. 9:27.

45. Chrysostom, *On the Statues,* xii (Migne, XLIX, col. 132).

46. Plutarch uses σφυρήλατος (wrought with a hammer) of friendship in *How to Tell a Flatterer from a Friend,* 65C; as Culverwell's remark suggests, he does not apply it directly to law.

47. Philo, *That Every Virtuous Man Is Free,* vii, 46–47, quoted in Grotius, *De Jure,* I, i, 10 (1).

48. I Tim. 3:15.

49. Plutarch, *To an Uneducated Ruler,* 780C.

50. These lines from Pindar, Frag. 169 (151), are quoted in Plato's *Gorgias,* 484B, from which the following discussion is drawn.

51. Plato, *Gorgias,* 482E; in the next three sentences Culverwell summarizes and paraphrases the discussion in 482E–488E.

52. Plato, *Republic,* II, 365D.

53. These four quotations are taken from Aristotle, *The Art of Rhetoric,* I, x, 3, and are quoted in Selden, *De Jure,* I, vi (75).

54. Aristotle, *Nicomachean Ethics*, X, ix, 12.

55. Aristotle, *Politics*, III, xi, 6; Culverwell's reference to the tenth book of *De Rep. (Nicomachean Ethics)* is incorrect.

56. Aristotle, *The Art of Rhetoric*, I, x, 3.

57. Rom. 2:15 and Aristotle, *Nicomachean Ethics*, X, ix, 14.

58. Cicero, *Pro Milone*, iv, 10.

59. Cicero, *De Legibus*, II, iv, 10, quoted in Selden, *De Jure*, I, viii (96).

60. Cicero, *De Republica*, III, 22, quoted in both Selden, *De Jure*, I, viii (96) and (in part) in Suárez, *De Legibus*, II, v, 11, and referred to in Grotius, *De Jure*, I, i, 10 (1), note.

61. Heb. 13:8.

62. Rom. 9:5.

63. Rom. 2:15.

64. The Latin phrase is, in fact, that of Suárez (*De Legibus*, II, v, 4); Culverwell simply repeats Suárez's summary (*De Legibus*, II, v, 2) of the argument of the Jesuit Gabriel Vasquez in his commentary (disp. 150, chap. iii) on Thomas Aquinas, *Summa Theologica*, I–II, qu. 90.

65. Suárez, *De Legibus*, II, vi, 3, summarizes Gregory of Rimini, *On the Sentences*, II, dist. xxxiv, qu. 1, art. 2.

66. Acts 17:28.

67. Suárez, *De Legibus*, II, x, 1.

68. Ibid., II, vi, 11.

69. Ibid., II, vi, 11.

70. Rom. 4:15, quoted in Suárez, *De Legibus*, II, v, 2 and II, vi, 7.

71. Suárez, *De Legibus*, II, vi, 11.

72. Ibid., II, v, 6: " . . . consequently, although the rational nature is the foundation of the objective goodness of the moral actions of human beings, it may not for that reason be termed law."

73. Suárez, *De Legibus*, II, vi, 23.

74. Ibid., II, vi, 12.

75. Culverwell is probably paraphrasing Suárez, *De Legibus*, II, ix, 3.

76. Suárez, *De Legibus*, II, xii, 1.

Chapter 7

1. See *Timaeus* 90A for the Platonic image of the inverted tree and *Of the Parts of Animals*, IV, 10, for Aristotle's version. A. B. Chalmers reviews the

history of this metaphor in "'I Was But an Inverted Tree': Notes towards the History of an Idea," *Studies in the Renaissance,* VIII, 291–99. Marvell's "Upon Appleton House," LXXI, makes use of the image.

2. These examples of first principles appear to be borrowed from Suárez, *De Legibus,* II, vii, 2; for the last one see Matt. 7:12.

3. Culverwell probably drew upon Selden's quotation in *De Jure,* I, ii (33), of a passage from Epictetus in which προλήψεις occurs and is translated by Selden as "anticipationis." Seneca's term for the same concept is found in his *Epistulae Morales,* 117, 6; the sentence containing it is quoted by Grotius, *De Jure,* II, xx, 46 (3), note.

4. Rom. 2:15.

5. Matt. 5:18.

6. αἱ Σποράδες are the islands off the west coast of Asia Minor; hence the transliterated word "sporades" means small, scattered bodies.

7. The phrase "crop the tops" is an echo of Pindar, *Olympian Odes,* I, 13; Culverwell quotes it in Greek in chap. 17, 174, and seems to have had it in mind in chap. 2, 19.

8. Edward Herbert, *De Veritate* (London, 1633), 113, 122. Since one of Culverwell's later quotations from this work (see chap. 11, n. 24) can be traced directly to the second edition of 1633, page numbers in the notes refer to that edition and not to the first (Paris, 1624).

9. Matt. 23:5.

10. Aristotle, *Nicomachean Ethics,* X, ix, 22, quoted in Selden, *De Jure,* I, i (3).

11. Culverwell echoes Selden, *De Jure,* I, i (2).

12. Both sets of examples are quoted from Suárez, *De Legibus,* II, vii, 5.

13. See Suárez, *De Legibus,* II, vii, 5. Culverwell substitutes falsehood for the original example of adultery and thus confuses one of Suárez's distinctions.

14. Herbert, *De Veritate,* 152–53.

15. This and the two subsequent Latin quotations are from Suárez, *De Legibus,* II, vii, 7.

16. See ibid., II, ix, 2: "legem naturalem obligare in conscientia."

17. Herbert, *De Veritate,* 104–5.

18. Suárez, *De Legibus,* II, v, 15; the following paragraph is a paraphrased version of this section of Suárez's work.

19. Ibid., II, x, chapter title.

20. See ibid., II, xii, 5.

21. Ibid., II, xii, 4.

22. See ibid., II, xii, 5.

23. Ibid., II, xvi, chapter title; Suárez uses the phrase "emendatio legis" in sections 9 and 13 of this chapter.

24. Ibid., II, xvi, 16.

25. A paraphrase of Suárez, *De Legibus,* II, xvii, 1.

26. See ibid., II xx, 7.

27. Grotius, *De Jure,* I, i, 14 (1).

28. See Suárez, *De Legibus,* II, xix, 5, 6: "autem jus gentium scriptum non esse."

29. Dio Chrysostom, *Orations,* LXXVI, quoted in Grotius, *De Jure,* I, i, 14 (2).

30. Justinian, *Institutes,* I, ii, 2, quoted in Suárez, *De Legibus,* II, xix, 6.

31. Cicero, *De Legibus,* II, 4, 9.

32. Culverwell found these Hebrew terms in Grotius, *De Jure,* I, i, 9 (2), where reference is correctly made to Maimonides, *Guide of the Perplexed,* III, xxvi.

33. *The Apostolical Constitutions,* I, 6, quoted in Selden, *De Jure,* I, iii (38).

34. Cf. Grotius, *De Jure,* I, i, 9 (2).

35. Both Greek terms (ἐντολαί and δικαιώματα) are attributed to "the Hellenists" by Grotius, *De Jure,* I, i, 9 (2); the Septuagint provides a number of examples of their use: Gen. 26:5; Exod. 15:26; Deut. 4:40.

36. For an example of such usage see Aristotle, *Nicomachean Ethics,* V, vii, 7; Grotius, in *De Jure,* I, i, 9 (2), refers to Aristotle and quotes one of the two phrases.

Chapter 8

1. Rom. 2:15.

2. The Schoolmen follow the Vulgate translation of Ps. 4:6, which Culverwell quotes below. See Suárez, *De Legibus,* I, iii, 9; Thomas Aquinas, *Summa Theologica,* I–II, qu. 91, art. 2, and Robert Bellarmine, *Explanatio in Psalmos* (London, 1611), 21.

3. Culverwell has Selden in mind; cf. *De Jure,* I, viii (102) and I, ix (116).

4. Ps. 4:6.

5. Ps. 4:6 (Vulgate 4:7).

6. Dionysius of Richel (the Carthusian), 1402–71, in his commentary on Prov. 20:27; Dionysius has been called "the last scholastic." *Enarrationes piae*

ac eruditae in quinque libros Sapientalis (Cologne, 1539), folio XLIX, v: "De quo lumine fertur in Psalmo: Signatum est super nos lumen vultus tui domine, quia hoc lumen naturale est quoddam signaculum atque impressio increatae lucis in anima. Porro anima appellatur spiraculum, juxta illud Geneseos: Inspiravit in faciem eius spiraculum vitae."

7. Culverwell quotes from the Greek translations of the OT by Aquila, who completed his version in 140, and Symmachus (late second century). See chap. 1, n. 1, and C. A. Briggs and E. G. Briggs, *A Critical and Exegetical Commentary on the Book of Psalms* (Edinburgh, 1906), I, 36.

8. This appears to be Culverwell's imaginative rendering of Ps. 4:7: "Thou has put gladness in my heart, more than in the time that their corn and their wine increased."

9. A phrase which Culverwell found in Selden, *De Jure,* sig. a4 (and elsewhere). The discussion of the Jewish view of the light of nature is in Selden, *De Jure,* I, ix (109–17). Selden's acceptance of Jewish claims to exclusive knowledge of the light of nature probably led Culverwell to include this chapter of the *Discourse.*

10. Mal. 3:17, and 1 Pet. 2:9; Selden quotes the Hebrew in *De Jure,* I, i (10).

11. Rom. 3:1, 2.

12. Gen. 6:5; this expression is commented upon by John Smith in his *Select Discourses* (London, 1660), 398: "We may say of that *Self-will* which is lodg'd in the heart of a wicked man, as the Jews speak of the . . . *figmentum malum*— so often mention'd in their Writings, that it is . . . the Prince of death and darkness. . . . This is the very heart of the old *Adam* that is within men."

13. See Rom. 2:15 and Prov. 7:3.

14. Mal. 3:17.

15. Theodoret, *Curatio Graecarum Affectionum,* 91, 5, quoted in Selden, *De Jure,* I, ii (16).

16. See Selden, *De Jure,* I, ii (17 ff.), who repeats Numenius' apothegm (Eusebius, *Preparation for the Gospel,* XI, x): "Quid enim est Plato aliud, quam Moses Attica lingua loquens?"

17. Rom. 2:15.

18. Pythagoras, *The Golden Verses,* 63, 64.

19. Hierocles, *On the Golden Verses of Pythagoras,* 64.

20. Selden tells the story in *De Jure,* I, ii (14).

21. See chap. 4, n. 11.

22. Eusebius (*Preparation for the Gospel,* IX, x) preserved these lines of Porphyry which Selden quotes in *De Jure,* I, ii (25).

23. Rom. 3:2.

24. From the anonymous *Life of Pythagoras,* 22 (66) in Iamblichus, *Vita Pythagorica,* ed. M. Theophilus Kiessling (Leipzig, 1815–16), II, 120, quoted in Selden, *De Jure,* I, ii (26–27).

25. Sir Thomas Browne, *Pseudodoxia Epidemica,* VI, i: "So did the Athenians term themselves αὐτόχθονες or Aborigines. . . . There was therefore never Autochthon or man arising from the earth, but Adam." See, e.g., Euripides, *Ion,* 520.

26. Plato, *Timaeus,* 22B, quoted in Selden, *De Jure,* I, ii (27), and in Bacon, *Novum Organum* (*Works,* I, 182).

27. See chap. 6, 48, and n. 41.

28. Rom. 3:29.

29. Col. 3:11.

Chapter 9

1. Pythagoras, *The Golden Verses,* 14.

2. Hierocles, *On the Golden Verses of Pythagoras,* 13–16.

3. Pythagoras, *The Golden Verses,* 29.

4. Hierocles, *On the Golden Verses of Pythagoras,* 29. Part of this passage is quoted in Selden, *De Jure,* I, viii (97).

5. Recorded by Epictetus, *Enchiridion,* 51.

6. Cicero, *De Legibus,* I, xvi, 44, quoted in Selden, *De Jure,* I, vii (87).

7. Marcus Aurelius Antoninus, *Meditations,* VII, 11: "To a rational creature the same act is at once according to nature and according to reason." The idea that living according to reason is obeying the gods appears frequently in the *Meditations,* as in I, 17.

8. Sextus Empiricus (circa A.D. 200) is the main authority for the history and doctrine of the Sceptics. Little is known about his life except that he was a Greek physician who succeeded Herodotus as head of the Sceptic School. His main works are *Outlines of Pyrrhonism, Against the Dogmatists, Against the Schoolmasters;* Culverwell draws heavily on the first of these books in chap. 14.

9. Selden, *De Jure,* I, ix (109); the passage expresses a view which Selden rejects.

10. *Plerophory:* full assurance or certainty. Common in the seventeenth century in theological use, this word finds its Greek original in Heb. 6:11; 10:22, and elsewhere.

11. This phrase is used by Bacon in *De Augmentis Scientiarum* (*Works,* I, 664, 839) to identify one of the deficiencies of learning: "it is possible for a man in a greater or less degree to revisit his own knowledge, and trace over again the footsteps both of his cognition and consent; and by that means to transplant it into another mind just as it grew in his own . . . if you will have the sciences grow, you need not much care about the body of the tree; only look well to this, that the roots be taken up uninjured, and with a little earth adhering to them . . . which kind of transmission . . . I note . . . as deficient, and term it the *Handing on of the Lamp,* or Method of Delivery to Posterity." (*Works,* IV, 449–50.)

12. Rom. 2:15.

13. The idea of the *intellectus agens* was elaborated in Avicenna's treatise *De Anima* and in the commentaries of both Avicenna and Averroes on Aristotle's *Metaphysics* and his work *On the Soul.* The Jewish philosopher Maimonides examines the doctrine at length in his *Guide of the Perplexed;* it is treated by the Schoolmen, particularly Thomas Aquinas in *Summa Theologica,* I, qu. 79, art. 4 and *Summa Contra Gentiles,* II, lix, by Bonaventura in *Expositio in Quattuor Libros Sententiarum,* II, dist. 24, qu. 4, and by Albertus Magnus, *Summa de Creaturis,* II, "Seu de homine"; Renaissance treatments of the subject can be found in J. C. Scaliger, *De Subtilitate,* cccviii, Selden, *De Jure,* I, ix, and Zabarella, *De Mente Agente.* In 1627 Fortunius Licetus offered an exhaustive survey in his *De Intellectu Agente.* Culverwell, although acknowledging the Arabians, draws his material largely from Selden, Maimonides, and Scaliger. Modern comment is to be found in Ernest Renan, *Averroes et l'Averroisme* (1852), 115 ff., and it is considered in the articles under "Avicenna" and "Averroes" in *Hastings' Encyclopedia of Religion and Ethics.* Isaac Husik, in *A History of Medieval Jewish Philosophy* (1916), provides the following account of the traditional view: "As the influence of the Arab Aristotelians, Alfarbi, Avicenna and especially Averroes, began to make itself felt, the discussions about the Active Intellect and its relation to the higher Intelligences on the one hand and to the human intellect on the other found their way also among the Jews and had their effect on the conception of prophecy. Aristotle's distinction of an active and a passive intellect in man, and his ideas about the spheral spirits as pure Intelligences endowing the heavenly spheres with their motions, were combined by the Arabian Aristotelians with the Neo-Platonic theory of emanation. The result was that they adopted as Aristotelian the view that from God emanated in succession ten Intelligences and their spheres. . . . From the Intelligence of the lunar sphere emanated the

Active Intellect. ... The Intelligences were identified with the angels of Scripture. ... The conversion of sense experience into immaterial concepts is accomplished through the aid of the Active Intellect. And at the end of the process a new intellect is produced in man, the Acquired Intellect. This alone is the immortal part in man and theoretical study creates it" (xlvi–xlvii). On the division of the understanding into "agent and patient," Robert Burton is illuminating: "The agent is that which is called the wit of man, acumen or subtlety, sharpness of invention, when he doth invent of himself without a teacher, or learns anew, which abstracts those intelligible species from the phantasy, and transfers them to passive understanding, 'because there is nothing in the understanding which was not first in the sense.' That which the imagination has taken from the sense, this agent judgeth of, whether it be true or false; and being so judged he commits it to the passible to be kept. This agent is a doctor or teacher, the passive a scholar; and his office is to keep and farther judge of such things as are committed to his charge; as a bare and razed table at first, capable of all forms and notions." (*The Anatomy of Melancholy,* pt. I, sec. 1, memb. 2, subsec. 10.)

14. Jacobus Zabarella discusses this topic in *De Mente Humana, De Speciebus Intelligibus,* and *De Mente Agente,* works which are contained in his *De Rebus Naturalibus* (1604). See particularly chap. x of *De Mente Agente* entitled "Confutatio omnium opinionum eorum, qui dicunt intellectum agentum et intellectum patientem esse unam et eandem substantiam."

15. J. C. Scaliger, *Exotericarum Exercitationum Liber XV De Subtilitate Ad Hieronymum Cardanum* (Paris, 1557), Exer. cccvii, 14. Although Scaliger's work was popular at Cambridge, Culverwell may have been led to this exercitation by Selden, who refers to it in *De Jure,* I, ix (n. 116).

16. Quoted in Scaliger, *De Subtilitate,* cccvii, 30; the entire section is a refutation of Cardan's "brutish tenet" concerning the *intellectus agens.*

17. Scaliger, *De Subtilitate,* cccvii, 18; Culverwell varies the list, adding "printing" and substituting "Pyxis Nautica" for "navigationis."

18. No exact source has been found for this view, but it follows logically from Maimonides' position concerning revelation: "All the prophets prophesied through the instrumentality of an angel; therefore what they saw, they saw in a parable and enigma. Not so our master Moses; for it was said of him, Mouth to mouth will I speak with him." *De Fundamentis Leges* (Amsterdam, 1638), VII, 7.

19. Maimonides, *Guide of the Perplexed,* II, vi.

20. In *De Subtilitate,* cccvii, 18. Scaliger cites this phrase from Averroes's commentary on the *Metaphysics* of Aristotle.

21. So Selden observes, *De Jure,* I, ix (116).

22. Maimonides, *Guide of the Perplexed,* II, iv, vi, xii; III, lii; see also Selden, *De Jure,* I, ix (110).

23. Ps. 36:9 (Vulgate 35:9). Maimonides comments on this passage in *Guide of the Perplexed,* II, xii. For the view of the Schoolmen see Thomas Aquinas, *In Psalmos Davidis Expositio Area,* Ps. 35, "Tertium est lumen gloriae," *Summa contra Gentiles,* III, liii, and Robert Bellarmine, *Explanatio in Psalmos.* See also chap. 18, n. 31. Selden, too, comments on this subject in *De Jure,* I, ix (110).

24. See Zabarella, *De Mente Agente,* xiii–xiv, xvi.

25. Quoted in Selden, *De Jure,* I, ix (114).

26. See n. 16 above.

27. The theory that the *intellectus agens* and *patiens* are aspects of the same soul is argued by Zabarella, *De Mente Agente,* x; see also Aristotle, *On the Soul,* III, v–viii.

28. On this vexed subject, see Zabarella, *De Speciebus Intelligibus,* v.

Chapter 10

1. Aristotle, *The Art of Rhetoric,* I, xiii, 2, and xv, 3, quoted in Selden, *De Jure,* I, vi (75).

2. Grotius, *De Jure,* I, i, 12 (1).

3. Acts 2:8–11.

4. Aristotle, *Nicomachean Ethics,* V, vii, 2.

5. Aristotle, *Physics,* II, viii.

6. Hesiod, *Works and Days,* 763–64, quoted in Grotius, *De Jure,* I, i, 12 (2).

7. Seneca, *Epistulae Morales,* 117, 6, quoted in Selden, *De Jure,* I, vi (76).

8. Cicero, *Tusculanarum Disputationum,* I, xiii, quoted in Selden, *De Jure,* I, vi (76).

9. Quintilian, *Institutionis Oratoriae,* V, x, 12, quoted in Grotius, *De Jure,* I, i, 12 (2).

10. Aristotle, *Eudemian Ethics,* I, vi, quoted in Grotius, *De Jure,* I, i, 12 (2).

11. Attributed to Heraclitus by Sextus Empiricus, *Against the Mathematicians,* vii, 34 (bk. IV of *Against the Schoolmasters*), and quoted in Grotius, *De Jure,* I, i, 12 (2).

12. Tertullian, *Prescriptione adversus Haereticos,* xxviii, quoted in Grotius, *De Jure,* I, i, 12 (2).

13. Mat. 7:6.

14. Culverwell's imagery echoes a passage from Andronicus of Rhodes quoted in Grotius, *De Jure,* I, i, 12 (2).

15. Aristotle, *Politics,* I, i, 8; *Topics,* V, 2.

16. Philo, *On the Ten Commandments,* xxv. In Grotius's notes to *De Jure,* I, i, 12 (2), however, the passage appears immediately after a citation from Chrysostom, *On the Statues,* Homily xi; Culverwell has mistakenly attributed the words of the Jewish philospher to the "sacred orator."

17. The Hebrew term is employed in Selden, *De Jure,* I, x (119).

18. Isa. 40:15.

19. Selden, *De Jure,* I, vi (75), chapter heading and opening sentence.

20. Ibid., I, vi (78).

21. Rom. 2:15.

22. Aristotle, *Nicomachean Ethics,* VII, v, 6, quoted in Selden, *De Jure,* I, vi (79).

23. The idea is found in Grotius, *De Jure,* I, i, 12 (1); the passage is quoted above, 80.

24. Salmasius, *Epistola ad Andream Colvium,* 715–16.

25. Rom. 2:15.

26. Aristotle, *Politics,* VIII, iii, 4, quoted in Selden, *De Jure,* I, vi (79).

Chapter 11

1. The Greek phrase occurs in the Nicene creed; see A. E. Burn, *An Introduction to the Creeds* (London, 1889), 79, 102.

2. The Latin phrase was probably suggested to Culverwell by bk. IX, chap. xvii (175 v) of *De Perenni Philosophia* (Lyon, 1540), by Augustinus Steuchus (1496–1549), also called Eugubinus. Culverwell drew many of the classical quotations in the present chapter from Steuchus's work, which was an impressive attempt to reconcile ancient philosophy and Christianity. Page numbers in the notes refer to the Venice edition (1590) of the *Opera Omnia,* vol. II.

3. Horace, *Sermonum,* II, ii, 79; although theologians were wary of the implications of the metaphor, this was a favourite quotation in discussions of the soul. Cf., e.g., Alexander Ross, *The Philosophicall Touch-stone* (London,

1645), 101 and Cornelius a Lapide, *Commentaria in Pentateuchum* (Antwerp, 1623), 68.

4. Plato, *Phaedo*, 75D.

5. Rom. 2:15.

6. See Origen, *On First Principles*, II, x; Thomas Aquinas refers to Origen's revision of Plato's theory in *Summa contra Gentiles*, II, xliv, lxxxiii.

7. Thomas Aquinas, *Summa contra Gentiles*, II, lxxxiii, lvii.

8. Plato, *Phaedo*, 77B, C; 75C.

9. See chap. 8, n. 9.

10. See n. 65 below.

11. A summarizing phrase (not in Aristotle's text) for the idea expressed in *On the Soul*, III, iv: "This would be in the same sense as when we say that a tablet which is empty is potentially written upon; which actually occurs in the case of the mind." For *abrasa tabula* see Thomas Aquinas, *Summa Theologica*, I, qu. 89, art. 1; and John Locke, *Essay concerning Human Understanding*, II, i, 2.

12. Persius, *Satires*, III, 1–3.

13. See the epistemological discussion of the active and passive mind in Aristotle, *On the Soul*, III, v–viii.

14. Culverwell's argument here parallels that of Thomas Aquinas (*Summa contra Gentiles*, II, lxxxiii), where the first of these common notions is quoted.

15. By "the Schoolmen" Culverwell probably means Suárez, but the sentence has not been discovered. The second quotation is from St. Jerome, *Letters*, cxxi, *Ad Algasiam* (Migne, XXII, col. 1022), quoted in Suárez, *De Legibus*, II, v, 11.

16. Rom. 2:15.

17. "For the Stoics, Logos was the principle of rationality in the universe, and as such it was identified with God and with the source of all activity. . . . It had various derivatives, which are better regarded as aspects of itself than separate entities. As active principle it was *logos spermaticos*, or seminal reason, which worked on passive matter to generate the world, and in plural form, as seminal reasons, it functioned as the universals which Plato and Aristotle had attempted to account for by their respective doctrines of transcendent and immanent Forms." *The Encyclopedia of Philosophy*, ed. Paul Edwards (New York, 1967), V, 83. See the discussion in E. Zeller, *Stoics, Epicureans and Sceptics* (London, 1870), 79–80, 162–63.

18. Sir Kenelm Digby, *Two Treatises . . . the Nature of Bodies . . . the Nature of Mans Soule* (Paris, 1644), 355–65.

19. Rom. 1:19.

20. A paraphrase of ibid., 1:20.

21. Ibid., 2:15.

22. Herbert, *De Veritate* (London, 1633), 37.

23. Ibid., 47, 49.

24. Ibid., 46; since "in quovis inarticulato licet & incauto" does not appear in the first edition (1624) of Herbert's work, it is clear that Culverwell was quoting from the revised second edition of 1633, or from the 1645 reprint of it; page numbers in the notes refer to the second edition.

25. Ibid., 79, 75.

26. Col. 3:2.

27. Herbert, *De Veritate,* 52.

28. Robert Greville, Lord Brooke, *The Nature of Truth* (London, 1640), 46: "And therefore I wholly subscribe to the Platonists, who make all *scientia* nothing but *reminiscentia.*" Greville was answered by the mathematician John Wallis, Culverwell's contemporary at Emmanuel, in *Truth Tried* (London, 1643), 45: "The understanding is not as a *Table.* . . . But rather as a *Glasse* which is able to Receive and Reflect whatsoever Colours fall upon it, though (before) it had none of them." This passage from *Truth Tried* is echoed at the end of the present paragraph.

29. Heb. 1:3.

30. See Thomas Aquinas, *Summa contra Gentiles,* II, lxxxv: "Quod anima non est de substantia Dei," and Ross, *The Philosophicall Touchstone,* 101: "[the] heresie which held the soule to be a part of the Divine Essence: such as were Carpocrates, Cerdon, the Gnosticks, Manichees, and Priscillianists."

31. Simplicius, *Commentary on the Enchiridion of Epictetus* (Leiden, 1640), 187.

32. Claudius Salmasius, *Notae et Animadversiones in Epictetum et Simplicium* (Leiden, 1640).

33. The following discussion of Stoic teaching is drawn from Salmasius (*Notae,* 161, 184–85, 191, 244 ff.) and repeats his quotation of terms from Porphyry and Nemesius.

34. Tertullian, *De Anima,* xiv, as summarized in Salmasius, *Notae,* 186.

35. Salmasius, *Notae,* 257.

36. Tertullian, *De Anima,* xiv, as summarized in Salmasius, *Notae,* 188.

37. Salmasius, *Notae,* 178, 311.

38. Ibid., 272, 176.

39. R[ichard] O[verton], *Mans Mortalitie; or, a treatise wherein 'tis proved both theologically and phylosophically, that whole man, as a rationall creature, is a compound wholly mortall, contrary to that common distinction of soule and body: and that the present going of the soule into Heaven or Hell is a meer fiction: and that at the Resurrection is the beginning of our immortality* (Amsterdam [London], 1644), 8. Overton's tract created a considerable stir and was responsible for the growth of a sect called "soul sleepers." See the DNB and David Masson's *Life of Milton* (London, 1859–80), III, 156, 164, and n. 73 in the present chapter.

40. Epictetus, *Discourses*, I, ix (chapter title), and Seneca, *Ad Helviam Matrem de Consolatione*, xi.

41. Epictetus, *Discourses*, I, xiv, 6, quoted in Steuchus, *De Perenni Philosophia*, IX, xvii (176 v).

42. Marcus Aurelius, *Meditations*, V, 27, quoted in Selden, *De Jure*, I, ix (112).

43. Pythagoras, *The Golden Verses*, 62.

44. Seneca, *Epistulae Morales*, 31, 11.

45. 1 Tim. 3:16.

46. Seneca, *Epistulae Morales*, 66, 12, quoted in Selden, *De Jure*, I, ix (112), and in Steuchus, *De Perenni Philosophia*, IX, xiii (173).

47. Selden argues so in *De Jure*, I, ix (111–12).

48. See n. 42 above.

49. Philo, *Concerning Noah's Work as a Planter*, II, 5 (18).

50. John of Damascus, *Exposition of the Orthodox Faith*, II, xii (Migne, XCIV, col. 924).

51. Gregory of Nyssa, *On the Words, Let us Make Man in our Image*, I (Migne, XLIV, col. 268).

52. Salmasius, *Notae*, 170.

53. Cf. Epictetus' use of these terms in his *Discourses*, I, iii.

54. Hermes Trismegistus, *Poimandres*, XII, 1, quoted in Steuchus, *De Perenni Philosophia*, IX, viii (169), and IX, xvii (176 v). This phrase, like many to follow in this section, is also quoted by Zanchius in *De Operibus Dei*, pt. III, II, V (Hanover, 1597, 772.)

55. See the discussions in Thomas Aquinas, *Summa contra Gentiles*, II, xvi, and Zanchius, *De Operibus Dei*, 773.

56. James 1:17.

57. Thomas Aquinas, *Summa contra Gentiles*, I, xvii, and I, xxvi, xxvii.

58. Rom. 9:21.

59. See Thomas Aquinas, *Summa contra Gentiles,* III, lxv, and I, xl, xli.

60. Carpocrates was a gnostic teacher of the second century.

61. James 1:17.

62. Gen. 1:3.

63. Sir Thomas Browne (*Religio Medici,* I, 36) and Milton (*De Doctrina Christiana,* I, vii) favour traducianism. For a survey of Renaissance discussions of the soul's origin see D. C. Allen, *Doubt's Boundless Sea* (Baltimore, 1964), v. This topic was debated publicly in the Schools at Cambridge on March 3, 1647, probably the year after Culverwell delivered his *Discourse.* See Charles Hotham, *Ad Philosophiam Teutonicam Manuductio* (London, 1648).

64. Galen, *That the Nature of the Soul Accords with the Temper of the Body,* in *Medicorum Graecorum Opera,* ed. D. C. G. Kuhn (Leipzig, 1821–30), IV, 766, quoted in Salmasius, *Notae,* 164.

65. The anecdote and the phrase come from Cicero, *Tusculanarum Disputationum,* I, x, and are quoted by Bacon in *The Advancement of Learning* (*Works,* III, 293).

66. Tertullian developed his view of traducianism in *De Origine Anima,* xxiii–xli. Nemesius is one of the authorities for the doctrine of Apollinaris; see *The Nature of Man,* ii, 5.

67. See chap. 9, n. 11.

68. Jerome, *Apologia adversus Libros Rufini,* III, 557 (Migne, XXIII, col. 478) and *Epistulae,* 126 (82) (Migne, XXII, col. 1086); the actual source of Culverwell's statement, however, was probably Zanchius, *De Operibus Dei,* 769.

69. Augustine, *De Origine Animae Hominis Liber* (Migne, XXXIII, cols. 724–25); Culverwell paraphrases Augustine's argument.

70. See, e.g., Peter Lombard, *Sentences,* II, dist. xvii, and Thomas Aquinas, *Summa Theologica,* I, qu. 118.

71. William Pemble, *De Formarum Origine* (London, 1629), 68–74; Pemble concludes his discussion of traducianism and the tract thus: "Res est non levis difficultatis, in qua, dum audiatur Doctorum judicium, ἀπέχω." Pemble employs the technical Sceptic term for suspension of judgment; see chap. 14, 137 and n. 5.

72. Sir Kenelm Digby, *Two Treatises . . . the Nature of Bodies . . . the Nature of Mans Soul* (Paris, 1644), 451. Digby was attacked by the relentless Alexander Ross in *The Philosophicall Touchstone* (London, 1645), 95–101, where the twenty arguments Culverwell mentions are to be found.

73. Cf. n. 39 above. Richard Overton's book was answered pseudonymously by Guy Holland (John Sergeant) in *The Prerogative of Man* (Oxford, 1645), 26: "It followeth then, that the soule neither generates a soule, nor againe is generated by any, and for this cause must be incorruptible, and by the principles of Nature, immortall." See F. Madan, *Oxford Books* (Oxford, 1895–1931), II, 417, and G. Williamson, "Milton and the Mortalist Heresy," in *Seventeenth-Century Contexts* (London, 1960).

74. Pythagoras, *The Golden Verses*, 63, quoted in Steuchus, *De Perenni Philosophia*, IX, xxi (178 v), and Zanchius, *De Operibus Dei*, 771.

75. Acts 17:28, quoted in Steuchus, *De Perenni Philosophia*, IX, xxi (178 v) and Zanchius, *De Operibus Dei*, 771. In 1634–37(?) John Sherman commonplaced on this text in Trinity College and published his remarks as *A Greek in the Temple* (Cambridge, 1641).

76. *De Oraculis Chaldaicis*, ed. W. Kroll (Hildesheim, 1962), 46, quoted in Steuchus, *De Perenni Philosophia*, IX, v (166).

77. *Oracula Magica Zoroastris cum Scholiis Plethonis et Pselli*, ed. J. Opsopoeus (Paris, 1607), 17, quoted in Steuchus, *De Perenni Philosophia*, IX, vii (168 v), and Zanchius, *De Operibus Dei*, 772.

78. The following three quotations from Hermes Trismegistus come from *Poimandres*, I, 12, and V, 7; they are all quoted in Steuchus, *De Perenni Philosophia*, IX, iii (165).

79. Epictetus, *The Discourses*, I, ix, 1, 6, quoted in Steuchus, *De Perenni Philosophia*, IX, xvii (176), and Zanchius, *De Operibus Dei*, 771–72.

80. Homer, *Odyssey*, I, 58.

81. Cicero, *Tusculanarum Disputationum*, V, xxxvii, and Diogenes Laertius, *Lives*, VI, 63; also Epictetus, *The Discourses*, I, ix, 1.

82. Cf. Steuchus, *De Perenni Philosophia*, IX, xiv (174), xxviii (185 v).

83. Heb. 1:3. Philo, *On the Creation*, 146 (51), quoted in Steuchus, *De Perenni Philosophia*, IX, xvii (176 v).

84. Plotinus, *Enneads*, IV, iv, 28, quoted and discussed in Steuchus, *De Perenni Philosophia*, IX, xxiii (180).

85. Plato, *Timaeus*, 41C, quoted in Steuchus, *De Perenni Philosophia*, IX, xix (177 v).

86. Epictetus, *The Discourses*, I, xvi, 14, quoted in Steuchus, *De Perenni Philosophia*, IX, xviii (177).

87. *Oracula Magica*, 93, quoted in Steuchus, *De Perenni Philosophia*, IX, xviii (177 v).

88. Gen. 1:27, quoted in Steuchus, *De Perenni Philosophia*, I, vii (6).

89. Steuchus in *De Perenni Philosophia,* IX, xix (177 v) attributes this remark to Thales, but it is not included in modern collections of fragments.

90. *Oracula Magica,* 18, quoted in Steuchus, *De Perenni Philosophia,* IX, xv (175). The following phrase is contained in Pletho's commentary on the oracles.

91. See n. 2 above.

92. Aristotle, *Nicomachean Ethics,* X, viii, 13.

93. Aristotle, *Generation of Animals,* II, iii, quoted in Zanchius, *De Operibus Dei,* 772.

94. Seneca, *Epistulae Morales,* 20, 15, quoted in Steuchus, *De Perenni Philosophia,* IX, xiii (173).

95. Simplicius, *Commentary on Aristotle's Physics,* ed. H. Diels (Berlin, 1882), I, 186, quoted in Steuchus, *De Perenni Philosophia,* IX, xv (175 v), and Zanchius, *De Operibus Dei,* 772.

96. The preceding six definitions Culverwell quotes from Steuchus, *De Perenni Philosophia:* Michael Psellus (*Oracula Magica,* 101), IX, viii (168 v); Plato (*Timaeus,* xliii, 90A), IX, xiv (174 v); the Sibyls (*Oracula Magica,* 18), IX, xv (175); "some others," i.e., Plutarch (*One Cannot Live Pleasurably in Accordance with the Doctrine of Epicurus,* 1107B), IX, xv (175 v); the Chaldaic oracle, IX, xxiii (180 v); Seneca the elder (*Suasoriae,* vi, 6), IX, xiii (172 v); Cicero (*Tusculanarum Disputationum,* V, xiii), IX, viii (168 v).

97. 1 Sam. 25:29.

98. Cicero, *Tusculanarum Disputationum,* I, xxvii; the first words of this passage appear in Steuchus, *De Perenni Philosophia,* IX, xii (171 v), and the entire paragraph is quoted in Zanchius, *De Operibus Dei,* 772–73.

99. The point is made by Steuchus, *De Perenni Philosophia,* IX, xiv (174).

100. Virgil, *Aeneid,* VI, 730, quoted in Bacon, *The Advancement of Learning* (*Works,* III, 426).

101. Ovid, *Ars Amatoria,* III, 550, quoted in Steuchus, *De Perenni Philosophia,* IX, x (170 v), and Zanchius, *De Operibus Dei,* 772.

102. See, e.g., Homer, *Iliad,* IV, 68.

103. Virgil, *Aeneid,* I, 256.

104. Gregory, *Epistolae,* IX, ii, 52 (Migne, LXXVII, 970), quoted in Zanchius, *De Operibus Dei,* 770.

105. Marcus Aurelius, *Meditations,* IV, 14, 21; VI, 24.

106. This line from Epicharmus occurs in Eusebius, *The Preparation for the Gospel,* XIII, xiii (682b) and is quoted in Selden, *De Jure,* I, ix (112).

107. Col. 2:3.

108. Ps. 94:9.

109. 1 Cor. 15:52.

110. Culverwell follows Thomas Aquinas's account of God's knowledge in *Summa contra Gentiles,* I, xlvi, xlviii–liv.

111. Rom. 1:19.

112. Thomas Aquinas, *Summa contra Gentiles,* I, xlv.

113. See ibid., I, liii, liv.

114. Ibid., I, liv.

115. Thomas Aquinas, *Summa Theologica,* I, qu. 103, art. 4, and *Summa contra Gentiles,* III, xix–xxi.

116. Cf. Sir Edward Coke, *The Second Part of the Institutes of the Laws of England* (London, 1642), 56: "The law is called *rectum,* because it discovereth, that which is tort, crooked, or wrong, for as right signifieth law, so tort, crooked, or wrong, signifieth injurie, and *injuria est contra jus,* against right: *recta linea est index sui, et obliqui.*"

117. A commonplace (see Bacon, *Novum Organum,* II, ii, *Works,* IV, 119) which had its origin in Aristotle, *Posterior Analytics,* I, 2.

118. See Thomas Aquinas, *Summa contra Gentiles,* I, lv, lvii, and chap. XVIII, n. 37, 38.

119. Ibid., I, lv, lvii.

120. Ibid., I, lv.

121. Ibid., I, lv, lvi.

122. Ibid., I, lxxxvi, lxxxvii (chapter titles).

123. Perhaps a paraphrase of a sentence in *Summa contra Gentiles,* I, lxxxi: "Bonum intellectum sit proprium objectum voluntatis."

124. Thomas Aquinas, *Summa contra Gentiles,* I, xlvii, lxxiv, lxxv.

125. Ibid., I, lxxxvi.

126. Ps. 85:10.

127. See chap. 4, n. 41.

128. This double definition of providence comes from Thomas Aquinas, *Summa Theologica,* I, qu. 22, art. 1. The first definition Thomas quotes from Boethius (*De Consolatione,* IV, 6); he then proceeds to analyze the relation between human prudence and divine providence.

129. 1 Cor. 2:10.

130. Unwillingness; this is the first cited occurrence of the word in the OED.

131. Zeno, as reported in Epictetus, *The Discourses,* I, xx, 15; see also Marcus Aurelius, *Meditations,* X, 11, and XII, 31.

132. Thomas Aquinas, *Summa contra Gentiles,* III, xix (title).

Chapter 12

1. Alluding to Job 38:11.

2. Isa. 14:12–15.

3. Gen. 3:22.

4. Prov. 20:27 and Gen. 2:7; see chap. 2, n. 8.

5. See Thomas Aquinas, *Summa Theologica*, I, qu. 94, art. 1.

6. Ibid., I, qu. 94, arts. 1, 2.

7. The idea is a commonplace in scholastic treatments of the subject; see Thomas Aquinas, *Summa Theologica*, I, qu. 94, art. 3, and Suárez, *De Opere Sex Dierum*, III, ix, 14. Suárez's account contains a survey of the views of other scholastic writers.

8. John Davenant, *Determinationes Quaestionum Quarundam Theologicarum* (Cambridge, 1634), 75; the Latin passage is the title of question xvi. John Davenant was educated at Queen's College, Cambridge, where he was first Fellow and then master before leaving to become bishop of Salisbury. Culverwell draws frequently from Davenant's *Praelectiones* in chap. 15.

9. This and the subsequent Latin quotation are from Robert Bellarmine, *De Gratia Primi Homini*, I, v–vii, in *De Controversiis*, IV (1619, 21–40), paraphrased in Davenant, *Determinationes*, 76.

10. Based on a passage by Hugh of St. Victor which Davenant quotes in *Determinationes*, 77: "nec fraeno, nec calcaribus instructum."

11. Davenant, *Determinationes*, 76. Culverwell continues to follow Davenant's argument, taking from p. 78 the idea of the *regno rationis*.

12. Thus Zanchius, for example, cites the opinion "Corpus quod corrumpiter, aggravat animam" in *De Operibus Dei*, pt. III, III, iii, thesis (Hanover, 1597, 890).

13. The proper object of the passions is discussed in Thomas Aquinas, *Summa Theologica*, I, qu. 95, art. 2, and Suárez, *De Opere Sex Dierum*, III, xii.

14. Cicero, *Epistularum ad Familiares*, VII, xxx; the narrative is treated freely.

15. Ps. 49:12. Alexander Gill (see chap. 16, 167, and n. 12) cites the same passage in a similar manner and context, *The Sacred Philosophie of the Holy Scripture* (London, 1635), 113.

16. Thomas Aquinas, *Summa Theologica*, I, qu. 94, art. 4. Culverwell omits the cautious qualifications.

17. Zanchius, *De Operibus Dei*, pt. III, III, iv, sec. 2, quaestio 3 (Hanover, 1597, 905): "Adamum non pecasse eo modo quo Angeli mali: ex mera malitia, et simplici voluntate: sed aliqua ex parte fuisse deceptum. . . ."

18. Zanchius, *De Operibus Dei*, pt. III, III, iv, sec. 2, quaestio 3 (Hanover, 1597, 905–6).

19. Davenant, *Determinationes*, 77.

20. See Plato, *Gorgias*, 525A.

21. Plato, *Timaeus*, 52B.

22. Plato, *Phaedrus*, 246C.

23. See chap. 11, n. 13.

24. Ibid., n. 11.

25. "We may say with *Aristotle*, at the brink of *Euripus*, not being able to give an account of the ebbes and flowes, *if I can't comprehend thee, thou shalt me*." Richard Culverwell, "Courteous Reader," 6 above. According to the legend, Aristotle then threw himself into the water.

26. The Stoa was the cloister at Athens in which Zeno and his successors taught.

27. Epictetus, *Enchiridion*, 42: "Everything has two handles, by one of which it ought to be carried and by the other not."

28. Although the passage has not been located, a particularly full discussion of divine knowledge can be found in his *Ordinis Minorum, Opere Omnia* (1639), vols. X, XI.

29. Ephraim Pagitt explained that "Antinomians are so called because they would have the law abolished" (OED *Antinomians*, B). They insisted that the whole Mosaic law (the moral parts as well as the ceremonial and judicial) had been abrogated by Christ, but most also urged (like Milton) that the outward commandments had been replaced by an inner law of love. The Seekers were forerunners of the Quakers: "Many," wrote Pagitt, "go under the name of Expecters and Seekers and doe deny that there is any true Church, or any true Minister, or any Ordinances: some of them assume the Church to be in the wildernesse, and they are seeking it there: others say it is in the smoke of the Temple, and that they are groping for it there." (OED *Seeker* 1, b) "Seraphic" appears to be a term used to mock those sects which placed a strong emphasis on evangelical love. John Saltmarsh mentions "Seraphinisme" in his *Groans for Liberty* (London, 1646), 27.

Chapter 13

1. See Sir Edward Coke, *The First Part of the Institutes of the Laws of England* (London, 1628), 56: "But against the king there shall be no *occupant*, because

nullum tempus occurrit regis. And therefore no man shall gain the king's land by priority of entry." The Nullum Tempus Act of 1769 limited to sixty years the ancient royal prerogative to sue for land or property without limitation of time.

2. Thomas Aquinas, *Summa contra Gentiles,* I, lxvii. The idea is a commonplace; see Suárez, *Opusculum,* pt. II, I, vii.

3. See, e.g., Thomas Aquinas, *Summa Theologica,* I, qu. 14, art. 13; Suárez, *De Angelorum Natura,* II, x, 3. Thomas points to the source in Aristotle, *Of Interpretation,* IX.

4. This argument is found in Thomas Aquinas, *Summa Theologica,* I, qu. 14, art. 13, and in *Summa contra Gentiles,* I, lxvii.

5. The idea is elaborated in slightly different language in Thomas Aquinas, *Summa Theologica,* I, qu. 14, arts. 7, 13.

6. The preceding discussion of knowledge owes its ideas and much of its phrasing to Thomas Aquinas, *Summa contra Gentiles,* I, lxvi–lxvii.

7. Horace, *Carmina,* II, i, 6.

8. Suárez, *De Angelorum Natura,* II, x, 8. Suárez's discussion of the angels' knowledge of the future is contained in chaps. ix–xi of bk. II.

9. This view is perhaps most fully stated by Suárez, *De Angelis,* II, x–xi, especially xi, 16–18; see also Thomas Aquinas, *Summa Theologica,* I, qu. 57, art. 3, and Zanchius, *De Operibus Dei,* pt. I, III, x (Hanover, 1597, 158).

10. See *On the Cessation of Oracles* and *On the Pythian Oracle.*

11. The following survey of methods of predicting the future is probably drawn from Francesco Pico della Mirandola, *De Rerum Praenotione,* VI, ii ("Adversus Cheiromantium"), iv ("Adversus Augria et Auspicia"), and vii ("Adversus Superstitiosa Somnia"). Culverwell quotes directly from Pico's book below.

12. Homer, *Odyssey,* XIX, 562–64; Virgil, *Aeneid,* VI, 893–95; Bacon cites the passage from the *Aeneid* and adds the following gloss: "Insignis sane magnificentia *portae eburneae;* tamen *somnia vera* per *corneam* commeant." *De Augmentis Scientiarum (Works,* I, 743).

13. Suetonius, *De Vita Caesarum,* I, *Divus Julius,* xxxii.

14. Thomas Aquinas, *Summa contra Gentiles,* III, cvi.

15. Francesco Pico della Mirandola, *De Rerum Praenotione,* I, viii (*Opera Omnia,* Basle, 1601, II, 264).

16. Heb. 1:1.

17. Bacon, *History of Henry VII* (*Works,* VI, 31).

18. Anacreon, *Odes,* xv, 9–10.

19. Horace, *Carmina,* I, ix, 13.

20. Virgil, *Aeneid,* X, 501.

21. Francesco Pico della Mirandola, *De Rerum Praenotione,* III, vi ("De Praenotionibus Pastoris et Nautae"), and vii ("De Praenotionibus Medicorum").

22. Roman historians record that Caligula sought divine honours by impersonating the gods and assuming their dress and attributes. He was particularly fond of the role of Jupiter; "He also consecrated himself to his own service and appointed his horse a fellow-priest; and dainty and expensive birds were sacrificed to him daily. He had a contrivance by which he gave answering peals when it thundered and sent return flashes when it lightened." Dion Cassius, *Roman History,* LIX, 28, 6.

23. The merriment of Democritus at the expense of the world is related by Hippocrates in his *Epistle to Demagetus;* the story was given currency by Juvenal, *Satires,* x, 33 ("Democritus his nimble lungs would tyre / With constant laughter," as Henry Vaughan translated the passage in 1646); both Milton (*Prolusion* vi) and Burton (Preface to *The Anatomy of Melancholy*) refer to the story.

24. Matt. 7:27.

25. See Thomas Aquinas, *Summa Theologica,* II, –II, qu. 172, art. 1; *De Veritate,* qu. xii, art. 3; *Summa contra Gentiles,* I, lxxxv.

26. Giovanni Pico della Mirandola, *De Astrologia Disputationum,* II, v (*Opera Omnia,* Basle, 1601, I, 297).

27. 2 Pet. 1:19.

28. Rev. 1:8.

29. Homer, *Iliad,* I, 70.

30. Virgil, *Georgics,* IV, 392–93.

31. See Thomas Aquinas, *Summa Theologica,* I, qu. 171, art. 2, and qu. 172, art. 1.

32. Maimonides, *Guide of the Perplexed,* II, xxxii (285). This work was translated as *'Doctor Perplexorum,* and the page numbers in parentheses refer to the Latin edition published at Basle in 1629. Maimonides' discussion of prophecy is found in II, xxxii–xlviii.

33. The following account of the views of Maimonides is a medley of summary and quotation drawn from chaps. xxxii, xxxvi, and xxxvii of bk. II (285–97).

34. It is worth noting that the *terrae filii* at Oxford were appointed by the procters and engaged in mock-serious and frequently scurrilous debate during the inceptors' disputations at the Vesperiae and Comitia; the same office at Cambridge was filled by the prevaricators.

35. Ps. 78:41.

Chapter 14

1. Sextus Empiricus, *Outlines of Pyrrhonism*, I, xxvi, 201.

2. Lucian, *Philosophies for Sale*, 27.

3. Sextus Empiricus, *Outlines*, I, i, 3, and elsewhere.

4. Sextus Empiricus, *Outlines*, I, xiv, 126; I, xxvi, 201; I, xxix, 212.

5. The Sceptic term for suspension of judgment; see Sextus Empiricus, *Outlines*, I, xxii, 196.

6. The ten modes or tropes described in Sextus Empiricus, *Outlines*, I, xiv, and Diogenes Laertius, *Lives*, IX, ii.

7. Sextus Empiricus, *Outlines*, I, iii, 7.

8. Ibid., I, xxiv, 198.

9. Ibid., I, xxvii, 204.

10. See ibid., I, xxvii, 202.

11. Lucian, *Philosophies for Sale*, 27.

12. Sextus Empiricus, *Outlines*, I, xix, and Diogenes Laertius, *Lives*, IX, 74.

13. 1 Pet. 1:17.

14. The Sceptic arguments for relativity in ethics are presented in Sextus Empiricus, *Outlines*, I, xiv, 145 ff.; III, xxiv, 188 ff.; *Against the Ethicists*, iii, 42.

15. Sextus Empiricus, *Outlines*, I, xxi, 194.

16. Ibid., I, iv, 10.

17. This fragment by Timo Phliasius appears in Eusebius, *Preparation for the Gospel*, xiv, and elsewhere.

18. Sextus Empiricus, *Outlines*, I, xvi, 179.

19. Diogenes Laertius, *Lives*, IX, ii, 66.

20. Sextus Empiricus, *Outlines*, I, x, 19.

21. Ibid., I, xi, 24.

22. Ibid., I, x.

23. Ibid., I, x, 20.

24. Cf. chap. 11, n. 65.

25. Ben Jonson employs this Latin phrase in *Discoveries*, 2418 (*Works*, eds.

Hereford and Simpson, Oxford, 1947, VII, 637), and attributes the saying to Aristotle. The ultimate source is probably the discussion of madness in Aristotle, *Problems*, 30, 1.

26. Francesco Pico della Mirandola, *Examen Vanitatis Doctrinae Gentium, et Veritatis Christianae Disciplinae*, II, v (*Opera Omnia*, Basle, 1601, II, 543–44).

27. Sextus Empiricus, *Outlines*, I, xxxii, 219.

28. Ibid., I, xxxii, 216.

29. The Greek phrase is not found in Aristotle, but it summarizes the attack which he directs against Protagoras in *Metaphysics* XI, vi, in a passage which identifies κριτήριον and μέτρον; "Protagoras . . . said that man is the measure of all things whereby he meant no more than that there really is what seems to any man to be. But if this is the case it follows that the same thing both is and is not, or is bad and good, and so with what is said in all other opposite statements; because what appears to each man is the measure, and things often appear to be beautiful to some and contrary to others."

30. Sextus Empiricus, *Outlines*, I, xiii, 33.

31. See the arguments for relativism in ibid., I, iv.

32. Sextus Empiricus, *Outlines*, I, xii, 25–26, 30.

33. On the seventeenth-century sect known as "Seekers," see chap. 12, n. 29.

34. Sextus Empiricus, *Outlines*, I, xiv, 152; III, xx, 177.

35. See ibid., II, i, 9; III, v, 22.

36. Plato uses the expression frequently; see, e.g., *Phaedrus*, 247E and *The Sophist*, 266E.

37. See chap. 4, n. 39.

38. Quoted in Sextus Empiricus, *Against the Logicians*, I, 126.

39. Sextus Empiricus, *Outlines*, I, xxxiii, 225 ff.

40. Culverwell criticizes the position which Descartes developed in *Discours de la methode*, IV (1637), and *Meditation* II (1638); his reference to this central theory is one of the earliest in England. Marjorie Nicolson, in "The Early Stage of Cartesianism in England," *SP*, 26 (1929), 356–74, does not mention Culverwell, but finds traces of Cartesianism in the work of John Hall of St. John's College, Cambridge, who published *Horae Vacivae* in 1646 and *An Humble Motion . . . Concerning the Advancement of Learning and Reformation of the University* in 1649. Henry More, who was to become chief spokesman for and critic of Cartesianism in England, first definitely refers to Descartes in his *Infinitie of Worlds*, 1647.

41. See chap. 9, n. 10.

42. Robert Greville, Lord Brooke, *The Nature of Truth* (London, 1640): "I fully conclude with *Aristotles* Adversaries *Anaxagoras, Democritus,* etc. That Contradictions may be *simul et semel* in the same Subject, same Instant, same notion (not onely in two distinct respects, or notions, as one thing may be *causa et effectus, Pater et Filius, respectu diversi;* but even in the same respect, under one and the same notion). For, *Non ens* is nothing; and so, the Being which it hath, may subsist with that which contradicts it. . . . Sin is onely a Privation, a Non-Entity: But, a Privation, a Non-Entity may subsist (according to the subsistence it hath) with Being. Such a co-existence of Entity and Non-Entity, was in his faith, who cried, *Lord, I beleeve, help my unbelief"* (100–101). This monism is central to Greville's argument; see 26, 164.

43. Sextus Empiricus, *Outlines,* I, xxii, 196; xx, 192; xxiv, 198.

Chapter 15

1. Rom. 2:15.

2. The authoritative part of the soul, reason, especially in Stoic philosophy. See Whichcote, *Aphorisms,* XI, 1042: "All objects affect; and all Faculties incline: God and Nature have appointed a *directing* Principle [τὸ ἡγεμονικόν] that there might be, in Multiplicity, a reduction to Unity; Harmony and Uniformity, in Variety."

3. Musaeus, *Hero and Leander,* 219.

4. The phrase appears in a story about Demosthenes which Bacon, drawing upon Plutarch's *Life of Demosthenes,* relates in *De Augmentis Scientiarum* (*Works,* I, 441).

5. Gal. 1:8.

6. 1 Pet. 2:2.

7. Acts 22:3.

8. Plato, *Republic,* VII, 528B, 535D, and elsewhere.

9. Jerome, *Epistolam ad Galatas,* Proemio, quoted in John Davenant, *Praelectiones de duobus in theologia controversis capitibus* (Cambridge, 1631), 169. Davenant's *Praelectiones* is a major source in the present chapter. On Davenant, see chap. 12, n. 8.

10. Acts 17:11.

11. Bacon, *The Advancement of Learning* (*Works,* III, 284): "Then did Car

of Cambridge, and Ascham, with their lectures and writings, almost deify Cicero and Demosthenes. . . ."

12. See chap. 4, n. 11.

13. See chap. 9, n. 13.

14. See chap. 12, n. 25.

15. Culverwell is in error in attributing this remark to Aristotle; it is found in Aelius Aristides, *Oratio Platonica, Prima pro Rhetorica,* in *Opera Omnia,* ed. Samuel Jebb (Oxford, 1722–30), II, 4.

16. Bacon, *De Augmentis Scientiarum* (*Works,* I, 457).

17. Ibid.

18. Herbert, *De Veritate,* 221–22: "such, then, are the Common Notions of which the true Catholic universal church is built. For the church which is built of clay or stone or living rock or even of marble cannot be claimed to be the infallible church. The true Catholic church is not supported on the inextricable confusion of oral and written tradition to which men have given their allegiance. Still less is it that which fights beneath any one particular standard, or is comprised in one organization so as to embrace only a restricted portion of the earth, or a single period of history. The only Catholic and uniform church is the doctrine of Common Notions which comprehends all places and all men." (M. H. Carré's translation)

19. Cf. Bacon, *Novum Organum* (*Works,* I, 191; IV, 82): "For rightly is truth called the daughter of time, not of authority."

20. Rev. 9:11.

21. 2 Tim. 3:16.

22. Aristotle, *Politics,* IV, iv, 7, quoted in Davenant, *Praelectiones,* 4.

23. The running title of bk. I of Davenant's *Praelectiones.*

24. This threefold distinction is drawn from Davenant, *Praelectiones,* I, iii, 3.

25. Davenant, *Praelectiones,* I, xxvi, 152.

26. Ibid., I, xxvii, 163.

27. Giovanni Pico della Mirandola, "De libertate credendi disputatio," in *Apologia* (*Opera Omnia,* Basle, 1601, I, 148); quoted by Davenant, *Praelectiones,* I, xxvii, 163.

28. Davenant, *Praelectiones,* I, xxvi, 149.

29. Persius, *Prologue,* 13–14.

30. This Latin tag from Plautus, *Poenulus,* 332, was apparently used in an animal fable.

31. Eccles. 12:13.

32. Virgil, *Aeneid*, III, 26, quoted in Davenant, *Praelectiones*, xxxi, 190.

33. So Davenant observes, *Praelectiones*, I, xxiii, 141.

34. Edmund Bonner was Bishop of London during the Marian persecutions. OED lists *Bonnering* as "Burning for heresy," and cites Bishop Hall: "No Bonnering or butchering of God's Saints."

35. John 3:19.

36. Rev. 17:4.

Chapter 16

1. Diogenes Laertius, *Lives*, VII, 110; the preceding Greek sentence is almost certainly Culverwell's invention, and not a quotation.

2. Cicero, *Tusculanarum Disputationum*, IV, vi; this is Cicero's translation of Zeno's definition of passion just quoted by Culverwell.

3. James 1:17.

4. Herbert, *De Veritate*, 225.

5. Ibid.

6. Rom. 2:15.

7. "Anti-Scripturists" is a derogatory term applied by orthodox Presbyterians to their more evangelical brethren. The catalogues of heresy which appeared in the mid-forties frequently employed the term, and it is found among the sixteen forms of heresy examined by Thomas Edwards in the first part of his famous *Gangraena* (London, 1646). The errors listed by Edwards as "Of the Scriptures" include the following: "That the Scriptures cannot be said to be the Word of God; there is no Word but Christ, the Scriptures are a dead letter; and no more to be credited then the writings of men, not divine, but humane invention; That the Scriptures are unsufficient and uncertain, there is no certainty to build any Doctrine upon them, they are not an infallible foundation of faith" (18).

8. Ps. 24:7–10.

9. Francesco Pico della Mirandola, *De Fide et Ordine Credendi*, theorem III (*Opera Omnia*, Basle, 1601, II, 173). Both the Latin phrase and the suggestion of movement to a centre are to be found in Pico's *De Fide*. Culverwell echoes Pico's Latin in the terms "inclination" and "propension."

10. Cf. Thomas Aquinas, *Summa Theologica*, II, –II, qu. 2, art. 3: "Whether it is necessary for salvation to believe anything above the natural reason," and II, –II, qu. 8, art. 2: "Whether the gift of understanding is compatible with faith." For a summary of the Thomistic synthesis of reason and faith see

Etienne Gilson, *The Christian Philosophy of St. Thomas Aquinas,* trans. L. K. Shook (London, 1957), 15–25.

11. 1 Cor. 5:12.

12. Alexander Gill, *The Sacred Philosophie of the Holy Scripture* (London, 1635), preface. Gill (1564–1635) was Milton's teacher at St. Paul's School and probably Culverwell's also. All four editions of the *Discourse* print "light" for the correct word "sight" in this quotation. The following sentence is based upon one from Gill's preface also.

13. Cant. 2:9.

14. John 1:14.

15. 1 Cor. 2:10.

16. The "solid Author" here has not been identified.

17. The story of Mahomet's loadstone is told by Sir Thomas Browne in his *Pseudodoxia Epidemica* (London, 1646), II, iii: "For the relation concerning Mahomet, it is generally believed his tomb, at Medina Talnabi, in Arabia, without any visible supporters, hangeth in the air between two loadstones artificially contrived both above and below; which conceit is fabulous and evidently false. . . ."

18. See n. 16 above.

19. 1 Cor. 13:12.

20. Heb. 12:18–22: "For ye are not come unto the mount that might be touched, and that burned with fire, nor unto blackness, and darkness, and tempest. . . . But ye are come unto mount Sion, and unto the city of the living God, the heavenly Jerusalem. . . ."

21. Luke 1:78.

22. Matt. 6:28, 29.

23. 1 Pet. 1:12: "Unto whom it was revealed, that not unto themselves, but unto us they did minister the things, which are now reported unto you by them that have preached the gospel unto you with the Holy Ghost sent down from heaven; which things the angels desire *to look into.*"

24. A paraphrase of John 1:27.

25. Ps. 85:10: "Mercy and truth are met together: righteousness and peace have kissed each other."

Chapter 17

1. Eccles. 11:7.

2. Sir Kenelm Digby, *Two Treatises . . . the Nature of Bodies . . . the Nature of Mans Soul* (Paris, 1644), 44–45.

3. Matt. 6:29.

4. Luke 16:19.

5. Plutarch, *One Cannot Live Pleasurably in Accordance with the Doctrine of Epicurus,* 1099D.

6. The common Greek phrase appears in Homer, *Iliad,* XXIV, 491, and elsewhere; the Latin phrase appears in Cicero, *Tusculanarum Disputationum,* III, xxi.

7. Diogenes Laertius, *Lives,* X.

8. Quoted in ibid., X, 6.

9. This and the two preceding Greek passages are taken from ibid., X, 131, 132.

10. Ibid., X, 14.

11. Plutarch.

12. A recurrent idea in Plutarch's criticism of Epicureanism; see *Doctrine of Epicurus,* 1088, 1090, 1092, 1096.

13. Plutarch, *Doctrine of Epicurus,* 1088E.

14. Diogenes Laertius, *Lives,* X, 128-29.

15. Lucretius, *De Rerum Natura,* II, 172.

16. Pindar, *Olympian Odes,* I, 13.

17. Ps. 37:35.

18. Diogenes Laertius, *Lives,* X, 6.

19. Ibid., X, 15-16.

20. *Tautopathy:* suffering caused by same thing as was habitually used previously.

21. Plutarch, *Doctrine of Epicurus,* 1087E-F.

22. Ibid., 1087F.

23. Lucretius, *De Rerum Natura,* IV, 627.

24. Plato, *Philebus,* 40B.

25. Ibid., 34A.

26. Exod. 15:23; 17:7.

27. Virgil, *Aeneid,* I, 203.

28. Plato, *Philebus,* 46C; 31E-32A.

29. See Plato, *Philebus,* 51B, 33D, 52D.

30. Lucretius, *De Rerum Natura,* IV, 1114.

31. Juvenal, *Satires,* VI, 130.

32. Plutarch, *Doctrine of Epicurus,* 1088B.

33. Juvenal, *Satires,* XI, 208.

34. The self-inflicted blindness of Democritus is described by Marcus Antonius Coccius (Sabellicus), *De Omnium gentium omniumque seculorum insignibus memoriamque dignis factis et dictis exemplorum libri X*, II (Basle, 1541), 65. Robert Burton refers to the legend in the preface to his *Anatomy of Melancholy*.

35. Plutarch, *Doctrine of Epicurus*, 1094C.

36. A paraphrase of Plato, *Gorgias*, 497E–498A.

37. Seneca, *Epistulae Moralaes*, 23, 4.

38. Plutarch, *Doctrine of Epicurus*, 1097D.

39. Horace, *Carmina*, III, xix, 21–22.

40. 2 Sam. 19:34, 35.

41. Plato, *Philebus*, 28C; the Latin phrase which follows the quotation states a main theme of the dialogue.

42. Possibly a free adaptation of Aristotle, *Nicomachean Ethics*, X, v.

43. Aristotle, *Nicomachean Ethics*, X, iv.

44. Ibid.

45. Ibid.

46. See the *Koran*, XXXVIII, 49–52; LXXVI, 5, 6; LXXXIII, 22–28.

47. Seneca, *Epistulae Morales*, 59, 12. Bacon tells this story in *The Advancement of Learning* (*Works*, III, 309).

48. Plato, *Republic*, II, III.

49. Aristotle, *Politics*, I, iii, 9.

50. Ps. 2:4.

51. Ibid., 11:7.

52. Prov. 8:31.

53. Plutarch, *Doctrine of Epicurus*; Culverwell's paraphrase is more extreme than the argument put forward in the closing sections of Plutarch's essay, 1102D–1107C.

54. The following criticism of Epicureanism is a summary of Plutarch, *Doctrine of Epicurus*, 1090A–C, 1103C–D; the five subsequent Greek quotations are from 1103C, 1101C, 1102A–B, 1100D.

55. *Swept* OED swoop, 2.

56. Diogenes Laertius, *Lives*, X, 120.

57. This and the following Greek passage are from Plutarch, *Doctrine of Epicurus*, 1106E–F.

58. This story of Lucretius' death is related by Jerome in his Chronicle under the year 94 B.C.

59. Homer, *Iliad,* XXII, 390, quoted in the "Moralist" Plutarch, *Doctrine of Epicurus,* 1104C.

60. Plutarch, *Doctrine of Epicurus,* 1106F; Plutarch cites Herodotus, *History,* vii, 46.

61. Plutarch, *Doctrine of Epicurus,* 1106E: "Wherefore it is neither the dog Cerberus nor the river Cocytus that has made our fear of death boundless; but the threatened danger of not being, representing it as impossible for such as are once extinct to shift back again into being."

62. Seneca, *Naturales Quaestiones,* I, Praefatio, 12.

63. Culverwell is probably not quoting a source here, but bringing together typical neo-Platonic terms; see Plotinus, *Enneads,* IV, viii, 2, 16; VI, ix, 3, 35; Plato, *Phaedo,* 80B; and chap. 5, n. 4.

Chapter 18

1. Musaeus, *Hero and Leander,* 8–9.

2. Augustine, *Confessions,* I, i.

3. Ovid, *Metamorphoses,* I, 85–86.

4. James 1:17.

5. Ps. 19:4.

6. Bacon, *Descriptio Globi Intellectualis* (*Works,* v, 538–39) and *Sylva Sylvarum* (*Works,* II, 352): "It appeareth also that the form of a pyramis in flame, which we usually see, is merely by accident, and that the air about, by quenching the sides of the flame, crusheth it, and extenuateth it into that form; for of itself it would be round."

7. Heb. 12:1.

8. Homer recounts the story of Vulcan's fall in books I, XIV, and XVIII of the *Iliad.*

9. Epictetus, *Discourses,* I, i.

10. Claudian, *Satires,* III, 215–16.

11. Sallust, *Bellum Jugurthinum,* 1.

12. Gerhard Jan Voss (1577–1649), author of *Historia Pelagiana* (London, 1618); Culverwell took the Latin phrase and the Greek word from p. 20 of this work, and he followed chap. iii in assigning Pelagius' nationality (incorrectly) and summarizing the opinions of Jerome, Chrysostom, and Augustine.

13. Thomas Bradwardine, *De Causa Dei* (London, 1618), sig. a6v.

14. Thomas Aquinas, *Summa contra Gentiles,* III, cxlix; this statement and

the preceding Latin sentence are quoted from one of Thomas's discussions of human merit and the necessity for grace.

15. Prosper of Aquitaine, *Liber contra Collatorem,* xii (337) (Migne, LI, col. 216).

16. Culverwell was probably reminded of this commonplace of Aristotelian physics (see *On the Heavens,* I, viii) by Thomas's use of it in *Summa contra Gentiles,* III, xxv, where he discusses man's movement toward God.

17. The source has not been identified; Robert Ferguson in his *The Interest of Reason in Religion* (London, 1675), 43, quotes the same sentence and translates it ("By the Light of Nature, they nodded after a Summum Bonum") in a manner which suggests that he might have read the *Discourse.*

18. Augustine, *De Verbis Apostoli,* sermon 14 (Migne, XXXVIII, col. 1338), quoted in Davenant, *Determinationes,* 235: "Pace eorum dicam, qui cuiquam salutem promittit sine Christo, nescio utrum ipse salutem habere possit in Christo." Anthony Tuckney repeats Culverwell's version of Augustine's statement on the title page of his *None but Christ* (London, 1654).

19. See the discussions of condign and congruous merit in Thomas Aquinas, *Summa Theologica,* I–II, qu. 114, art. 3 and Davenant, *Determinationes,* 66–69 and 151–55.

20. Mal. 4:2.

21. Zanchius, *De Operibus Dei,* pt. III, III, iii, thesis I.

22. *Manu-tenncy:* maintenance.

23. Virgil, *Georgics,* II, 490; Culverwell's eye may have fallen upon this proverbial line from Virgil when he was reading Bradwardine (see n. 13 above), where it appears on the page he quotes.

24. Ovid, *Metamorphoses,* III, 137.

25. Thomas Aquinas, *Summa contra Gentiles,* III, xlvii.

26. Ibid., III, xl; see also Rom. 10:17.

27. A close paraphrase of Thomas Aquinas, *Summa contra Gentiles,* III, xl.

28. Both the phrase and the idea come from Thomas Aquinas, *Summa Theologica,* I, qu. 12, art. 12: "Whether God can be known in this life by natural reason."

29. Defined and discussed by Thomas in the *Summa contra Gentiles,* III, liii, from which chapter Culverwell excerpts three of the following four quotations.

30. See Dionysius the Pseudo-Areopagite, *Divine Names,* I, 4, in *Opera Omnia* (Paris, 1644), I, where the idea is abundantly illustrated, although the exact quotation has not been discovered.

31. Ps. 36:9, quoted in Thomas Aquinas, *Summa contra Gentiles,* III, liii.

32. Quoted in Thomas Aquinas, *Summa contra Gentiles,* III, liii.

33. Rev. 21:23, quoted in ibid. III, liii.

34. Thomas Aquinas, *Summa contra Gentiles,* III, lviii.

35. This statement and the previous two Latin phrases are quoted from ibid., III, liii.

36. Both Latin phrases are quoted from ibid., III, lix.

37. A close summary of the concluding paragraphs of ibid., III, lix.

38. Ibid., III, lx; the second half of the quotation is Culverwell's expression of Thomas's concept.

39. Ibid., III, lxi.

40. See, e.g., ibid., III, xxvi: "That happiness does not consist in an act of the will."

TEXTUAL NOTES

The textual notes list all departures in this edition from the first edition of 1652. Emendations by the editors are marked (ed.); all other preferred readings are from the edition of 1654 (see Foreword: "The Text").

page	line	
13	18	Its] It's (ed.)
16	6	them,] them
18	12	wearied,] wearied;
19	10	men] men, (ed.)
23	24	*Natural;*] *Natural,*
23	25	*Fortune;*] *Fortune,*
25	14	being,] being
25	17	Providence,] Providence; (ed.)
31	29	speaks,] speaks. (ed.)
33	12	*leges;*] *leges,*
35	20	νόμος, ὁ νόμος] νόμος ὁ νόμος,
36	28	lineage] linage
36	30	*neque*] *nemque*
38	13	means.] means,
38	23	*ideas*] *idea's* (ed.)
38	24	*Ideas*] *Idea's* (ed.)
41	20	φυσικόν:] φυσικόν.
42	4	counterfeit] cunterfeit
42	9	pleased,] pleased;
43	2	*Hesiod*] *Hesiod.*

page	line	
45	15	this,] this;
46	4	remarkable,] remarkable
48	1	twelfth and thirteenth] 12 & 13
48	3	τοιόυτων,] τοιούτων;
48	6	principles,] principles
48	16	δικασταὶ,] δικασταὶ;
49	18	Church:] Church;
50	2	νόμος:] νόμος. (ed.)
50	17	follow] follow, (ed.)
52	18	them] them,
52	19	inexcusable] inexcusable,
53	31	Creature] Creature,
54	31	forbidden,] forbidden;
55	8	also,] also;
55	27	being] being; (ed.)
56	15	operations,] operations;
57	13	it,] it; (ed.)
58	23	warming] warning
59	7	before,] before:, (ed.)
59	10	(which] which (ed.)
60	3	Precepts,] Precepts. (ed.)

60	21	falsities] falsities,
62	20	*Nature,*] *Nature*
62	35	*Durantem,*] *Durantem;* (ed.)
65	14	them,] them; (ed.)
70	18	Gentile.] Gentile: (ed.)
73	25	What,] What (ed.)
75	32	opinion] opinion,
81	10	language] languge
82	31	notwithstanding,] notwithstanding
84	31	appear,] appear
85	6	them] him (ed.)
85	12	Heathen,] Heathen; (ed.)
85	14	*Individuums*] *Individuum's* (ed.)
89	10	this,] this.
90	11	maxime:] maxime.
91	28	organical] origanical
91	32	*Ideas*] *Idea's* (ed.)
92	2	determining:] determining.
93	16	*Ideas*] *Idea's* (ed.)
94	1	them:] them.
94	5	*rerum,*] *rerum;*
95	11	noetical] noentical
95	21	Ideas] Idea's (ed.)
95	25	Ideas] Idea's (ed.)
95	27	ingenuously] ingeniously
96	12	God,] God.
96	13	Manichees] Maniche's (ed.)
99	1	notwithstanding,] notwithstanding (ed.)
102	6	semi-Deity;] semi-Deity,
103	4	word,] word.
103	15	soul,] soul (ed.)

104	3	another,] another; (ed.)
106	18	it;] it,
108	12	συγγενέστατον] συγγενέστατον) (ed.)
109	21	spark;] spark,
109	28	Deity;] Deity, (ed.)
119	32	knowledge,] knowledge (ed.)
122	21	time,] time;
124	30	invalidate that,] invalidate, that
132	10	*errato.* Did] *errato,* did
132	20	times] tims
134	9	he] he,
134	19	*apex,*] *apex*
139	17	*infinitum;*] *infinitum,*
141	2	rest,] rest
142	1	minde] minde, (ed.)
142	1	unprejudic'd,] unprejudic'd; (ed.)
142	1	perturbations,] perturbations
143	23	God] God, (ed.)
144	17	sense,] sense (ed.)
149	34	*Anathema;*] *Anathema*
151	6	proportionable] proportionable,
154	13	*Constantine*] *Constantines*
155	27	contradictions,] contradictions
161	14	testimony;] testimony
162	26	it;] it
163	30	them [and] will] them; will (ed.)
166	13	Antichrist,] Antichrist
166	28	contradiction;] contradiction?

166	32	remarkable:] remarkable;	179	5	though] (though (ed.)
167	5	sight] light (ed.)	179	7	he] he) (ed.)
168	8	them;] them,	180	25	tenent] tenent,
170	21	it;] it,	182	17	pleasure);] pleasure; (ed.)
171	20	peculiar] pecular	182	18	it,] it,) (ed.)
172	22	call] calls	182	33	connexion] connexion;
172	28	faculties,] faculties;			(ed.)
173	14	others] other (ed.)	186	12	excesse] excesse,
175	16	*juvabit*] *jutabit*	186	34	minde,—] minde.—
176	21	when,] when	190	9	grace;] grace.

INDEX

References to the Notes are included when the author or source of a quotation is not given in Culverwell's text, or when the note provides information in addition to the identification of source.

This book is set in Adobe Garamond, a modern adaptation by Robert Slimbach of the typeface originally cut around 1540 by the French typographer and printer Claude Garamond. The Garamond face, with its small lowercase height and restrained contrast between thick and thin strokes, is a classic "old-style" face and has long been one of the most influential and widely used typefaces.

Printed on paper that is acid free and meets the requirements of the American National Standard for Permanence of Paper for Printed Library Materials, z39.48-1992. ⊗

Book design by Louise OFarrell, Gainesville, Florida
Typography by Impressions Book and Journal Services, Inc., Madison, Wisconsin
Books printed and bound by Edwards Brothers, Inc., Ann Arbor, Michigan
Paperback covers printed by Commercial Printing Company, Inc., Birmingham, Alabama